Praise for *Building Machine Learning Pipelines*

"I wish this book had existed when I started working in production ML! It's an outstanding resource for getting a comprehensive view of production ML systems in general, and TFX in particular. Hannes and Catherine have worked directly with the TensorFlow team to get the most accurate information available for including in this book, and then explained it in clear, concise explanations and examples."

—*Robert Crowe, TensorFlow Developer Advocate, Google*

"The data science practitioner knows that real-world machine learning involves more than just machine learning model training. This book demystifies the hidden technical debt in modern machine learning workflows such that you can put the lab and factory data science patterns into production as repeatable workflows."

—*Josh Patterson, CEO, Patterson Consulting,*
Coauthor of Deep Learning: A Practitioner's Approach
and Kubeflow Operations Guide

"This is definitely the book to read if you would like to understand how to build ML pipelines that are automated, scalable, and reproducible! You will learn something useful from it whether you are a data scientist, machine learning engineer, software engineer, or DevOps. It also covers the latest features of TFX and its components."

—*Margaret Maynard-Reid, Machine Learning Engineer,*
Tiny Peppers, ML GDE (Google Developer Expert), GDG Seattle Lead Organizer

Building Machine Learning Pipelines

Automating Model Life Cycles with TensorFlow

Hannes Hapke and Catherine Nelson

Beijing · Boston · Farnham · Sebastopol · Tokyo

Building Machine Learning Pipelines

by Hannes Hapke and Catherine Nelson

Published by O'Reilly Media, Inc., 1005 Gravenstein Highway North, Sebastopol, CA 95472.

O'Reilly books may be purchased for educational, business, or sales promotional use. Online editions are also available for most titles (*http://oreilly.com*). For more information, contact our corporate/institutional sales department: 800-998-9938 or *corporate@oreilly.com*.

Acquisitions Editor: Jonathan Hassell
Developmental Editors: Amelia Blevins, Nicole Tachè
Production Editor: Katherine Tozer
Copyeditor: Tom Sullivan
Proofreader: Piper Editorial, LLC

Indexer: Ellen Troutman-Zaig
Interior Designer: David Futato
Cover Designer: Karen Montgomery
Illustrator: Rebecca Demarest

August 2020:   First Edition

Revision History for the First Edition
2020-07-13:   First Release

See *http://oreilly.com/catalog/errata.csp?isbn=9781492053194* for release details.

978-1-492-05319-4

[LSI]

Table of Contents

Foreword

When Henry Ford's company built its first moving assembly line in 1913 to produce its legendary Model T, it cut the time it took to build each car from 12 to 3 hours. This drastically reduced costs, allowing the Model T to become the first affordable automobile in history. It also made mass production possible: soon, roads were flooded with Model Ts.

Since the production process was now a clear sequence of well-defined steps (aka, a *pipeline*), it became possible to automate some of these steps, saving even more time and money. Today, cars are mostly built by machines.

But it's not just about time and money. For many repetitive tasks, a machine will produce much more consistent results than humans, making the final product more predictable, consistent, and reliable. Lastly, by keeping humans away from heavy machinery, safety is greatly improved, and many workers went on to perform higher-level jobs (although to be fair, many others just lost their jobs).

On the flip side, setting up an assembly line can be a long and costly process. And it's not ideal if you want to produce small quantities or highly customized products. Ford famously said, "Any customer can have a car painted any color that he wants, so long as it is black."

The history of car manufacturing has repeated itself in the software industry over the last couple of decades: every significant piece of software nowadays is typically built, tested, and deployed using automation tools such as Jenkins or Travis. However, the Model T metaphor isn't sufficient anymore. Software doesn't just get deployed and forgotten; it must be monitored, maintained, and updated regularly. Software pipelines now look more like dynamic loops than static production lines. It's crucial to be able to quickly update the software (or the pipeline itself) without ever breaking it. And software is much more customizable than the Model T ever was: *software can be painted any color* (e.g., try counting the number of MS Office variants that exist).

Unfortunately, "classical" automation tools are not well suited to handle a full machine learning pipeline. Indeed, an ML model is not a regular piece of software.

For one, a large part of its behavior is driven by the data it trains on. Therefore, the training data itself must be treated as code (e.g., versioned). This is quite a tricky problem because new data pops up every day (often in large quantities), usually evolves and drifts over time, often includes private data, and must be labelled before you can feed it to supervised learning algorithms.

Second, the behavior of a model is often quite opaque: it may pass all the tests on some data but fail entirely on others. So you must ensure that your tests cover all the data domains on which your model will be used in production. In particular, you must make sure that it doesn't discriminate against a subset of your users.

For these (and other) reasons, data scientists and software engineers first started building and training ML models manually, "in their garage," so to speak, and many of them still do. But new automation tools have been developed in the past few years that tackle the challenges of ML pipelines, such as TensorFlow Extended (TFX) and Kubeflow. More and more organizations are starting to use these tools to create ML pipelines that automate most (or all) of the steps involved in building and training ML models. The benefits of this automation are mostly the same as for the car industry: save time and money; build better, more reliable, and safer models; and spend more time doing more useful tasks than copying data or staring at learning curves. However, building an ML pipeline is not trivial. So where should you start?

Well, right here!

In this book, Hannes and Catherine provide a clear guide to start automating your ML pipelines. As a firm believer in the hands-on approach, especially for such a technical topic, I particularly enjoyed the way this book guides you step by step through a concrete example project from start to finish. Thanks to the many code examples and the clear, concise explanations, you should have your own ML pipeline up and running in no time, as well as all the conceptual tools required to adapt these ML pipelines to your own use cases. I highly recommend you grab your laptop and actually try things out as you read; you will learn much faster.

I first met Hannes and Catherine in October 2019 at the TensorFlow World conference in Santa Clara, CA, where I was speaking on building ML pipelines using TFX. They were working on this book on the same topic, and we shared the same editor, so naturally we had a lot to talk about. Some participants in my course had asked very technical questions about TensorFlow Serving (which is part of TFX), and Hannes and Catherine had all the answers I was looking for. Hannes even kindly accepted my invitation to give a talk on advanced features of TensorFlow Serving at the end of my course on very short notice. His talk was a treasure trove of insights and helpful tips, all of which you will find in this book, along with many, many more.

Now it's time to start building professional ML pipelines!

— Aurélien Géron
Former YouTube Video Classification Team Lead
Author of Hands-On Machine Learning with
Scikit-Learn, Keras, and TensorFlow *(O'Reilly)*
Auckland, New Zealand, June 18, 2020

Preface

Everybody's talking about machine learning. It's moved from an academic discipline to one of the most exciting technologies around. From understanding video feeds in self-driving cars to personalizing medications, it's becoming important in every industry. While the model architectures and concepts have received a lot of attention, machine learning has yet to go through the standardization of processes that the software industry experienced in the last two decades. In this book, we'd like to show you how to build a standardized machine learning system that is automated and results in models that are reproducible.

What Are Machine Learning Pipelines?

During the last few years, the developments in the field of machine learning have been astonishing. With the broad availability of graphical processing units (GPUs) and the rise of new deep learning concepts like Transformers such as BERT (*https://arxiv.org/abs/1810.04805*), or Generative Adversarial Networks (GANs) such as deep convolutional GANs, the number of AI projects has skyrocketed. The number of AI startups is enormous. Organizations are increasingly applying the latest machine learning concepts to all kinds of business problems. In this rush for the most performant machine learning solution, we have observed a few things that have received less attention. We have seen that data scientists and machine learning engineers are lacking good sources of information for concepts and tools to accelerate, reuse, manage, and deploy their developments. What is needed is the standardization of machine learning pipelines.

Machine learning pipelines implement and formalize processes to accelerate, reuse, manage, and deploy machine learning models. Software engineering went through the same changes a decade or so ago with the introduction of continuous integration (CI) and continuous deployment (CD). Back in the day, it was a lengthy process to test and deploy a web app. These days, these processes have been greatly simplified by a few tools and concepts. Previously, the deployment of web apps required collaboration between a DevOps engineer and the software developer. Today, the app can be tested and deployed reliably in a matter of minutes. Data scientists and machine learning engineers can learn a lot about workflows from software engineering. Our intention with this book is to contribute to the standardization of machine learning projects by walking readers through an entire machine learning pipeline, end to end.

From our personal experience, most data science projects that aim to deploy models into production do not have the luxury of a large team. This makes it difficult to build an entire pipeline in-house from scratch. It may mean that machine learning projects turn into one-off efforts where performance degrades after time, the data scientist spends much of their time fixing errors when the underlying data changes, or the model is not used widely. An automated, reproducible pipeline reduces the effort required to deploy a model. The pipeline should include steps that:

- Version your data effectively and kick off a new model training run
- Validate the received data and check against data drift
- Efficiently preprocess data for your model training and validation
- Effectively train your machine learning models
- Track your model training
- Analyze and validate your trained and tuned models
- Deploy the validated model
- Scale the deployed model
- Capture new training data and model performance metrics with feedback loops

This list leaves out one important point: choosing the model architecture. We assume that you already have a good working knowledge of this step. If you are getting started with machine or deep learning, these resources are a great starting point to familiarize yourself with machine learning:

- *Fundamentals of Deep Learning: Designing Next-Generation Machine Intelligence Algorithms*, 1st edition by Nikhil Buduma and Nicholas Locascio (O'Reilly)
- *Hands-On Machine Learning with Scikit-Learn, Keras, and TensorFlow*, 2nd edition by Aurélien Géron (O'Reilly)

Who Is This Book For?

The primary audience for the book is data scientists and machine learning engineers who want to go beyond training a one-off machine learning model and who want to successfully productize their data science projects. You should be comfortable with basic machine learning concepts and familiar with at least one machine learning framework (e.g., PyTorch, TensorFlow, Keras). The machine learning examples in this book are based on TensorFlow and Keras, but the core concepts can be applied to any framework.

A secondary audience for this book is managers of data science projects, software developers, or DevOps engineers who want to enable their organization to accelerate their data science projects. If you are interested in better understanding automated machine learning life cycles and how they can benefit your organization, the book will introduce a toolchain to achieve exactly that.

Why TensorFlow and TensorFlow Extended?

Throughout this book, all our pipeline examples will use tools from the TensorFlow ecosystem, and in particular TensorFlow Extended (TFX). There are a number of reasons behind our choice of this framework:

- The TensorFlow ecosystem is the most extensively available for machine learning at the time of writing. It includes multiple useful projects and support libraries beyond its core focus, such as TensorFlow Privacy and TensorFlow Probability.

- It is popular and widely used in small and large production setups, and there is an active community of interested users.

- The supported use cases span from academic research to machine learning in production. TFX is tightly integrated with the core TensorFlow platform for production use cases.

- Both TensorFlow and TFX are open source tools, and there are no restrictions on their usage.

However, all the principles we describe in this book are relevant to other tools and frameworks as well.

Overview of the Chapters

In each chapter, we will introduce specific steps for building machine learning pipelines and demonstrate how these work with an example project.

Chapter 1: Introduction gives an overview of machine learning pipelines, discusses when you should use them, and describes all the steps that make up a pipeline. We also introduce the example project we will use throughout the book.

Chapter 2: Introduction to TensorFlow Extended introduces the TFX ecosystem, explains how tasks communicate with each other, and describes how TFX components work internally. We also take a look at the ML MetadataStore and how it is used in the context of TFX, and how Apache Beam runs the TFX components behind the scenes.

Chapter 3: Data Ingestion discusses how to get data into our pipelines in a consistent way and also covers the concept of data versioning.

Chapter 4: Data Validation explains how the data that flows into your pipeline can be validated efficiently using TensorFlow Data Validation. This will alert you if new data changes substantially from previous data in a way that may affect your model's performance.

Chapter 5: Data Preprocessing focuses on preprocessing data (the feature engineering) using TensorFlow Transform to convert raw data to features suitable for training a machine learning model.

Chapter 6: Model Training discusses how you can train models within machine learning pipelines. We also explain the concept of model tuning.

Chapter 7: Model Analysis and Validation introduces useful metrics for understanding your model in production, including those that may allow you to uncover biases in the model's predictions, and discusses methods to explain your model's predictions. "Analysis and Validation in TFX" on page 124 explains how to control the versioning of your model when a new version improves on a metric. The model in the pipeline can be automatically updated to the new version.

Chapter 8: Model Deployment with TensorFlow Serving focuses on how to deploy your machine learning model efficiently. Starting off with a simple Flask implementation, we highlight the limitations of such custom model applications. We will introduce TensorFlow Serving and how to configure your serving instances. We also discuss its batching functionality and guide you through the setup of clients for requesting model predictions.

Chapter 9: Advanced Model Deployments with TensorFlow Serving discusses how to optimize your model deployments and how to monitor them. We cover strategies for optimizing your TensorFlow models to increase your performance. We also guide you through a basic deployment setup with Kubernetes.

Chapter 10: Advanced TensorFlow Extended introduces the concept of custom components for your machine learning pipelines so that you aren't limited by the standard components in TFX. Whether you want to add extra data ingestion steps or convert your exported models to TensorFlow Lite (TFLite), we will guide you through the necessary steps for creating such components.

Chapter 11: Pipelines Part I: Apache Beam and Apache Airflow connects all the dots from the previous chapters. We discuss how you can turn your components into pipelines and how you'll need to configure them for the orchestration platform of your choice. We also guide you through an entire end-to-end pipeline running on Apache Beam and Apache Airflow.

Chapter 12: Pipelines Part 2: Kubeflow Pipelines continues from the previous chapter and walks through end-to-end pipelines using Kubeflow Pipelines and Google's AI Platform.

Chapter 13: Feedback Loops discusses how to turn your model pipeline into a cycle that can be improved by feedback from users of the final product. We'll discuss what type of data to capture to improve the model for future versions and how to feed data back into the pipeline.

Chapter 14: Data Privacy for Machine Learning introduces the rapidly growing field of privacy-preserving machine learning and discusses three important methods for this: differential privacy, federated learning, and encrypted machine learning.

Chapter 15: The Future of Pipelines and Next Steps provides an outlook of technologies that will have an impact on future machine learning pipelines and how we will think about machine learning engineering in the years to come.

Appendix A: Introduction to Infrastructure for Machine Learning gives a brief introduction to Docker and Kubernetes.

Appendix B: Setting Up a Kubernetes Cluster on Google Cloud has some supplementary material on setting up Kubernetes on Google Cloud.

Appendix C: Tips for Operating Kubeflow Pipelines has some useful tips for operating your Kubeflow Pipelines setup, including an overview of the TFX command-line interface.

Conventions Used in This Book

The following typographical conventions are used in this book:

Italic
> Indicates new terms, URLs, email addresses, filenames, and file extensions.

`Constant width`
> Used for program listings, as well as within paragraphs to refer to program elements such as variable or function names, databases, data types, environment variables, statements, and keywords.

`Constant width bold`
> Shows commands or other text that should be typed literally by the user.

`Constant width italic`
> Shows text that should be replaced with user-supplied values or by values determined by context.

This element signifies a tip or suggestion.

This element signifies a general note.

This element indicates a warning or caution.

Using Code Examples

Supplemental material (code examples, etc.) is available for download at *https://oreil.ly/bmlp-git*.

If you have a technical question or a problem using the code examples, please email *bookquestions@oreilly.com* and *buildingmlpipelines@gmail.com*.

This book is here to help you get your job done. In general, if example code is offered with this book, you may use it in your programs and documentation. You do not need to contact us for permission unless you're reproducing a significant portion of the code. For example, writing a program that uses several chunks of code from this book does not require permission. Selling or distributing examples from O'Reilly books does require permission. Answering a question by citing this book and quoting example code does not require permission. Incorporating a significant amount of example code from this book into your product's documentation does require permission.

We appreciate, but do not require, attribution. An attribution usually includes the title, author, publisher, and ISBN. For example: "*Building Machine Learning Pipelines* by Hannes Hapke and Catherine Nelson (O'Reilly). Copyright 2020 Hannes Hapke and Catherine Nelson, 978-1-492-05319-4."

If you feel your use of code examples falls outside fair use or the permission given above, feel free to contact us at *permissions@oreilly.com*.

O'Reilly Online Learning

 For more than 40 years, *O'Reilly Media* has provided technology and business training, knowledge, and insight to help companies succeed.

Our unique network of experts and innovators share their knowledge and expertise through books, articles, and our online learning platform. O'Reilly's online learning platform gives you on-demand access to live training courses, in-depth learning paths, interactive coding environments, and a vast collection of text and video from O'Reilly and 200+ other publishers. For more information, visit *http://oreilly.com*.

How to Contact Us

Both authors would like to thank you for picking up this book and giving it your attention. If you would like to get in touch with them, you can contact them via their website *www.buildingmlpipelines.com* or via email at *buildingmlpipelines@gmail.com*. They wish you every success in building your own machine learning pipelines!

Please address comments and questions concerning this book to the publisher:

O'Reilly Media, Inc.
1005 Gravenstein Highway North
Sebastopol, CA 95472
800-998-9938 (in the United States or Canada)
707-829-0515 (international or local)
707-829-0104 (fax)

We have a web page for this book, where we list errata, examples, and any additional information. You can access this page at *https://oreil.ly/build-ml-pipelines*.

Email *bookquestions@oreilly.com* to comment or ask technical questions about this book.

For news and information about our books and courses, visit *http://oreilly.com*.

Find us on Facebook: *http://facebook.com/oreilly*

Follow us on Twitter: *http://twitter.com/oreillymedia*

Watch us on YouTube: *http://www.youtube.com/oreillymedia*

Acknowledgments

We've had so much support from many wonderful people throughout the process of writing this book. Thank you so much to everyone who helped make it a reality! We would like to give an especially big thank you to the following people.

Everyone at O'Reilly has been fantastic to work with throughout the whole life cycle of this book. To our editors, Melissa Potter, Nicole Taché, and Amelia Blevins, thank you for your amazing support, constant encouragement, and thoughtful feedback. Thank you also to Katie Tozer and Jonathan Hassell for their support along the way.

Thank you to Aurélien Géron, Robert Crowe, Margaret Maynard-Reid, Sergii Khomenko, and Vikram Tiwari, who reviewed the entire book and provided many helpful suggestions and insightful comments. Your reviews have made the final draft a better book. Thank you for your hours reviewing the book in such detail.

Thank you to Yann Dupis, Jason Mancuso, and Morten Dahl for your thorough and in-depth review of the machine learning privacy chapter.

We have had fantastic support from many wonderful people at Google. Thank you for helping us find and fix bugs, and thank you for making these tools available as open-source packages! As well as the Googlers mentioned, thanks especially to Amy Unruh, Anusha Ramesh, Christina Greer, Clemens Mewald, David Zats, Edd Wilder-James, Irene Giannoumis, Jarek Wilkiewicz, Jiayi Zhao, Jiri Simsa, Konstantinos Katsiapis, Lak Lakshmanan, Mike Dreves, Paige Bailey, Pedram Pejman, Sara Robinson, Soonson Kwon, Thea Lamkin, Tris Warkentin, Varshaa Naganathan, Zhitao Li, and Zohar Yahav.

Thanks go out to the TensorFlow and Google Developer Expert community and its amazing members. We owe deep gratitude to the community. Thank you for supporting this endeavor.

Thank you to the other contributors who helped in the various stages: Barbara Fusinska, Hamel Husain, Michał Jastrzębski, and Ian Hensel.

Thank you to the people at Concur Labs (past and present) and elsewhere in SAP Concur for great discussions and helpful ideas. In particular, thank you to John Dietz and Richard Puckett for your amazing support of the book.

Hannes

    I would like to thank my wonderful partner, Whitney, for her tremendous support throughout the course of writing this book. Thank you for your constant encouragement and feedback, as well as putting up with me spending long hours writing. Thank you to my family, especially my parents, who let me follow my dreams throughout the world.

This book would not have been possible without amazing friends. Thank you, Cole Howard for being a wonderful friend and teacher. Our collaboration back in the day kick-started this publication and my thinking about machine learning pipelines. To my friends, Timo Metzger and Amanda Wright: thank you for teaching me about the power of language. And thank you to Eva and Kilian Rambach as well as Deb and David Hackleman. Without your help, I wouldn't have made it all the way to Oregon.

I would like to thank my previous employers like Cambia Health, Caravel, and Talentpair for letting me implement concepts of this publication in production settings, even though the concepts were novel.

This publication would not have been possible without my coauthor, Catherine. Thank you for your friendship, your encouragement, and your endless patience. I am glad we met due to sheer randomness in life. I am very happy we accomplished this publication together.

Catherine

I've written a lot of words in this book, but there aren't words to express how much I appreciate the support I've had from my husband, Mike. Thank you for all your encouragement, cooking, helpful discussions, sarcasm, and insightful feedback. Thank you to my parents for planting the seed of programming so long ago—it took a while to grow, but you were right all along!

Thank you to all the wonderful communities I have been fortunate to be a part of. I've met so many great people through Seattle PyLadies, Women in Data Science, and the wider Python community. I really appreciate your encouragement.

And thank you to Hannes for inviting me on this journey! It wouldn't have happened without you! Your depth of knowledge, attention to detail, and persistence have made this whole project a success. And it's been a lot of fun, too!

## CHAPTER 1

Introduction

In this first chapter, we will introduce machine learning pipelines and outline all the steps that go into building them. We'll explain what needs to happen to move your machine learning model from an experiment to a robust production system. We'll also introduce our example project that we will use throughout the rest of the book to demonstrate the principles we describe.

Why Machine Learning Pipelines?

The key benefit of machine learning pipelines lies in the automation of the model life cycle steps. When new training data becomes available, a workflow which includes data validation, preprocessing, model training, analysis, and deployment should be triggered. We have observed too many data science teams manually going through these steps, which is costly and also a source of errors. Let's cover some details of the benefits of machine learning pipelines:

Ability to focus on new models, not maintaining existing models
> Automated machine learning pipelines will free up data scientists from maintaining existing models. We have observed too many data scientists spending their days on keeping previously developed models up to date. They run scripts manually to preprocess their training data, they write one-off deployment scripts, or they manually tune their models. Automated pipelines allow data scientists to develop new models, the fun part of their job. Ultimately, this will lead to higher job satisfaction and retention in a competitive job market.

Prevention of bugs
> Automated pipelines can prevent bugs. As we will see in later chapters, newly created models will be tied to a set of versioned data and preprocessing steps will be tied to the developed model. This means that if new data is collected, a new

model will be generated. If the preprocessing steps are updated, the training data will become invalid and a new model will be generated. In manual machine learning workflows, a common source of bugs is a change in the preprocessing step after a model was trained. In this case, we would deploy a model with different processing instructions than what we trained the model with. These bugs might be really difficult to debug since an inference of the model is still possible, but simply incorrect. With automated workflows, these errors can be prevented.

Useful paper trail

The experiment tracking and the model release management generate a paper trail of the model changes. The experiment will record changes to the model's hyperparameters, the used datasets, and the resulting model metrics (e.g., loss or accuracy). The model release management will keep track of which model was ultimately selected and deployed. This paper trail is especially valuable if the data science team needs to re-create a model or track the model's performance.

Standardization

Standardized machine learning pipelines improve the experience of a data science team. Due to the standardized setups, data scientists can be onboarded quickly or move across teams and find the same development environments. This improves efficiency and reduces the time spent getting set up on a new project. The time investment of setting up machine learning pipelines can also lead to an improved retention rate.

The business case for pipelines

The implementation of automated machine learning pipelines will lead to three key impacts for a data science team:

- More development time for novel models
- Simpler processes to update existing models
- Less time spent to reproduce models

All these aspects will reduce the costs of data science projects. But furthermore, automated machine learning pipelines will:

- Help detect potential biases in the datasets or in the trained models. Spotting biases can prevent harm to people who interact with the model. For example, Amazon's machine learning–powered resume screener (*https://oreil.ly/39rEg*) was found to be biased against women.

- Create a paper trail (via experiment tracking and model release management) that will assist if questions arise around data protection laws, such as Europe's General Data Protection Regulation (GDPR).

- Free up development time for data scientists and increase their job satisfaction.

When to Think About Machine Learning Pipelines

Machine learning pipelines provide a variety of advantages, but not every data science project needs a pipeline. Sometimes data scientists simply want to experiment with a new model, investigate a new model architecture, or reproduce a recent publication. Pipelines wouldn't be useful in these cases. However, as soon as a model has users (e.g., it is being used in an app), it will require continuous updates and fine-tuning. In these situations, we are back in the scenarios we discussed earlier about continuously updating models and reducing the burden of these tasks for data scientists.

Pipelines also become more important as a machine learning project grows. If the dataset or resource requirements are large, the approaches we discuss allow for easy infrastructure scaling. If repeatability is important, this is provided through the automation and the audit trail of machine learning pipelines.

Overview of the Steps in a Machine Learning Pipeline

A machine learning pipeline starts with the ingestion of new training data and ends with receiving some kind of feedback on how your newly trained model is performing. This feedback can be a production performance metric or feedback from users of your product. The pipeline includes a variety of steps, including data preprocessing, model training, and model analysis, as well as the deployment of the model. You can imagine that going through these steps manually is cumbersome and very error-prone. In the course of this book, we will introduce tools and solutions to automate your machine learning pipeline.

As you can see in Figure 1-1, the pipeline is actually a recurring cycle. Data can be continuously collected and, therefore, machine learning models can be updated. More data generally means improved models. And because of this constant influx of data, automation is key. In real-world applications, you want to retrain your models frequently. If you don't, in many cases accuracy will decrease because the training data is different from the new data that the model is making predictions on. If retraining is a manual process, where it is necessary to manually validate the new training data or analyze the updated models, a data scientist or machine learning engineer would have no time to develop new models for entirely different business problems.

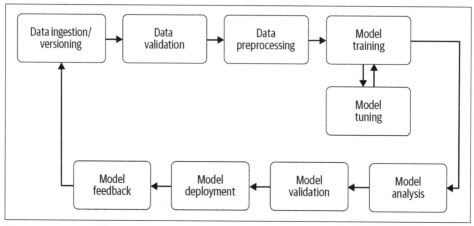

Figure 1-1. Model life cycle

A machine learning pipeline commonly includes the steps in the following sections.

Data Ingestion and Data Versioning

Data ingestion, as we describe in Chapter 3, is the beginning of every machine learning pipeline. In this pipeline step, we process the data into a format that the following components can digest. The data ingestion step does not perform any feature engineering (this happens after the data validation step). It is also a good moment to version the incoming data to connect a data snapshot with the trained model at the end of the pipeline.

Data Validation

Before training a new model version, we need to validate the new data. Data validation (Chapter 4) focuses on checking that the statistics of the new data are as expected (e.g., the range, number of categories, and distribution of categories). It also alerts the data scientist if any anomalies are detected. For example, if you are training a binary classification model, your training data could contain 50% of Class X samples and 50% of Class Y samples. Data validation tools provide alerts if the split between these classes changes, where perhaps the newly collected data is split 70/30 between the two classes. If a model is being trained with such an imbalanced training set and the data scientist hasn't adjusted the model's loss function, or over/under sampled category X or Y, the model predictions could be biased toward the dominant category.

Common data validation tools will also allow you to compare different datasets. If you have a dataset with a dominant label and you split the dataset into a training and validation set, you need to make sure that the label split is roughly the same between the two datasets. Data validation tools will allow you to compare datasets and highlight anomalies.

If the validation highlights anything out of the ordinary, the pipeline can be stopped here and the data scientist can be alerted. If a shift in the data is detected, the data scientist or the machine learning engineer can either change the sampling of the individual classes (e.g., only pick the same number of examples from each class), or change the model's loss function, kick off a new model build pipeline, and restart the life cycle.

Data Preprocessing

It is highly likely that you cannot use your freshly collected data and train your machine learning model directly. In almost all cases, you will need to preprocess the data to use it for your training runs. Labels often need to be converted to one or multi-hot vectors.[1] The same applies to the model inputs. If you train a model from text data, you want to convert the characters of the text to indices or the text tokens to word vectors. Since preprocessing is only required prior to model training and not with every training epoch, it makes the most sense to run the preprocessing in its own life cycle step before training the model.

Data preprocessing tools can range from a simple Python script to elaborate graph models. While most data scientists focus on the processing capabilities of their preferred tools, it is also important that modifications of preprocessing steps can be linked to the processed data and vice versa. This means if someone modifies a processing step (e.g., allowing an additional label in a one-hot vector conversion), the previous training data should become invalid and force an update of the entire pipeline. We describe this pipeline step in Chapter 5.

Model Training and Tuning

The model training step (Chapter 6) is the core of the machine learning pipeline. In this step, we train a model to take inputs and predict an output with the lowest error possible. With larger models, and especially with large training sets, this step can quickly become difficult to manage. Since memory is generally a finite resource for our computations, the efficient distribution of the model training is crucial.

Model tuning has seen a great deal of attention lately because it can yield significant performance improvements and provide a competitive edge. Depending on your machine learning project, you may choose to tune your model before starting to

---

1 In supervised classification problems with multiple classes as outputs, it's often necessary to convert from a category to a vector such as (0,1,0), which is a one-hot vector, or from a list of categories to a vector such as (1,1,0), which is a multi-hot vector.

think about machine learning pipelines or you may want to tune it as part of your pipeline. Because our pipelines are scalable, thanks to their underlying architecture, we can spin up a large number of models in parallel or in sequence. This lets us pick out the optimal model hyperparameters for our final production model.

Model Analysis

Generally, we would use accuracy or loss to determine the optimal set of model parameters. But once we have settled on the final version of the model, it's extremely useful to carry out a more in-depth analysis of the model's performance (described in Chapter 7). This may include calculating other metrics such as precision, recall, and AUC (area under the curve), or calculating performance on a larger dataset than the validation set used in training.

Another reason for an in-depth model analysis is to check that the model's predictions are fair. It's impossible to tell how the model will perform for different groups of users unless the dataset is sliced and the performance is calculated for each slice. We can also investigate the model's dependence on features used in training and explore how the model's predictions would change if we altered the features of a single training example.

Similar to the model-tuning step and the final selection of the best performing model, this workflow step requires a review by a data scientist. However, we will demonstrate how the entire analysis can be automated with only the final review done by a human. The automation will keep the analysis of the models consistent and comparable against other analyses.

Model Versioning

The purpose of the model versioning and validation step is to keep track of which model, set of hyperparameters, and datasets have been selected as the next version to be deployed.

Semantic versioning in software engineering requires you to increase the major version number when you make an incompatible change in your API or when you add major features. Otherwise, you increase the minor version number. Model release management has another degree of freedom: the dataset. There are situations in which you can achieve a significant difference of model performance without changing a single model parameter or architecture description by providing significantly more and/or better data for the training process. Does that performance increase warrant a major version upgrade?

While the answer to this question might be different for every data science team, it is essential to document all inputs into a new model version (hyperparameters, datasets, architecture) and track them as part of this release step.

Model Deployment

Once you have trained, tuned, and analyzed your model, it is ready for prime time. Unfortunately, too many models are deployed with one-off implementations, which makes updating models a brittle process.

Modern model servers allow you to deploy your models without writing web app code. Often, they provide multiple API interfaces like representational state transfer (REST) or remote procedure call (RPC) protocols and allow you to host multiple versions of the same model simultaneously. Hosting multiple versions at the same time will allow you to run A/B tests on your models and provide valuable feedback about your model improvements.

Model servers also allow you to update a model version without redeploying your application, which will reduce your application's downtime and reduce the communication between the application development and the machine learning teams. We describe model deployment in Chapters 8 and 9.

Feedback Loops

The last step of the machine learning pipeline is often forgotten, but it is crucial to the success of data science projects. We need to close the loop. We can then measure the effectiveness and performance of the newly deployed model. During this step, we can capture valuable information about the performance of the model. In some situations, we can also capture new training data to increase our datasets and update our model. This may involve a human in the loop, or it may be automatic. We discuss feedback loops in Chapter 13.

Except for the two manual review steps (the model analysis step and the feedback step), we can automate the entire pipeline. Data scientists should be able to focus on the development of new models, not on updating and maintaining existing models.

Data Privacy

At the time of writing, data privacy considerations sit outside the standard machine learning pipeline. We expect this to change in the future as consumer concerns grow over the use of their data and new laws are brought in to restrict the usage of personal data. This will lead to privacy-preserving methods being integrated into tools for building machine learning pipelines.

We discuss several current options for increasing privacy in machine learning models in Chapter 14:

- Differential privacy, where math guarantees that model predictions do not expose a user's data

- Federated learning, where the raw data does not leave a user's device

- Encrypted machine learning, where either the entire training process can run in the encrypted space or a model trained on raw data can be encrypted

Pipeline Orchestration

All the components of a machine learning pipeline described in the previous section need to be executed or, as we say, *orchestrated*, so that the components are being executed in the correct order. Inputs to a component must be computed before a component is executed. The orchestration of these steps is performed by tools such as Apache Beam, Apache Airflow (discussed in Chapter 11), or Kubeflow Pipelines for Kubernetes infrastructure (discussed in Chapter 12).

While data pipeline tools coordinate the machine learning pipeline steps, pipeline artifact stores like the TensorFlow ML MetadataStore capture the outputs of the individual processes. In Chapter 2, we will provide an overview of TFX's MetadataStore and look behind the scenes of TFX and its pipeline components.

Why Pipeline Orchestration?

In 2015, a group of machine learning engineers at Google concluded that one of the reasons machine learning projects often fail is that most projects come with custom code to bridge the gap between machine learning pipeline steps.[2] However, this custom code doesn't transfer easily from one project to the next. The researchers summarized their findings in the paper "Hidden Technical Debt in Machine Learning Systems."[3] The authors argue in this paper that the *glue code* between the pipeline steps is often brittle and that custom scripts don't scale beyond specific cases. Over time, tools like Apache Beam, Apache Airflow, or Kubeflow Pipelines have been developed. These tools can be used to manage the machine learning pipeline tasks; they allow a standardized orchestration and an abstraction of the glue code between tasks.

While it might seem cumbersome at first to learn a new tool (e.g., Beam or Airflow) or a new framework (e.g., Kubeflow) and set up an additional machine learning

---

2 Google started an internal project called Sibyl in 2007 to manage an internal machine learning production pipeline. However, in 2015, the topic gained wider attention when D. Sculley et al. published their learnings of machine learning pipelines, "Hidden Technical Debt in Machine Learning Systems" (*https://oreil.ly/qVlYb*).

3 D. Sculley et al., "Hidden Technical Debt in Machine Learning Systems," *Google, Inc.* (2015).

infrastructure (e.g., Kubernetes), the time investment will pay off very soon. By not adopting standardized machine learning pipelines, data science teams will face unique project setups, arbitrary log file locations, unique debugging steps, etc. The list of complications can be endless.

Directed Acyclic Graphs

Pipeline tools like Apache Beam, Apache Airflow, and Kubeflow Pipelines manage the flow of tasks through a graph representation of the task dependencies.

As the example graph in Figure 1-2 shows, the pipeline steps are directed. This means that a pipeline starts with Task A and ends with Task E, which guarantees that the path of execution is clearly defined by the tasks' dependencies. Directed graphs avoid situations where some tasks start without all dependencies fully computed. Since we know that we must preprocess our training data before training a model, the representation as a directed graph prevents the training task from being executed before the preprocessing step is completed.

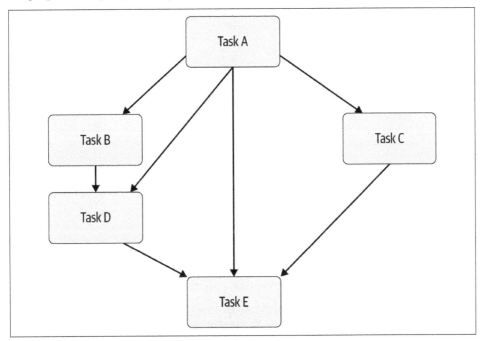

Figure 1-2. Example directed acyclic graph

Pipeline graphs must also be acyclic, meaning that a graph isn't linking to a previously completed task. This would mean that the pipeline could run endlessly and therefore wouldn't finish the workflow.

Because of the two conditions (being *directed* and *acyclic*), pipeline graphs are called *directed acyclic graphs* (DAGs). You will discover DAGs are a central concept behind most workflow tools. We will discuss more details about how these graphs are executed in Chapters 11 and 12.

Our Example Project

To follow along with this book, we have created an example project using open source data. The dataset is a collection of consumer complaints about financial products in the United States, and it contains a mixture of structured data (categorical/numeric data) and unstructured data (text). The data is taken from the Consumer Finance Protection Bureau (*https://oreil.ly/0RVBG*).

Figure 1-3 shows a sample from this dataset.

	product	issue	consumer_complaint_narrative	company	state	company_response	timely_response	consumer_disputed
0	Mortgage	Loan servicing, payments, escrow account	My mortgage servicing provider (XXXX) transf...	SunTrust Banks, Inc.	TX	Closed with non-monetary relief	Yes	No
1	Debt collection	Cont'd attempts collect debt not owed	I HAVE NEVER RECEIVED ANY FORM OF NOTIFICATION...	ERC	CA	Closed with non-monetary relief	Yes	No
2	Debt collection	Disclosure verification of debt	i contacted walmart and the manager there said...	Synchrony Financial	MA	Closed with non-monetary relief	Yes	No
3	Credit reporting	Credit reporting company's investigation	I have filed multiple complaints XXXX on this ...	TransUnion Intermediate Holdings, Inc.	NY	Closed with explanation	Yes	Yes
4	Bank account or service	Account opening, closing, or management	Sofi has ignored my request to stop sending me...	Social Finance, Inc.	TX	Closed with explanation	Yes	No

Figure 1-3. Data sample

The machine learning problem is, given data about the complaint, to predict whether the complaint was disputed by the consumer. In this dataset, 30% of complaints are disputed, so the dataset is not balanced.

Project Structure

We have provided our example project as a GitHub repo (*https://oreil.ly/bmlp-git*), and you can clone it as normal using the following command:

```
$ git clone https://github.com/Building-ML-Pipelines/\
        building-machine-learning-pipelines.git
```

Python Package Versions

To build our example project, we used Python 3.6–3.8. We used TensorFlow version 2.2.0 and TFX version 0.22.0. We will do our best to update our GitHub repo with future versions, but we cannot guarantee that the project will work with other language or package versions.

Our example project contains the following:

- A *chapters* folder containing notebooks for standalone examples from Chapters 3, 4, 7, and 14
- A *components* folder with the code for common components such as the model definition
- A complete interactive pipeline
- An example of a machine learning experiment, which is the starting point for the pipeline
- Complete example pipelines orchestrated by Apache Beam, Apache Airflow, and Kubeflow Pipelines
- A *utility* folder with a script to download the data

In the following chapters. we will guide you through the necessary steps to turn the example machine learning experiment, in our case a Jupyter Notebook with a Keras model architecture, into a complete end-to-end machine learning pipeline.

Our Machine Learning Model

The core of our example deep learning project is the model generated by the function get_model in the components/module.py script of our example project. The model predicts whether a consumer disputed a complaint using the following features:

- The financial product
- The subproduct
- The company's response to the complaint
- The issue that the consumer complained about
- The US state
- The zip code
- The text of the complaint (the narrative)

For the purpose of building the machine learning pipeline, we assume that the model architecture design is done and we won't modify the model. We discuss the model architecture in more detail in Chapter 6. But for this book, the model architecture is a very minor point. This book is all about what you can do with your model once you have it.

Goal of the Example Project

Over the course of this book, we will demonstrate the necessary frameworks, components, and infrastructure elements to continuously train our example machine learning model. We will use the stack in the architecture diagram shown in Figure 1-4.

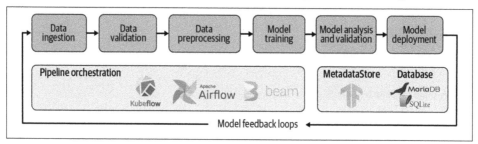

Figure 1-4. Machine learning pipeline architecture for our example project

We have tried to implement a generic machine learning problem that can easily be replaced with your specific machine learning problem. The structure and the basic setup of the machine learning pipeline remains the same and can be transferred to your use case. Each component will require some customization (e.g., where to ingest the data from), but as we will discuss, the customization needs will be limited.

Summary

In this chapter, we have introduced the concept of machine learning pipelines and explained the individual steps. We have also shown the benefits of automating this process. In addition, we have set the stage for the following chapters and included a brief outline of every chapter along with an introduction of our example project. In the next chapter, we will start building our pipeline!

## CHAPTER 2

Introduction to TensorFlow Extended

In the previous chapter, we introduced the concept of machine learning pipelines and discussed the components that make up a pipeline. In this chapter, we introduce *TensorFlow Extended* (TFX). The TFX library supplies all the components we will need for our machine learning pipelines. We define our pipeline tasks using TFX, and they can then be executed with a pipeline orchestrator such as Airflow or Kubeflow Pipelines. Figure 2-1 gives an overview of the pipeline steps and how the different tools fit together.

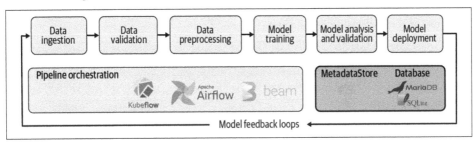

Figure 2-1. TFX as part of ML pipelines

In this chapter, we will guide you through the installation of TFX, explaining basic concepts and terminology that will set the stage for the following chapters. In those chapters, we take an in-depth look at the individual components that make up our pipelines. We also introduce Apache Beam (*https://beam.apache.org*) in this chapter. Beam is an open source tool for defining and executing data-processing jobs. It has two uses in TFX pipelines: first, it runs under the hood of many TFX components to carry out processing steps like data validation or data preprocessing. Second, it can be used as a pipeline orchestrator, as we discussed in Chapter 1. We introduce Beam here because it will help you understand TFX components, and it is essential if you wish to write custom components, as we discuss in Chapter 10.

What Is TFX?

Machine learning pipelines can become very complicated and consume a lot of overhead to manage task dependencies. At the same time, machine learning pipelines can include a variety of tasks, including tasks for data validation, preprocessing, model training, and any post-training tasks. As we discussed in Chapter 1, the connections between tasks are often brittle and cause the pipelines to fail. These connections are also known as the glue code from the publication "Hidden Technical Debt in Machine Learning Systems" (*https://oreil.ly/SLttH*). Having brittle connections ultimately means that production models will be updated infrequently, and data scientists and machine learning engineers loathe updating *stale* models. Pipelines also require well-managed distributed processing, which is why TFX leverages Apache Beam. This is especially true for large workloads.

Google faced the same problem internally and decided to develop a platform to simplify the pipeline definitions and to minimize the amount of task boilerplate code to write. The open source version of Google's internal ML pipeline framework is TFX.

Figure 2-2 shows the general pipeline architecture with TFX. Pipeline orchestration tools are the foundation for executing our tasks. Besides the orchestration tools, we need a data store to keep track of the intermediate pipeline results. The individual components communicate with the data store to receive their inputs, and they return the results to the data store. These results can then be inputs to following tasks. TFX provides the layer that combines all of these tools, and it provides the individual components for the major pipeline tasks.

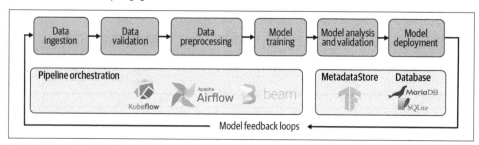

Figure 2-2. ML pipeline architecture

Initially, Google released some of the pipeline functionality as open source TensorFlow libraries (e.g., TensorFlow Serving is discussed in Chapter 8) under the umbrella of TFX libraries. In 2019, Google then published the open source glue code containing all the required pipeline components to tie the libraries together and to automatically create pipeline definitions for orchestration tools like Apache Airflow, Apache Beam, and Kubeflow Pipelines.

TFX provides a variety of pipeline components that cover a good number of use cases. At the time of writing, the following components were available:

- Data ingestion with `ExampleGen`
- Data validation with `StatisticsGen`, `SchemaGen`, and the `ExampleValidator`
- Data preprocessing with `Transform`
- Model training with `Trainer`
- Checking for previously trained models with `ResolverNode`
- Model analysis and validation with `Evaluator`
- Model deployments with `Pusher`

Figure 2-3 shows how the components of the pipeline and the libraries fit together.

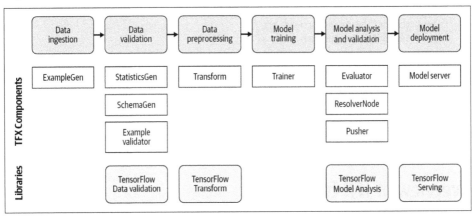

Figure 2-3. TFX components and libraries

We will discuss the components and libraries in greater detail in the following chapters. In case you need some nonstandard functionality, in Chapter 10 we discuss how to create custom pipeline components.

Stable Release of TFX

At the time of writing this chapter, a stable 1.X version of TFX hasn't been released. The TFX API mentioned in this and the following chapters might be subject to future updates. To the best of our knowledge, all the examples in this book will work with TFX version 0.22.0.

Installing TFX

TFX can easily be installed by running the following Python installer command:

```
$ pip install tfx
```

The tfx package comes with a variety of dependencies that will be installed automatically. It installs not only the individual TFX Python packages (e.g., TensorFlow Data Validation), but also their dependencies like Apache Beam.

After installing TFX, you can import the individual Python packages. We recommend taking this approach if you want to use the individual TFX packages (e.g., you want to validate a dataset using TensorFlow Data Validation, see Chapter 4):

```
import tensorflow_data_validation as tfdv
import tensorflow_transform as tft
import tensorflow_transform.beam as tft_beam
...
```

Alternatively, you can import the corresponding TFX component (if using the components in the context of a pipeline):

```
from tfx.components import ExampleValidator
from tfx.components import Evaluator
from tfx.components import Transform
...
```

Overview of TFX Components

A component handles a more complex process than just the execution of a single task. All machine learning pipeline components read from a channel to get input artifacts from the metadata store. The data is then loaded from the path provided by the metadata store and processed. The output of the component, the processed data, is then provided to the next pipeline components. The generic internals of a component are always:

- Receive some input
- Perform an action
- Store the final result

In TFX terms, the three internal parts of the component are called the *driver, executor*, and *publisher*. The driver handles the querying of the metadata store. The executor performs the actions of the components. And the publisher manages the saving of the output metadata in the MetadataStore. The driver and the publisher aren't moving any data. Instead, they read and write references from the MetadataStore. Figure 2-4 shows the structure of a TFX component.

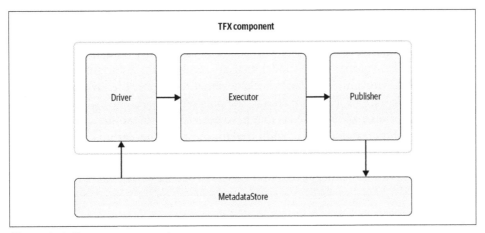

Figure 2-4. Component overview

The inputs and outputs of the components are called *artifacts*. Examples of artifacts include raw input data, preprocessed data, and trained models. Each artifact is associated with metadata stored in the MetadataStore. The artifact metadata consists of an artifact type as well as artifact properties. This artifact setup guarantees that the components can exchange data effectively. TFX currently provides ten different types of artifacts, which we review in the following chapters.

What Is ML Metadata?

The components of TFX "communicate" through *metadata*; instead of passing artifacts directly between the pipeline components, the components consume and publish references to pipeline artifacts. An artifact could be, for example, a raw dataset, a transform graph, or an exported model. Therefore, the metadata is the backbone of our TFX pipelines. One advantage of passing the metadata between components instead of the direct artifacts is that the information can be centrally stored.

In practice, the workflow goes as follows: when we execute a component, it uses the ML Metadata (MLMD) API to save the metadata corresponding to the run. For example, the component driver receives the reference for a raw dataset from the metadata store. After the component execution, the component publisher will store the references of the component outputs in the metadata store. MLMD saves the metadata consistently to a MetadataStore, based on a storage backend. Currently, MLMD supports three types of backends:

- In-memory database (via SQLite)
- SQLite
- MySQL

Because the TFX components are so consistently tracked, ML Metadata provides a variety of useful functions. We can compare two artifacts from the same component. For example, we see this in Chapter 7 when we discuss model validation. In this particular case, TFX compares the model analysis results from a current run with the results from the previous run. This checks whether the more recently trained model has a better accuracy or loss compared to the previous model. The metadata can also be used to determine all the artifacts that have been based on another, previously created artifact. This creates a kind of audit trail for our machine learning pipelines.

Figure 2-5 shows that each component interacts with the MetadataStore, and the MetadataStore stores the metadata on the provided database backend.

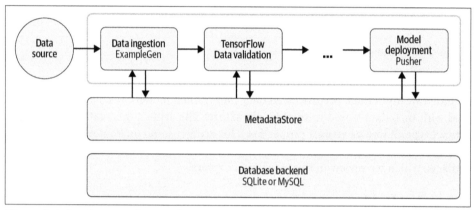

Figure 2-5. Storing metadata with MLMD

Interactive Pipelines

Designing and implementing machine learning pipelines can be frustrating at times. It is sometimes challenging to debug components within a pipeline, for example. This is why the TFX functionality around interactive pipelines is beneficial. In fact, in the following chapters, we will implement a machine learning pipeline step by step and demonstrate its implementations through an interactive pipeline. The pipeline runs in a Jupyter Notebook, and the components' artifacts can be immediately reviewed. Once you have confirmed the full functionality of your pipeline, in Chapters 11 and 12, we discuss how you can convert your interactive pipeline to a production-ready pipeline, for example, for execution on Apache Airflow.

Any interactive pipeline is programmed in the context of a Jupyter Notebook or a Google Colab session. In contrast to the orchestration tools we will discuss in Chapters 11 and 12, interactive pipelines are orchestrated and executed by the user.

You can start an interactive pipeline by importing the required packages:

```
import tensorflow as tf
from tfx.orchestration.experimental.interactive.interactive_context import \
    InteractiveContext
```

Once the requirements are imported, you can create a context object. The context object handles component execution and displays the component's artifacts. At this point, the InteractiveContext also sets up a simple in-memory ML MetadataStore:

```
context = InteractiveContext()
```

After setting up your pipeline component(s) (e.g., StatisticsGen), you can then execute each component object through the run function of the context object, as shown in the following example:

```
from tfx.components import StatisticsGen

statistics_gen = StatisticsGen(
    examples=example_gen.outputs['examples'])
context.run(statistics_gen)
```

The component itself receives the outputs of the previous component (in our case, the data ingestion component ExampleGen) as an instantiation argument. After executing the component's tasks, the component automatically writes the metadata of the output artifact to the metadata store. The output of some components can be displayed in your notebook. The immediate availability of the results and the visualizations is very convenient. For example, you can use the StatisticsGen component to inspect the features of the dataset:

```
context.show(statistics_gen.outputs['statistics'])
```

After running the previous context function, you can see a visual overview of the statistics of the dataset in your notebook, as shown in Figure 2-6.

Sometimes it can be advantageous to inspect the output artifacts of a component programmatically. After a component object has been executed, we can access the artifact properties, as shown in the following example. The properties depend on the specific artifact:

```
for artifact in statistics_gen.outputs['statistics'].get():
    print(artifact.uri)
```

This gives the following result:

```
'/tmp/tfx-interactive-2020-05-15T04_50_16.251447/StatisticsGen/statistics/2'
```

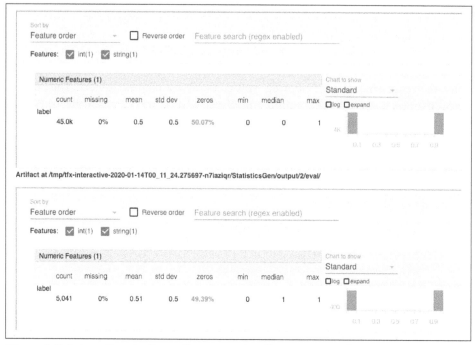

Figure 2-6. Interactive pipelines allow us to visually inspect our dataset

Throughout the following chapters, we will show how each component can be run in an interactive context. Then in Chapters 11 and 12, we will show the full pipeline and how it can be orchestrated by both Airflow and Kubeflow.

Alternatives to TFX

Before we take a deep dive into TFX components in the following chapters, let's take a moment to look at alternatives to TFX. The orchestration of machine learning pipelines has been a significant engineering challenge in the last few years, and it should come as no surprise that many major Silicon Valley companies have developed their own pipeline frameworks. In the following table, you can find a small selection of frameworks:

Company	Framework	Link
AirBnb	AeroSolve	*https://github.com/airbnb/aerosolve*
Stripe	Railyard	*https://stripe.com/blog/railyard-training-models*
Spotify	Luigi	*https://github.com/spotify/luigi*
Uber	Michelangelo	*https://eng.uber.com/michelangelo-machine-learning-platform/*
Netflix	Metaflow	*https://metaflow.org/*

Since the frameworks originated from corporations, they were designed with specific engineering stacks in mind. For example, AirBnB's AeroSolve focuses on Java-based inference code, and Spotify's Luigi focuses on efficient orchestration. TFX is no different in this regard. At this point, TFX architectures and data structures assume that you are using TensorFlow (or Keras) as your machine learning framework. Some TFX components can be used in combination with other machine learning frameworks. For example, data can be analyzed with TensorFlow Data Validation and later consumed by a scikit-learn model. However, the TFX framework is closely tied to TensorFlow or Keras models. Since TFX is backed by the TensorFlow community and more companies like Spotify are adopting TFX, we believe it is a stable and mature framework that will ultimately be adopted by a broader base of machine learning engineers.

Introduction to Apache Beam

A variety of TFX components and libraries (e.g., TensorFlow Transform) rely on Apache Beam to process pipeline data efficiently. Because of the importance for the TFX ecosystem, we would like to provide a brief introduction into how Apache Beam works behind the scenes of the TFX components. In Chapter 11, we will then discuss how to use Apache Beam for a second purpose: as a pipeline orchestrator tool.

Apache Beam offers you an open source, vendor-agnostic way to describe data processing steps that then can be executed on various environments. Since it is incredibly versatile, Apache Beam can be used to describe batch processes, streaming operations, and data pipelines. In fact, TFX relies on Apache Beam and uses it under the hood for a variety of components (e.g., TensorFlow Transform or TensorFlow Data Validation). We will discuss the specific use of Apache Beam in the TFX ecosystem when we talk about TensorFlow Data Validation in Chapter 4 and TensorFlow Transform in Chapter 5.

While Apache Beam abstracts away the data processing logic from its supporting runtime tools, it can be executed on multiple distributed processing runtime environments. This means that you can run the same data pipeline on Apache Spark or Google Cloud Dataflow without a single change in the pipeline description. Also, Apache Beam was not just developed to describe batch processes but to support streaming operations seamlessly.

Setup

The installation of Apache Beam is straightforward. You can install the latest version with:

```
$ pip install apache-beam
```

If you plan to use Apache Beam in the context of Google Cloud Platform—for example, if you want to process data from Google BigQuery or run our data pipelines on Google Cloud Dataflow (as described in "Processing Large Datasets with GCP" on page 57)—you should install Apache Beam as follows:

```
$ pip install 'apache-beam[gcp]'
```

If you plan to use Apache Beam in the context of Amazon Web Services (AWS) (e.g., if you want to load data from S3 buckets), you should install Apache Beam as follows:

```
$ pip install 'apache-beam[boto]'
```

If you install TFX with the Python package manager `pip`, Apache Beam will be automatically installed.

Basic Data Pipeline

Apache Beam's abstraction is based on two concepts: collections and transformations. On the one hand, Beam's collections describe operations where data is being read or written from or to a given file or stream. On the other hand, Beam's transformations describe ways to manipulate the data. All collections and transformations are executed in the context of a pipeline (expressed in Python through the context manager command `with`). When we define our collections or transformations in our following example, no data is actually being loaded or transformed. This only happens when the pipeline is executed in the context of a runtime environment (e.g., Apache Beam's DirectRunner, Apache Spark, Apache Flink, or Google Cloud Dataflow).

Basic collection example

Data pipelines usually start and end with data being read or written, which is handled in Apache Beam through collections, often called `PCollections`. The collections are then transformed, and the final result can be expressed as a collection again and written to a filesystem.

The following example shows how to read a text file and return all lines:

```
import apache_beam as beam

with beam.Pipeline() as p:  ❶
    lines = p | beam.io.ReadFromText(input_file)  ❷
```

❶ Use the context manager to define the pipeline.

❷ Read the text into a `PCollection`.

Similar to the `ReadFromText` operation, Apache Beam provides functions to write collections to a text file (e.g., `WriteToText`). The write operation is usually performed after all transformations have been executed:

```
with beam.Pipeline() as p:
    ...
    output | beam.io.WriteToText(output_file) ❶
```

❶ Write the output to the file *output_file*.

Basic transformation example

In Apache Beam, data is manipulated through transformations. As we see in this example and later in Chapter 5, the transformations can be chained by using the pipe operator |. If you chain multiple transformations of the same type, you have to provide a name for the operation, noted by the string identifier between the pipe operator and the right-angle brackets. In the following example, we apply all transformations sequentially on our lines extracted from the text file:

```
counts = (
    lines
    | 'Split' >> beam.FlatMap(lambda x: re.findall(r'[A-Za-z\']+', x))
    | 'PairWithOne' >> beam.Map(lambda x: (x, 1))
    | 'GroupAndSum' >> beam.CombinePerKey(sum))
```

Let's walk through this code in detail. As an example, we'll take the phrases *"Hello, how do you do?"* and *"I am well, thank you."*

The `Split` transformation uses `re.findall` to split each line into a list of tokens, giving the result:

```
["Hello", "how", "do", "you", "do"]
["I", "am", "well", "thank", "you"]
```

`beam.FlatMap` maps the result into a PCollection:

```
"Hello" "how" "do" "you" "do" "I" "am" "well" "thank" "you"
```

Next, the `PairWithOne` transformation uses `beam.Map` to create a tuple out of every token and the count (1 for each result):

```
("Hello", 1) ("how", 1) ("do", 1) ("you", 1) ("do", 1) ("I", 1) ("am", 1)
("well", 1) ("thank", 1) ("you", 1)
```

Finally, the `GroupAndSum` transformation sums up all individual tuples for each token:

```
("Hello", 1) ("how", 1) ("do", 2) ("you", 2) ("I", 1) ("am", 1) ("well", 1)
("thank", 1)
```

You can also apply Python functions as part of a transformation. The following example shows how the function `format_result` can be applied to earlier produced summation results. The function converts the resulting tuples into a string that then can be written to a text file:

```
def format_result(word_count):
    """Convert tuples (token, count) into a string"""
```

```
    (word, count) = word_count
    return "{}: {}".format(word, count)

output = counts | 'Format' >> beam.Map(format_result)
```

Apache Beam provides a variety of predefined transformations. However, if your preferred operation isn't available, you can write your own transformations by using the Map operators. Just keep in mind that the operations should be able to run in a distributed way to fully take advantage of the capabilities of the runtime environments.

Putting it all together

After discussing the individual concepts of Apache Beam's pipelines, let's put them all together in one example. The previous snippets and following examples are a modified version of the Apache Beam introduction (*https://oreil.ly/e0tj-*). For readability, the example has been reduced to the bare minimum Apache Beam code:

```
import re

import apache_beam as beam
from apache_beam.io import ReadFromText
from apache_beam.io import WriteToText
from apache_beam.options.pipeline_options import PipelineOptions
from apache_beam.options.pipeline_options import SetupOptions

input_file = "gs://dataflow-samples/shakespeare/kinglear.txt"  ❶
output_file = "/tmp/output.txt"

# Define pipeline options object.
pipeline_options = PipelineOptions()

with beam.Pipeline(options=pipeline_options) as p:  ❷
    # Read the text file or file pattern into a PCollection.
    lines = p | ReadFromText(input_file)  ❸

    # Count the occurrences of each word.
    counts = (  ❹
        lines
        | 'Split' >> beam.FlatMap(lambda x: re.findall(r'[A-Za-z\']+', x))
        | 'PairWithOne' >> beam.Map(lambda x: (x, 1))
        | 'GroupAndSum' >> beam.CombinePerKey(sum))

    # Format the counts into a PCollection of strings.
    def format_result(word_count):
        (word, count) = word_count
        return "{}: {}".format(word, count)

    output = counts | 'Format' >> beam.Map(format_result)

    # Write the output using a "Write" transform that has side effects.
    output | WriteToText(output_file)
```

❶ The text is stored in a Google Cloud Storage bucket.

❷ Set up the Apache Beam pipeline.

❸ Create a data collection by reading the text file.

❹ Perform the transformations on the collection.

The example pipeline downloads Shakespeare's *King Lear* and performs the token count pipeline on the entire corpus. The results are then written to the text file located at */tmp/output.txt*.

Executing Your Basic Pipeline

As an example, you can run the pipeline with Apache Beam's DirectRunner by executing the following command (assuming that the previous example code was saved as `basic_pipeline.py`). If you want to execute this pipeline on different Apache Beam runners like Apache Spark or Apache Flink, you will need to set the pipeline configurations through the `pipeline_options` object:

```
python basic_pipeline.py
```

The results of the transformations can be found in the designated text file:

```
$ head /tmp/output.txt*
KING: 243
LEAR: 236
DRAMATIS: 1
PERSONAE: 1
king: 65
...
```

Summary

In this chapter, we presented a high-level overview of TFX and discussed the importance of a metadata store as well as the general internals of a TFX component. We also introduced Apache Beam and showed you how to carry out a simple data transformation using Beam.

Everything we discussed in this chapter will be useful to you as you read through Chapters 3–7 on the pipeline components and the pipeline orchestration expalined in Chapters 11 and 12. The first step is to get your data into the pipeline, and we will cover this in Chapter 3.

## CHAPTER 3

Data Ingestion

With the basic TFX setup and the ML MetadataStore in place, in this chapter, we focus on how to ingest your datasets into a pipeline for consumption in various components, as shown in Figure 3-1.

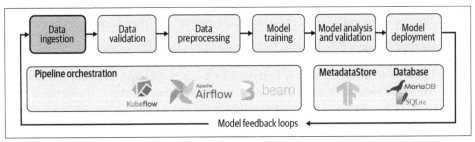

Figure 3-1. Data ingestion as part of ML pipelines

TFX provides us components to ingest data from files or services. In this chapter, we outline the underlying concepts, explain ways to split the datasets into training and evaluation subsets, and demonstrate how to combine multiple data exports into one all-encompassing dataset. We then discuss some strategies to ingest different forms of data (structured, text, and images), which have proven helpful in previous use cases.

Concepts for Data Ingestion

In this step of our pipeline, we read data files or request the data for our pipeline run from an external service (e.g., Google Cloud BigQuery). Before passing the ingested dataset to the next component, we divide the available data into separate datasets (e.g., training and validation datasets) and then convert the datasets into TFRecord files containing the data represented as tf.Example data structures.

TFRecord

TFRecord is a lightweight format optimized for *streaming* large datasets. While in practice, most TensorFlow users store serialized example Protocol Buffers in TFRecord files, the TFRecord file format actually supports any binary data, as shown in the following:

```
import tensorflow as tf

with tf.io.TFRecordWriter("test.tfrecord") as w:
    w.write(b"First record")
    w.write(b"Second record")

for record in tf.data.TFRecordDataset("test.tfrecord"):
    print(record)

tf.Tensor(b'First record', shape=(), dtype=string)
tf.Tensor(b'Second record', shape=(), dtype=string)
```

If TFRecord files contain tf.Example records, each record contains one or more features that would represent the columns in our data. The data is then stored in binary files, which can be digested efficiently. If you are interested in the internals of TFRecord files, we recommend the TensorFlow documentation (*https://oreil.ly/2-MuJ*).

Storing your data as *TFRecord* and tf.Examples provides a few benefits:

1. The data structure is system independent since it relies on Protocol Buffers, a cross-platform, cross-language library, to serialize data.

2. TFRecord is optimized for downloading or writing large amounts of data quickly.

3. tf.Example, the data structure representing every data row within TFRecord, is also the default data structure in the TensorFlow ecosystem and, therefore, is used in all TFX components.

The process of ingesting, splitting, and converting the datasets is performed by the ExampleGen component. As we see in the following examples, datasets can be read from local and remote folders as well as requested from data services like Google Cloud BigQuery.

Ingesting Local Data Files

The ExampleGen component can ingest a few data structures, including *comma-separated value* files (CSVs), precomputed TFRecord files, and serialization outputs from Apache Avro and Apache Parquet.

Converting comma-separated data to tf.Example

Datasets for structured data or text data are often stored in CSV files. TFX provides functionality to read and convert these files to `tf.Example` data structures. The following code example demonstrates the ingestion of a folder containing the CSV data of our example project:

```
import os
from tfx.components import CsvExampleGen
from tfx.utils.dsl_utils import external_input

base_dir = os.getcwd()
data_dir = os.path.join(os.pardir, "data")
examples = external_input(os.path.join(base_dir, data_dir)) ❶
example_gen = CsvExampleGen(input=examples) ❷

context.run(example_gen) ❸
```

❶ Define the data path.

❷ Instantiate the pipeline component.

❸ Execute the component interactively.

If you execute the component as part of an interactive pipeline, the metadata of the run will be shown in the Jupyter Notebook. The outputs of the component are shown in Figure 3-2, highlighting the storage locations of the training and the evaluation datasets.

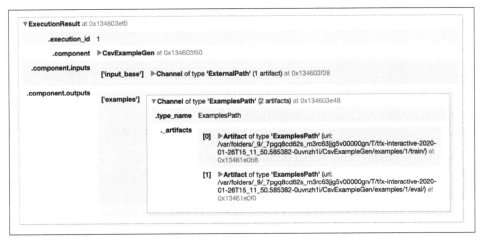

Figure 3-2. ExampleGen component output

Folder Structure

It is expected that the input path of *ExampleGen* only contains the data files. The component tries to consume all existing files within the path level. Any additional files (e.g., metadata files) can't be consumed by the component and make the component step fail. The component is also not stepping through existing subdirectories unless it is configured as an input pattern.

Importing existing TFRecord Files

Sometimes our data can't be expressed efficiently as CSVs (e.g., when we want to load images for computer vision problems or large corpora for natural language processing problems). In these cases, it is recommended to convert the datasets to TFRecord data structures and then load the saved TFRecord files with the `ImportExampleGen` component. If you would like to perform the conversion of your data to TFRecord files as part of the pipeline, take a look at Chapter 10, in which we discuss the development of custom TFX components including a data ingestion component. TFRecord files can be ingested as shown in the following example:

```
import os
from tfx.components import ImportExampleGen
from tfx.utils.dsl_utils import external_input

base_dir = os.getcwd()
data_dir = os.path.join(os.pardir, "tfrecord_data")
examples = external_input(os.path.join(base_dir, data_dir))
example_gen = ImportExampleGen(input=examples)

context.run(example_gen)
```

Since the datasets are already stored as `tf.Example` records within the TFRecord files, they can be imported and don't need any conversion. The `ImportExampleGen` component handles this import step.

Converting Parquet-serialized data to tf.Example

In Chapter 2, we discussed the internal architecture of TFX components and the behavior of a component, which is driven by its executor. If we would like to load new file types into our pipeline, we can override the `executor_class` instead of writing a completely new component.

TFX includes `executor` classes for loading different file types, including Parquet serialized data. The following example shows how you can override the `executor_class` to change the loading behavior. Instead of using the `CsvExampleGen` or `ImportExampleGen` components, we will use a generic file loader component `FileBasedExampleGen`, which allows an override of the `executor_class`:

```
from tfx.components import FileBasedExampleGen ❶
from tfx.components.example_gen.custom_executors import parquet_executor ❷
from tfx.utils.dsl_utils import external_input

examples = external_input(parquet_dir_path)
example_gen = FileBasedExampleGen(
    input=examples,
    executor_class=parquet_executor.Executor) ❸
```

❶ Import generic file loader component.

❷ Import Parquet-specific executor.

❸ Override the executor.

Converting Avro-serialized data to tf.Example

The concept of overriding the `executor_class` can, of course, be expanded to almost any other file type. TFX provides additional classes, as shown in the following example for loading Avro-serialized data:

```
from tfx.components import FileBasedExampleGen ❶
from tfx.components.example_gen.custom_executors import avro_executor ❷
from tfx.utils.dsl_utils import external_input

examples = external_input(avro_dir_path)
example_gen = FileBasedExampleGen(
    input=examples,
    executor_class=avro_executor.Executor) ❸
```

❶ Import generic file loader component.

❷ Import the Avro-specific executor.

❸ Override the executor.

In case we want to load a different file type, we could write our custom executor specific to our file type and apply the same concepts of overriding the executor earlier. In Chapter 10, we will guide you through two examples of how to write your own custom data ingestion component and executor.

Converting your custom data to TFRecord data structures

Sometimes it is simpler to convert existing datasets to TFRecord data structures and then ingest them with the `ImportExampleGen` component as we discussed in "Importing existing TFRecord Files" on page 30. This approach is useful if our data is not available through a data platform that allows efficient data streaming. For example, if we are training a computer vision model and we load a large number of images into our pipeline, we have to convert the images to TFRecord data structures in the first place (more on this in the later section on "Image Data for Computer Vision Problems" on page 41).

In the following example, we convert our structured data into TFRecord data structures. Imagine our data isn't available in a CSV format, only in JSON or XML. The following example can be used (with small modifications) to convert these data formats before ingesting them to our pipeline with the `ImportExampleGen` component.

To convert data of any type to TFRecord files, we need to create a `tf.Example` structure for every data record in the dataset. `tf.Example` is a simple but highly flexible data structure, which is a key-value mapping:

```
{"string": value}
```

In the case of TFRecord data structure, a `tf.Example` expects a `tf.Features` object, which accepts a dictionary of features containing key-value pairs. The key is always a string identifier representing the feature column, and the value is a `tf.train.Feature` object.

Example 3-1. TFRecord data structure

```
Record 1:
tf.Example
    tf.Features
        'column A': tf.train.Feature
        'column B': tf.train.Feature
        'column C': tf.train.Feature
```

`tf.train.Feature` allows three data types:

- `tf.train.BytesList`
- `tf.train.FloatList`
- `tf.train.Int64List`

To reduce code redundancy, we'll define helper functions to assist with converting the data records into the correct data structure used by `tf.Example`:

```
import tensorflow as tf

def _bytes_feature(value):
    return tf.train.Feature(bytes_list=tf.train.BytesList(value=[value]))

def _float_feature(value):
    return tf.train.Feature(float_list=tf.train.FloatList(value=[value]))

def _int64_feature(value):
    return tf.train.Feature(int64_list=tf.train.Int64List(value=[value]))
```

With the helper functions in place, let's take a look at how we could convert our demo dataset to files containing the TFRecord data structure. First, we need to read our original data file and convert every data record into a `tf.Example` data structure and then save all records in a TFRecord file. The following code example is an abbreviated version. The complete example can be found in the book's GitHub repository (*https://oreil.ly/bmlp-git-convert_data_to_tfrecordspy*) under *chapters/data_ingestion*.

```
import csv
import tensorflow as tf

original_data_file = os.path.join(
    os.pardir, os.pardir, "data",
    "consumer-complaints.csv")
tfrecord_filename = "consumer-complaints.tfrecord"
tf_record_writer = tf.io.TFRecordWriter(tfrecord_filename) ❶

with open(original_data_file) as csv_file:
    reader = csv.DictReader(csv_file, delimiter=",", quotechar='"')
    for row in reader:
        example = tf.train.Example(features=tf.train.Features(feature={ ❷
            "product": _bytes_feature(row["product"]),
            "sub_product": _bytes_feature(row["sub_product"]),
            "issue": _bytes_feature(row["issue"]),
            "sub_issue": _bytes_feature(row["sub_issue"]),
            "state": _bytes_feature(row["state"]),
            "zip_code": _int64_feature(int(float(row["zip_code"]))),
            "company": _bytes_feature(row["company"]),
            "company_response": _bytes_feature(row["company_response"]),
            "consumer_complaint_narrative": \
                _bytes_feature(row["consumer_complaint_narrative"]),
            "timely_response": _bytes_feature(row["timely_response"]),
            "consumer_disputed": _bytes_feature(row["consumer_disputed"]),
        }))
        tf_record_writer.write(example.SerializeToString()) ❸
    tf_record_writer.close()
```

❶ Creates a `TFRecordWriter` object that saves to the path specified in *tfrecord_filename*

❷ `tf.train.Example` for every data record

❸ Serializes the data structure

The generated TFRecord file *consumer-complaints.tfrecord* can now be imported with the `ImportExampleGen` component.

Ingesting Remote Data Files

The `ExampleGen` component can read files from remote cloud storage buckets like Google Cloud Storage or AWS Simple Storage Service (S3).[1] TFX users can provide the bucket path to the `external_input` function, as shown in the following example:

```
examples = external_input("gs://example_compliance_data/")
example_gen = CsvExampleGen(input=examples)
```

Access to private cloud storage buckets requires setting up the cloud provider credentials. The setup is provider specific. AWS is authenticating users through a user-specific *access key* and *access secret*. To access private AWS S3 buckets, you need to create a user access key and secret.[2] In contrast, the Google Cloud Platform (GCP) authenticates users through *service accounts*. To access private GCP Storage buckets, you need to create a service account file with the permission to access the storage bucket.[3]

Ingesting Data Directly from Databases

TFX provides two components to ingest datasets directly from databases. In the following sections, we introduce the `BigQueryExampleGen` component to query data from BigQuery tables and the `PrestoExampleGen` component to query data from Presto databases.

Google Cloud BigQuery

TFX provides a component to ingest data from Google Cloud's BigQuery tables. This is a very efficient way of ingesting structured data if we execute our machine learning pipelines in the GCP ecosystem.

Google Cloud Credentials

Executing the `BigQueryExampleGen` component requires that we have set the necessary Google Cloud credentials in our local environment. We need to create a service account with the required roles (at least *BigQuery Data Viewer* and *BigQuery Job User*). If you execute the component in the interactive context with Apache Beam or Apache Airflow, you have to specify the path to the service account credential file through the environment variable `GOOGLE_APPLICATION_CREDENTIALS`, as shown in the following code snippet. If you execute the component through Kubeflow Pipe-

---

1 Reading files from AWS S3 requires Apache Beam 2.19 or higher, which is supported since TFX version 0.22.

2 See the documentation for more details on managing AWS Access Keys (*https://oreil.ly/Dow7L*).

3 See the documentation for more details on how to create and manage service accounts (*https://oreil.ly/6y8WX*).

lines, you can provide the service account information through OpFunc functions introduced at "OpFunc Functions" on page 239.

You can do this in Python with the following:

```
import os
os.environ["GOOGLE_APPLICATION_CREDENTIALS"] =
    "/path/to/credential_file.json"
```

For more details, see the Google Cloud documentation (*https://oreil.ly/EPEs3*).

The following example shows the simplest way of querying our BigQuery tables:

```
from tfx.components import BigQueryExampleGen

query = """
    SELECT * FROM `<project_id>.<database>.<table_name>`
"""

example_gen = BigQueryExampleGen(query=query)
```

Of course, we can create more complex queries to select our data, for example, joining multiple tables.

Changes to the BigQueryExampleGen Component

In TFX versions greater than 0.22.0, the *BigQueryExampleGen* component needs to be imported from `tfx.extensions.goo gle_cloud_big_query`:

```
from tfx.extensions.google_cloud_big_query.example_gen \
    import component as big_query_example_gen_component
big_query_example_gen_component.BigQueryExampleGen(query=query)
```

Presto databases

If we want to ingest data from a Presto database, we can use `PrestoExampleGen`. The usage is very similar to `BigQueryExampleGen`, in which we defined a database query and then executed the query. The `PrestoExampleGen` component requires additional configuration to specify the database's connection details:

```
from proto import presto_config_pb2
from presto_component.component import PrestoExampleGen

query = """
    SELECT * FROM `<project_id>.<database>.<table_name>`
"""
presto_config = presto_config_pb2.PrestoConnConfig(
    host='localhost',
    port=8080)
example_gen = PrestoExampleGen(presto_config, query=query)
```

PrestoExampleGen Requires Separate Installation

Since TFX version 0.22, the *PrestoExampleGen* requires a separate installation process. After installing the protoc compiler,[4] you can install the component from source with the steps below:

```
$ git clone git@github.com:tensorflow/tfx.git && cd tfx/
$ git checkout v0.22.0
$ cd tfx/examples/custom_components/presto_example_gen
$ pip install -e .
```

After the installation, you will be able to import the *PrestoExample-Gen* component and its protocol buffer definitions.

Data Preparation

Each of the introduced ExampleGen components allows us to configure input settings (input_config) and output settings (output_config) for our dataset. If we would like to ingest datasets incrementally, we can define a span as the input configuration. At the same time, we can configure how the data should be split. Often we would like to generate a training set together with an evaluation and test set. We can define the details with the output configuration.

Splitting Datasets

Later in our pipeline, we will want to evaluate our machine learning model during the training and test it during the model analysis step. Therefore, it is beneficial to split the dataset into the required subsets.

Splitting one dataset into subsets

The following example shows how we can extend our data ingestion by requiring a three-way split: training, evaluation, and test sets with a ratio of 6:2:2. The ratio settings are defined through the hash_buckets:

```
from tfx.components import CsvExampleGen
from tfx.proto import example_gen_pb2
from tfx.utils.dsl_utils import external_input

base_dir = os.getcwd()
data_dir = os.path.join(os.pardir, "data")
output = example_gen_pb2.Output(
    split_config=example_gen_pb2.SplitConfig(splits=[ ❶
        example_gen_pb2.SplitConfig.Split(name='train', hash_buckets=6), ❷
        example_gen_pb2.SplitConfig.Split(name='eval', hash_buckets=2),
        example_gen_pb2.SplitConfig.Split(name='test', hash_buckets=2)
```

---

4 Visit the proto-lens GitHub for details on the protoc installation (*https://oreil.ly/h6FtO*).

```
    ]))

    examples = external_input(os.path.join(base_dir, data_dir))
    example_gen = CsvExampleGen(input=examples, output_config=output) ❸

    context.run(example_gen)
```

❶ Define preferred splits.

❷ Specify the ratio.

❸ Add `output_config` argument.

After the execution of the `example_gen` object, we can inspect the generated artifacts
by printing the list of the artifacts:

```
for artifact in example_gen.outputs['examples'].get():
    print(artifact)

Artifact(type_name: ExamplesPath,
    uri: /path/to/CsvExampleGen/examples/1/train/, split: train, id: 2)
Artifact(type_name: ExamplesPath,
    uri: /path/to/CsvExampleGen/examples/1/eval/, split: eval, id: 3)
Artifact(type_name: ExamplesPath,
    uri: /path/to/CsvExampleGen/examples/1/test/, split: test, id: 4)
```

In the following chapter, we will discuss how we investigate the produced datasets for
our data pipeline.

Default Splits

If we don't specify any output configuration, the `ExampleGen` component splits the dataset into a training and evaluation split with a
ratio of 2:1 by default.

Preserving existing splits

In some situations, we have already generated the subsets of the datasets externally,
and we would like to preserve these splits when we ingest the datasets. We can achieve this by providing an input configuration.

For the following configuration, let's assume that our dataset has been split externally
and saved in subdirectories:

```
└ data
    ├── train
    │   └ 20k-consumer-complaints-training.csv
    ├── eval
    │   └ 4k-consumer-complaints-eval.csv
```

```
└─ test
    └─ 2k-consumer-complaints-test.csv
```

We can preserve the existing input split by defining this input configuration:

```
import os

from tfx.components import CsvExampleGen
from tfx.proto import example_gen_pb2
from tfx.utils.dsl_utils import external_input

base_dir = os.getcwd()
data_dir = os.path.join(os.pardir, "data")

input = example_gen_pb2.Input(splits=[
    example_gen_pb2.Input.Split(name='train', pattern='train/*'),  ❶
    example_gen_pb2.Input.Split(name='eval', pattern='eval/*'),
    example_gen_pb2.Input.Split(name='test', pattern='test/*')
])

examples = external_input(os.path.join(base_dir, data_dir))
example_gen = CsvExampleGen(input=examples, input_config=input)  ❷
```

❶ Set existing subdirectories.

❷ Add the input_config argument.

After defining the input configuration, we can pass the settings to the ExampleGen component by defining the input_config argument.

Spanning Datasets

One of the significant use cases for machine learning pipelines is that we can update our machine learning models when new data becomes available. For this scenario, the ExampleGen component allows us to use *spans*. Think of a span as a snapshot of data. Every hour, day, or week, a batch *extract, transform, load* (ETL) process could make such a data snapshot and create a new span.

A span can replicate the existing data records. As shown in the following, *export-1* contains the data from the previous *export-0* as well as newly created records that were added since the *export-0* export:

```
└─ data
    ├─ export-0
    │   └─ 20k-consumer-complaints.csv
    ├─ export-1
    │   └─ 24k-consumer-complaints.csv
    └─ export-2
        └─ 26k-consumer-complaints.csv
```

We can now specify the patterns of the spans. The input configuration accepts a {SPAN} placeholder, which represents the number (0, 1, 2, …) shown in our folder structure. With the input configuration, the ExampleGen component now picks up the "latest" span. In our example, this would be the data available under folder *export-2*:

```
from tfx.components import CsvExampleGen
from tfx.proto import example_gen_pb2
from tfx.utils.dsl_utils import external_input

base_dir = os.getcwd()
data_dir = os.path.join(os.pardir, "data")

input = example_gen_pb2.Input(splits=[
    example_gen_pb2.Input.Split(pattern='export-{SPAN}/*')
])

examples = external_input(os.path.join(base_dir, data_dir))
example_gen = CsvExampleGen(input=examples, input_config=input)
context.run(example_gen)
```

Of course, the input definitions can also define subdirectories if the data is already split:

```
input = example_gen_pb2.Input(splits=[
    example_gen_pb2.Input.Split(name='train',
                                pattern='export-{SPAN}/train/*'),
    example_gen_pb2.Input.Split(name='eval',
                                pattern='export-{SPAN}/eval/*')
])
```

Versioning Datasets

In machine learning pipelines, we want to track the produced models together with the used datasets, which were used to train the machine learning model. To do this, it is useful to version our datasets.

Data versioning allows us to track the ingested data in more detail. This means that we not only store the file name and path of the ingested data in the ML MetadataStore (because it's currently supported by the TFX components) but also that we track more metainformation about the raw dataset, such as a hash of the ingested data. Such version tracking would allow us to verify that the dataset used during the training is still the dataset at a later point in time. Such a feature is critical for end-to-end ML reproducibility.

However, such a feature is currently not supported by the TFX ExampleGen component. If you would like to version your datasets, you can use third-party data versioning tools and version the data before the datasets are ingested into the pipeline.

Unfortunately, none of the available tools will write the metadata information to the TFX ML MetadataStore directly.

If you would like to version your datasets, you can use one of the following tools:

Data Version Control (DVC) (https://dvc.org)
DVC is an open source version control system for machine learning projects. It lets you commit hashes of your datasets instead of the entire dataset itself. Therefore, the state of the dataset is tracked (e.g., via `git`), but the repository isn't cluttered with the entire dataset.

Pachyderm (https://www.pachyderm.com)
Pachyderm is an open source machine learning platform running on Kubernetes. It originated with the concept of versioning for data ("Git for data") but has now expanded into an entire data platform, including pipeline orchestration based on data versions.

Ingestion Strategies

So far, we have discussed a variety of ways to ingest data into our machine learning pipelines. If you are starting with an entirely new project, it might be overwhelming to choose the right data ingestion strategy. In the following sections, we will provide a few suggestions for three data types: structured, text, and image data.

Structured Data

Structured data is often stored in a database or on a disk in file format, supporting tabular data. If the data exists in a database, we can either export it to CSVs or consume the data directly with the `PrestoExampleGen` or the `BigQueryExampleGen` components (if the services are available).

Data available on a disk stored in file formats supporting tabular data should be converted to CSVs and ingested into the pipeline with the `CsvExampleGen` component. Should the amount of data grow beyond a few hundred megabytes, you should consider converting the data into TFRecord files or store the data with Apache Parquet.

Text Data for Natural Language Problems

Text corpora can snowball to a considerable size. To ingest such datasets efficiently, we recommend converting the datasets to TFRecord or Apache Parquet representations. Using performant data file types allows an efficient and incremental loading of the corpus documents. The ingestion of the corpora from a database is also possible; however, we recommend considering network traffic costs and bottlenecks.

Image Data for Computer Vision Problems

We recommend converting image datasets from the image files to TFRecord files, but not to decode the images. Any decoding of highly compressed images only increases the amount of disk space needed to store the intermediate tf.Example records. The compressed images can be stored in tf.Example records as byte strings:

```
import tensorflow as tf

base_path = "/path/to/images"
filenames = os.listdir(base_path)

def generate_label_from_path(image_path):
    ...
    return label

def _bytes_feature(value):
    return tf.train.Feature(bytes_list=tf.train.BytesList(value=[value]))

def _int64_feature(value):
    return tf.train.Feature(int64_list=tf.train.Int64List(value=[value]))

tfrecord_filename = 'data/image_dataset.tfrecord'

with tf.io.TFRecordWriter(tfrecord_filename) as writer:
    for img_path in filenames:
        image_path = os.path.join(base_path, img_path)
        try:
            raw_file = tf.io.read_file(image_path)
        except FileNotFoundError:
            print("File {} could not be found".format(image_path))
            continue
        example = tf.train.Example(features=tf.train.Features(feature={
            'image_raw': _bytes_feature(raw_file.numpy()),
            'label': _int64_feature(generate_label_from_path(image_path))
        }))
        writer.write(example.SerializeToString())
```

The example code reads images from a provided path */path/to/images* and stores the image as byte strings in the tf.Example. We aren't preprocessing our images at this point in the pipeline. Even though we might save a considerable amount of disk space, we want to perform these tasks later in our pipeline. Avoiding the preprocessing at this point helps us to prevent bugs and potential training/serving skew later on.

We store the raw image together with labels in the tf.Examples. We derive the label for each image from the file name with the function generate_label_from_path in our example. The label generation is dataset specific; therefore, we haven't included it in this example.

After converting the images to TFRecord files, we can consume the datasets efficiently with the `ImportExampleGen` component and apply the same strategies we discussed in "Importing existing TFRecord Files" on page 30.

Summary

In this chapter, we discussed various ways of ingesting data into our machine learning pipeline. We highlighted the consumption of datasets stored on a disk as well as in databases. In the process, we also discussed that ingested data records, which are converted to `tf.Example` (store in TFRecord files) for the consumption of the downstream components.

In the following chapter, we will take a look at how we can consume the generated `tf.Example` records in our data validation step of the pipeline.

Data Validation

In Chapter 3, we discussed how we can ingest data from various sources into our pipeline. In this chapter, we now want to start consuming the data by validating it, as shown in Figure 4-1.

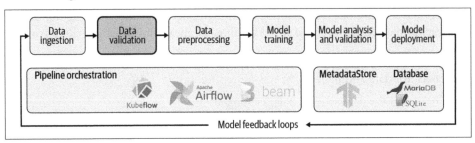

Figure 4-1. Data validation as part of ML pipelines

Data is the basis for every machine learning model, and the model's usefulness and performance depend on the data used to train, validate, and analyze the model. As you can imagine, without robust data, we can't build robust models. In colloquial terms, you might have heard the phrase: "garbage in, garbage out"—meaning that our models won't perform if the underlying data isn't curated and validated. This is the exact purpose of our first workflow step in our machine learning pipeline: data validation.

In this chapter, we first motivate the idea of data validation, and then we introduce you to a Python package from the TensorFlow Extended ecosystem called *Tensor-Flow Data Validation* (TFDV). We show how you can set up the package in your data science projects, walk you through the common use cases, and highlight some very useful workflows.

The data validation step checks that the data in your pipelines is what your feature engineering step expects. It assists you in comparing multiple datasets. It also highlights if your data changes over time, for example, if your training data is significantly different from the new data provided to your model for inference.

At the end of the chapter, we integrate our first workflow step into our TFX pipeline.

Why Data Validation?

In machine learning, we are trying to learn from patterns in datasets and to generalize these learnings. This puts data front and center in our machine learning workflows, and the quality of the data becomes fundamental to the success of our machine learning projects.

Every step in our machine learning pipeline determines whether the workflow can proceed to the next step or if the entire workflow needs to be abandoned and restarted (e.g., with more training data). Data validation is an especially important checkpoint because it catches changes in the data coming into the machine learning pipeline before it reaches the time-consuming preprocessing and training steps.

If our goal is to automate our machine learning model updates, validating our data is essential. In particular, when we say validating, we mean three distinct checks on our data:

- Check for data anomalies.
- Check that the data schema hasn't changed.
- Check that the statistics of our new datasets still align with statistics from our previous training datasets.

The data validation step in our pipeline performs these checks and highlights any failures. If a failure is detected, we can stop the workflow and address the data issue by hand, for example, by curating a new dataset.

It is also useful to refer to the data validation step from the data processing step, the next step in our pipeline. Data validation produces statistics around your data features and highlights whether a feature contains a high percentage of missing values or if features are highly correlated. This is useful information when you are deciding which features should be included in the preprocessing step and what the form of the preprocessing should be.

Data validation lets you compare the statistics of different datasets. This simple step can assist you in debugging your model issues. For example, data validation can compare the statistics of your training against your validation data. With a few lines of code, it brings any difference to your attention. You might train a binary classification model with a perfect label split of 50% positive labels and 50% negative labels, but the label split isn't 50/50 in your validation set. This difference in the label distribution ultimately will affect your validation metrics.

In a world where datasets continuously grow, data validation is crucial to make sure that our machine learning models are still up to the task. Because we can compare schemas, we can quickly detect if the data structure in newly obtained datasets has changed (e.g., when a feature is deprecated). It can also detect if your data starts to *drift*. This means that your newly collected data has different underlying statistics than the initial dataset used to train your model. This drift could mean that new features need to be selected or that the data preprocessing steps need to be updated (e.g., if the minimum or maximum of a numerical column changes). Drift can happen for a number of reasons: an underlying trend in the data, seasonality of the data, or as a result of a feedback loop, as we discuss in Chapter 13.

In the following sections, we will walk through these different use cases. However, before that, let's take a look at the required installation steps to get TFDV up and running.

TFDV

The TensorFlow ecosystem offers a tool that can assist you in data validation, TFDV. It is part of the TFX project. TFDV allows you to perform the kind of analyses we discussed previously (e.g., generating schemas and validating new data against an existing schema). It also offers visualizations based on the Google PAIR project *Facets* (*https://oreil.ly/ZXbqa*), as shown in Figure 4-2.

TFDV accepts two input formats to start the data validation: TensorFlow's TFRecord and CSV files. In common with other TFX components, it distributes the analysis using Apache Beam.

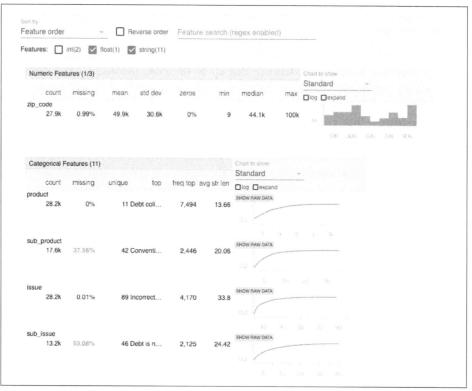

Figure 4-2. Screenshot of a TFDV visualization

Installation

When we installed the `tfx` package introduced in Chapter 2, TFDV was already installed as a dependency. If we would like to use TFDV as a standalone package, we can install it with this command:

```
$ pip install tensorflow-data-validation
```

After installing `tfx` or `tensorflow-data-validation`, we can now integrate our data validation into your machine learning workflows or analyze our data visually in a Jupyter Notebook. Let's walk through a couple of use cases in the following sections.

Generating Statistics from Your Data

The first step in our data validation process is to generate some summary statistics for our data. As an example, we can load our consumer complaints CSV data directly with TFDV and generate statistics for each feature:

```
import tensorflow_data_validation as tfdv
stats = tfdv.generate_statistics_from_csv(
```

```
    data_location='/data/consumer_complaints.csv',
    delimiter=',')
```

We can generate feature statistics from TFRecord files in a very similar way using the following code:

```
stats = tfdv.generate_statistics_from_tfrecord(
    data_location='/data/consumer_complaints.tfrecord')
```

We discuss how to generate TFRecord files in Chapter 3.

Both TFDV methods generate a data structure that stores the summary statistics for each feature, including the minimum, maximum, and average values.

The data structure looks like this:

```
datasets {
  num_examples: 66799
  features {
    type: STRING
    string_stats {
      common_stats {
        num_non_missing: 66799
        min_num_values: 1
        max_num_values: 1
        avg_num_values: 1.0
        num_values_histogram {
          buckets {
            low_value: 1.0
            high_value: 1.0
            sample_count: 6679.9
    ...
}}}}}
```

For numerical features, TFDV computes for every feature:

- The overall count of data records
- The number of missing data records
- The mean and standard deviation of the feature across the data records
- The minimum and maximum value of the feature across the data records
- The percentage of zero values of the feature across the data records

In addition, it generates a histogram of the values for each feature.

For categorical features, TFDV provides:

- The overall count of data records
- The percentage of missing data records
- The number of unique records

- The average string length of all records of a feature
- For each category, TFDV determines the sample count for each label and its rank

In a moment, you'll see how we can turn these statistics into something actionable.

Generating Schema from Your Data

Once we have generated our summary statistics, the next step is to generate a schema of our dataset. Data schema are a form of describing the representation of your datasets. A schema defines which features are expected in your dataset and which type each feature is based on (float, integer, bytes, etc.). Besides, your schema should define the boundaries of your data (e.g., outlining minimums, maximums, and thresholds of allowed missing records for a feature).

The schema definition of your dataset can then be used to validate future datasets to determine if they are in line with your previous training sets. The schemas generated by TFDV can also be used in the following workflow step when you are preprocessing your datasets to convert them to data that can be used to train machine learning models.

As shown in the following, you can generate the schema information from your generated statistics with a single function call:

```
schema = tfdv.infer_schema(stats)
```

`tfdv.infer_schema` generates a schema protocol defined by TensorFlow:[1]

```
feature {
  name: "product"
  type: BYTES
  domain: "product"
  presence {
    min_fraction: 1.0
    min_count: 1
  }
  shape {
    dim {
      size: 1
    }
  }
}
```

You can display the schema with a single function call in any Jupyter Notebook:

```
tfdv.display_schema(schema)
```

---

[1] You can find the protocol buffer definitions for the schema protocol in the TensorFlow repository (*https://oreil.ly/Qi263*).

And the results are shown in Figure 4-3.

Feature name	Type	Presence	Valency	Domain
'product'	STRING	required		'product'
'sub_product'	STRING	optional	single	'sub_product'
'issue'	STRING	required		'issue'
'sub_issue'	STRING	optional	single	'sub_issue'
'consumer_complaint_narrative'	BYTES	required		-
'company'	BYTES	required		-
'state'	STRING	optional	single	'state'
'zip_code'	BYTES	optional	single	-
'company_response'	STRING	required		'company_response'
'timely_response'	STRING	required		'timely_response'
'consumer_disputed'	INT	required		-

Figure 4-3. Screenshot of a schema visualization

In this visualization, `Presence` means whether the feature must be present in 100% of data examples (`required`) or not (`optional`). `Valency` means the number of values required per training example. In the case of categorical features, `single` would mean each training example must have exactly one category for the feature.

The schema that has been generated here may not be exactly what we need because it assumes that the current dataset is exactly representative of all future data as well. If a feature is present in all training examples in this dataset, it will be marked as `required`, but in reality it may be `optional`. We will show you how to update the schema according to your own knowledge of the dataset in "Updating the Schema" on page 52.

With the schema now defined, we can compare our training or evaluation datasets, or check our datasets for any problems that may affect our model.

Recognizing Problems in Your Data

In the previous sections, we discussed how to generate summary statistics and a schema for our data. These describe our data, but they don't spot potential issues with it. In the next few sections, we will describe how TFDV can help us spot problems in our data.

Comparing Datasets

Let's say we have two datasets: training and validation datasets. Before training our machine learning model, we would like to determine how representative the validation set is in regards to the training set. Does the validation data follow our training data schema? Are any feature columns or a significant number of feature values missing? With TFDV, we can quickly determine the answer.

As shown in the following, we can load both datasets and then visualize both datasets. If we execute the following code in a Jupyter Notebook, we can compare the dataset statistics easily:

```
train_stats = tfdv.generate_statistics_from_tfrecord(
    data_location=train_tfrecord_filename)
val_stats = tfdv.generate_statistics_from_tfrecord(
    data_location=val_tfrecord_filename)

tfdv.visualize_statistics(lhs_statistics=val_stats, rhs_statistics=train_stats,
                          lhs_name='VAL_DATASET', rhs_name='TRAIN_DATASET')
```

Figure 4-4 shows the difference between the two datasets. For example, the validation dataset (containing 4,998 records) has a lower rate of missing sub_issue values. This could mean that the feature is changing its distribution in the validation set. More importantly, the visualization highlighted that over half of all records don't contain sub_issue information. If the sub_issue is an important feature for our model training, we need to fix our data-capturing methods to collect new data with the correct issue identifiers.

The schema of the training data we generated earlier now becomes very handy. TFDV lets us validate any data statistics against the schema, and it reports any anomalies.

Figure 4-4. Comparison between training and validation datasets

Anomalies can be detected using the following code:

```
anomalies = tfdv.validate_statistics(statistics=val_stats, schema=schema)
```

And we can then display the anomalies with:

```
tfdv.display_anomalies(anomalies)
```

This displays the result shown in Table 4-1.

Table 4-1. Visualize the anomalies in a Jupyter Notebook

Feature name	Anomaly short description	Anomaly long description
"company"	Column dropped	The feature was present in fewer examples than expected.

The following code shows the underlying anomaly protocol. This contains useful information that we can use to automate our machine learning workflow:

```
anomaly_info {
  key: "company"
  value {
    description: "The feature was present in fewer examples than expected."
    severity: ERROR
    short_description: "Column dropped"
    reason {
      type: FEATURE_TYPE_LOW_FRACTION_PRESENT
      short_description: "Column dropped"
```

```
    description: "The feature was present in fewer examples than expected."
  }
  path {
    step: "company"
  }
}
}
```

Updating the Schema

The preceding anomaly protocol shows us how to detect variations from the schema that is autogenerated from our dataset. But another use case for TFDV is manually setting the schema according to our domain knowledge of the data. Taking the sub_issue feature discussed previously, if we decide that we need to require this feature to be present in greater than 90% of our training examples, we can update the schema to reflect this.

First, we need to load the schema from its serialized location:

```
schema = tfdv.load_schema_text(schema_location)
```

Then, we update this particular feature so that it is required in 90% of cases:

```
sub_issue_feature = tfdv.get_feature(schema, 'sub_issue')
sub_issue_feature.presence.min_fraction = 0.9
```

We could also update the list of US states to remove Alaska:

```
state_domain = tfdv.get_domain(schema, 'state')
state_domain.value.remove('AK')
```

Once we are happy with the schema, we write the schema file to its serialized location with the following:

```
tfdv.write_schema_text(schema, schema_location)
```

We then need to revalidate the statistics to view the updated anomalies:

```
updated_anomalies = tfdv.validate_statistics(eval_stats, schema)
tfdv.display_anomalies(updated_anomalies)
```

In this way, we can adjust the anomalies to those that are appropriate for our dataset.[2]

Data Skew and Drift

TFDV provides a built-in "skew comparator" that detects large differences between the statistics of two datasets. This isn't the statistical definition of skew (a dataset that is asymmetrically distributed around its mean). It is defined in TFDV as the

---

2 You can also adjust the schema so that different features are required in the training and serving environments. See the documentation (*https://oreil.ly/iSgKL*) for more details.

L-infinity norm of the difference between the `serving_statistics` of two datasets. If the difference between the two datasets exceeds the threshold of the L-infinity norm for a given feature, TFDV highlights it as an anomaly using the anomaly detection defined earlier in this chapter.

L-infinity Norm

The *L-infinity norm* is an expression used to define the difference between two vectors (in our case, the serving statistics). The L-infinity norm is defined as the maximum absolute value of the vector's entries.

For example, the L-infinity norm of the vector [3, –10, –5] is 10. Norms are often used to compare vectors. If we wish to compare the vectors [2, 4, –1] and [9, 1, 8], we first compute their difference, which is [–7, 3, –9], and then we compute the L-infinity norm of this vector, which is 9.

In the case of TFDV, the two vectors are the summary statistics of the two datasets. The norm returned is the biggest difference between these two sets of statistics.

The following code shows how you can compare the skew between datasets:

```
tfdv.get_feature(schema,
                'company').skew_comparator.infinity_norm.threshold = 0.01
skew_anomalies = tfdv.validate_statistics(statistics=train_stats,
                                        schema=schema,
                                        serving_statistics=serving_stats)
```

And Table 4-2 shows the results.

Table 4-2. Visualization of the data skew between the training and serving datasets

Feature name	Anomaly short description	Anomaly long description
"company"	High L-infinity distance between training and serving	The L-infinity distance between training and serving is 0.0170752 (up to six significant digits), above the threshold 0.01. The feature value with maximum difference is: Experian

TFDV also provides a `drift_comparator` for comparing the statistics of two datasets of the same type, such as two training sets collected on two different days. If drift is detected, the data scientist should either check the model architecture or determine whether feature engineering needs to be performed again.

Similar to this skew example, you should define your `drift_comparator` for the features you would like to watch and compare. You can then call `validate_statistics` with the two dataset statistics as arguments, one for your baseline (e.g., yesterday's dataset) and one for a comparison (e.g., today's dataset):

```
tfdv.get_feature(schema,
                 'company').drift_comparator.infinity_norm.threshold = 0.01
drift_anomalies = tfdv.validate_statistics(statistics=train_stats_today,
                                           schema=schema,
                                           previous_statistics=\
                                               train_stats_yesterday)
```

And this gives the result shown in Table 4-3.

Table 4-3. Visualization of the data drift between two training sets

Feature name	Anomaly short description	Anomaly long description
"company"	High L-infinity distance between current and previous	The L-infinity distance between current and previous is 0.0170752 (up to six significant digits), above the threshold 0.01. The feature value with maximum difference is: Experian

The L-infinity norm in both the `skew_comparator` and the `drift_comparator` is useful for showing us large differences between datasets, especially ones that may show us that something is wrong with our data input pipeline. Because the L-infinity norm only returns a single number, the schema may be more useful for detecting variations between datasets.

Biased Datasets

Another potential problem with an input dataset is bias. We define bias here as data that is in some way not representative of the real world. This is in contrast to fairness, which we define in Chapter 7 as predictions made by our model that have disparate impacts on different groups of people.

Bias can creep into data in a number of different ways. A dataset is always, by necessity, a subset of the real world—we can't hope to capture all the details about everything. The way that we sample the real world is always biased in some way. One of the types of bias we can check for is *selection bias*, in which the distribution of the dataset is not the same as the real-world distribution of data.

We can use TFDV to check for selection bias using the statistics visualizations that we described previously. For example, if our dataset contains Gender as a categorical feature, we can check that this is not biased toward the *male* category. In our consumer complaints dataset, we have State as a categorical feature. Ideally, the distribution of example counts across the different US states would reflect the relative population in each state.

We can see in Figure 4-5 that it doesn't (e.g., Texas, in third place, has a larger population than Florida in second place). If we find this type of bias in our data and we believe this bias may harm our model's performance, we can go back and collect more data or over/undersample our data to get the correct distribution.

Categorical Features (1/11)							Chart to show
							Standard
	count	missing	unique	top	freq top	avg str len	☐ log ☑ expand
State							
	9,282	1.45%	57	CA	1,359	2	

SHOW CHART

Value	lhs_statist...
CA	1359
FL	870
TX	751
NY	620
GA	375
NJ	372
PA	351
OH	327
IL	320
VA	312

Figure 4-5. Visualization of a biased feature in our dataset

You can also use the anomaly protocol described previously to automatically alert you to these kinds of problems. Using the domain knowledge you have of your dataset, you can enforce limits on numeric values that mean your dataset is as unbiased as possible—for example, if your dataset contains people's wages as a numeric feature, you can enforce that the mean of the feature value is realistic.

For more details and definitions of bias, Google's Machine Learning Crash Course (*https://oreil.ly/JtX5b*) has some useful material.

Slicing Data in TFDV

We can also use TFDV to slice datasets on features of our choice to help show whether they are biased. This is similar to the calculation of model performance on sliced features that we describe in Chapter 7. For example, a subtle way for bias to enter data is when data is missing. If data is not missing at random, it may be missing more frequently for one group of people within the dataset than for others. This can mean that when the final model is trained, its performance is worse for these groups.

In this example, we'll look at data from different US states. We can slice the data so that we only get statistics from California using the following code:

```
from tensorflow_data_validation.utils import slicing_util

slice_fn1 = slicing_util.get_feature_value_slicer(
    features={'state': [b'CA']}) ❶
slice_options = tfdv.StatsOptions(slice_functions=[slice_fn1])
slice_stats = tfdv.generate_statistics_from_csv(
    data_location='data/consumer_complaints.csv',
    stats_options=slice_options)
```

❶ Note that the feature value must be provided as a list of binary values.

We need some helper code to copy the sliced statistics to the visualization:

```
from tensorflow_metadata.proto.v0 import statistics_pb2

def display_slice_keys(stats):
    print(list(map(lambda x: x.name, slice_stats.datasets)))

def get_sliced_stats(stats, slice_key):
    for sliced_stats in stats.datasets:
        if sliced_stats.name == slice_key:
            result = statistics_pb2.DatasetFeatureStatisticsList()
            result.datasets.add().CopyFrom(sliced_stats)
            return result
    print('Invalid Slice key')

def compare_slices(stats, slice_key1, slice_key2):
    lhs_stats = get_sliced_stats(stats, slice_key1)
    rhs_stats = get_sliced_stats(stats, slice_key2)
    tfdv.visualize_statistics(lhs_stats, rhs_stats)
```

And we can visualize the results with the following code:

```
tfdv.visualize_statistics(get_sliced_stats(slice_stats, 'state_CA'))
```

And then compare the statistics for California with the overall results:

```
compare_slices(slice_stats, 'state_CA', 'All Examples')
```

The results of this are shown in Figure 4-6.

Figure 4-6. Visualization of data sliced by feature values

In this section, we have shown some useful features of TFDV that allow you to spot problems in your data. Next, we'll look at how to scale up your data validation using a product from Google Cloud.

Processing Large Datasets with GCP

As we collect more data, the data validation becomes a more time-consuming step in our machine learning workflow. One way of reducing the time to perform the validation is by taking advantage of available cloud solutions. By using a cloud provider, we aren't limited to the computation power of our laptop or on-premise computing resources.

As an example, we'll introduce how to run TFDV on Google Cloud's product Dataflow. TFDV runs on Apache Beam, which makes a switch to GCP Dataflow very easy.

Dataflow lets us accelerate our data validation tasks by parallelizing and distributing them across the allocated nodes for our data-processing task. While Dataflow charges for the number of CPUs and the gigabytes of memory allocated, it can speed up our pipeline step.

We'll demonstrate a minimal setup to distribute our data validation tasks. For more information, we highly recommend the extended GCP documentation (*https:// oreil.ly/X3cdi*). We assume that you have a Google Cloud account created, the billing details set up, and the `GOOGLE_APPLICATION_CREDENTIALS` environment variable set in your terminal shell. If you need help to get started, see Chapter 3 or the Google Cloud documentation (*https://oreil.ly/p4VTx*).

We can use the same method we discussed previously (e.g., `tfdv.generate_statis tics_from_tfrecord`), but the methods require the additional arguments `pipe line_options` and `output_path`. While `output_path` points at the Google Cloud bucket where the data validation results should be written, `pipeline_options` is an object that contains all the Google Cloud details to run our data validation on Google Cloud. The following code shows how we can set up such a pipeline object:

```
from apache_beam.options.pipeline_options import (
    PipelineOptions, GoogleCloudOptions, StandardOptions)

options = PipelineOptions()
google_cloud_options = options.view_as(GoogleCloudOptions)
google_cloud_options.project = '<YOUR_GCP_PROJECT_ID>'        ❶
google_cloud_options.job_name = '<YOUR_JOB_NAME>'             ❷
google_cloud_options.staging_location = 'gs://<YOUR_GCP_BUCKET>/staging'  ❸
google_cloud_options.temp_location = 'gs://<YOUR_GCP_BUCKET>/tmp'
options.view_as(StandardOptions).runner = 'DataflowRunner'
```

❶ Set your project's identifier.

❷ Give your job a name.

❸ Point toward a storage bucket for staging and temporary files.

We recommend creating a storage bucket for your Dataflow tasks. The storage bucket will hold all the datasets and temporary files.

Once we have configured the Google Cloud options, we need to configure the setup for the Dataflow workers. All tasks are executed on workers that need to be provisioned with the necessary packages to run their tasks. In our case, we need to install TFDV by specifying it as an additional package.

To do this, download the latest TFDV package (the binary `.whl` file)[3] to your local system. Choose a version which can be executed on a Linux system (e.g., `tensorflow_data_validation-0.22.0-cp37-cp37m-manylinux2010_x86_64.whl`).

---

3 Download TFDV packages (*https://oreil.ly/lhExZ*).

To configure the worker setup options, specify the path to the downloaded package in the `setup_options.extra_packages` list as shown:

```
from apache_beam.options.pipeline_options import SetupOptions

setup_options = options.view_as(SetupOptions)
setup_options.extra_packages = [
    '/path/to/tensorflow_data_validation'
    '-0.22.0-cp37-cp37m-manylinux2010_x86_64.whl']
```

With all the option configurations in place, you can kick off the data validation tasks from your local machine. They are executed on the Google Cloud Dataflow instances:

```
data_set_path = 'gs://<YOUR_GCP_BUCKET>/train_reviews.tfrecord'
output_path = 'gs://<YOUR_GCP_BUCKET>/'
tfdv.generate_statistics_from_tfrecord(data_set_path,
                                       output_path=output_path,
                                       pipeline_options=options)
```

After you have started the data validation with Dataflow, you can switch back to the Google Cloud console. Your newly kicked off job should be listed in a similar way to the one in Figure 4-7.

Figure 4-7. Google Cloud Dataflow Jobs console

You can then check the details of the running job, its status, and its autoscaling details, as shown in Figure 4-8.

You can see that with a few steps you can parallelize and distribute the data validation tasks in a cloud environment. In the next section, we'll discuss the integration of the data validation tasks into our automated machine learning pipelines.

Figure 4-8. Google Cloud Dataflow Job details

Integrating TFDV into Your Machine Learning Pipeline

So far, all methods we have discussed can be used in a standalone setup. This can be helpful to investigate datasets outside of the pipeline setup.

TFX provides a pipeline component called `StatisticsGen`, which accepts the output of the previous `ExampleGen` components as input and then performs the generation of statistics:

```
from tfx.components import StatisticsGen

statistics_gen = StatisticsGen(
    examples=example_gen.outputs['examples'])
context.run(statistics_gen)
```

Just like we discussed in Chapter 3, we can visualize the output in an interactive context using:

```
context.show(statistics_gen.outputs['statistics'])
```

This gives us the visualization shown in Figure 4-9.

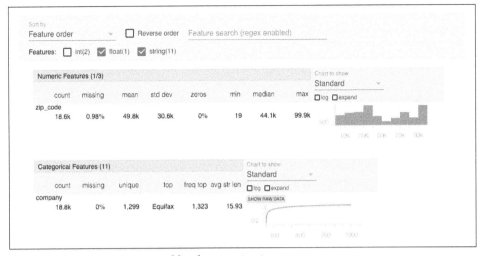

Figure 4-9. Statistics generated by the StatisticsGen component

Generating our schema is just as easy as generating the statistics:

```
from tfx.components import SchemaGen

schema_gen = SchemaGen(
    statistics=statistics_gen.outputs['statistics'],
    infer_feature_shape=True)
context.run(schema_gen)
```

The SchemaGen component only generates a schema if one doesn't already exist. It's a good idea to review the schema on the first run of this component and then manually adjust it if required as we discussed in "Updating the Schema" on page 52. We can then use this schema until it's necessary to change it, for example, if we add a new feature.

With the statistics and schema in place, we can now validate our new dataset:

```
from tfx.components import ExampleValidator

example_validator = ExampleValidator(
    statistics=statistics_gen.outputs['statistics'],
    schema=schema_gen.outputs['schema'])
context.run(example_validator)
```

 The ExampleValidator can automatically detect the anomalies against the schema by using the skew and drift comparators we described previously. However, this may not cover all the potential anomalies in your data. If you need to detect some other specific anomalies, you will need to write your own custom component as we describe in Chapter 10.

If the `ExampleValidator` component detects a misalignment in the dataset statistics or schema between the new and the previous dataset, it will set the status to *failed* in the metadata store, and the pipeline ultimately stops. Otherwise, the pipeline moves on to the next step, the data preprocessing.

Summary

In this chapter, we discussed the importance of data validation and how you can efficiently perform and automate the process. We discussed how to generate data statistics and schemas and how to compare two different datasets based on their statistics and schemas. We stepped through an example of how you could run your data validation on Google Cloud with Dataflow, and ultimately we integrated this machine learning step in our automated pipeline. This is a really important go/no go step in our pipeline, as it stops dirty data getting fed through to the time-consuming preprocessing and training steps.

In the following chapters, we will extend our pipeline setup by starting with data preprocessing.

Data Preprocessing

The data we use to train our machine learning models is often provided in formats our machine learning models can't consume. For example, in our example project, a feature we want to use to train our model is available only as *Yes* and *No* tags. Any machine learning model requires a numerical representation of these values (e.g., *1* and *0*). In this chapter, we will explain how to convert features into consistent numerical representations so that your machine learning model can be trained with the numerical representations of the features.

One major aspect that we discuss in this chapter is focusing on consistent preprocessing. As shown in Figure 5-1, the preprocessing takes place after data validation, which we discussed in Chapter 4. *TensorFlow Transform* (TFT), the TFX component for data preprocessing, allows us to build our preprocessing steps as TensorFlow graphs. In the following sections, we will discuss why and when this is a good workflow and how to export the preprocessing steps. In Chapter 6, we will use the preprocessed datasets and the preserved transformation graph to train and export our machine learning model, respectively.

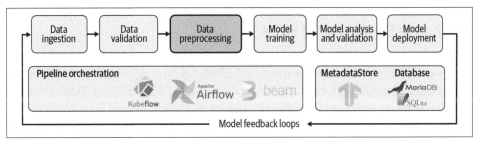

Figure 5-1. Data preprocessing as part of ML pipelines

Data scientists might see the preprocessing steps expressed as TensorFlow operations (operations) as too much overhead. After all, it requires different implementations than you might be used to when you write your preprocessing step with Python's pandas or numpy. We aren't advocating the use of TFT during the experimentation phase. However, as we demonstrate in the following sections, converting your preprocessing steps to TensorFlow operations when you bring your machine learning model to a production environment will help avoid training-serving skews as we discussed in Chapter 4.

Why Data Preprocessing?

In our experience, TFT requires the steepest learning curve of any TFX library because expressing preprocessing steps through TensorFlow operations is required. However, there are a number of good reasons why data preprocessing should be standardized in a machine learning pipeline with TFT, including:

- Preprocessing your data efficiently in the context of the entire dataset
- Scaling the preprocessing steps effectively
- Avoiding a potential training-serving skew

Preprocessing the Data in the Context of the Entire Dataset

When we want to convert our data into numerical representations, we often have to do it in the context of the entire dataset. For example, if we want to normalize a numerical feature, we have to first determine the minimum and maximum values of the feature in the training set. With the determined boundaries, we can then normalize our data to values between 0 and 1. This normalization step usually requires two passes over the data: one pass to determine the boundaries and one to convert each feature value. TFT provides functions to manage the passes over the data behind the scenes for us.

Scaling the Preprocessing Steps

TFT uses Apache Beam under the hood to execute preprocessing instructions. This allows us to distribute the preprocessing if needed on the Apache Beam backend of our choice. If you don't have access to Google Cloud's Dataflow product or an Apache Spark or Apache Flink cluster, Apache Beam will default back to its Direct Runner mode.

Avoiding a Training-Serving Skew

TFT creates and saves a TensorFlow graph of the preprocessing steps. First, it will create a graph to process the data (e.g., determine minimum/maximum values). Afterwards, it will preserve the graph with the determined boundaries. This graph can then be used during the inference phase of the model life cycle. This process guarantees that the model in the inference life cycle step sees the same preprocessing steps as the model used during the training.

What Is a Training-Serving Skew?

We speak of a training-serving skew when the preprocessing steps used during model training get out of line with the steps used during inference. In many cases, the data used to train models is processed in Python notebooks with pandas or in Spark jobs. When the model is deployed to a production setup, the preprocessing steps are implemented in an API before the data hits the model for the prediction. As you can see in Figure 5-2, these two processes require coordination to make sure the steps are always aligned.

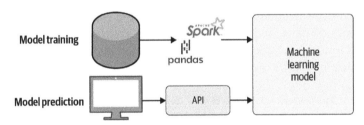

Figure 5-2. A commonly used machine learning setup

With TFT, we can avoid a misalignment of the preprocessing steps. As shown in Figure 5-3, the prediction-requesting client can now submit the raw data, and the preprocessing happens on the deployed model graph.

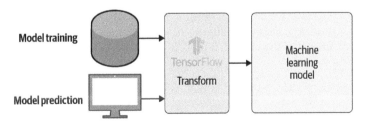

Figure 5-3. Avoiding the training-serving skew with TFT

Such a setup reduces the amount of coordination needed and simplifies deployments.

Deploying Preprocessing Steps and the ML Model as One Artifact

To avoid a misalignment between the preprocessing steps and the trained model, the exported model of our pipeline should include the preprocessing graph and the trained model. We can then deploy the model like any other TensorFlow model, but during our inference, the data will be preprocessed on the model server as part of the model inference. This avoids the requirement that preprocessing happen on the client side and simplifies the development of clients (e.g., web or mobile apps) that request the model predictions. In Chapters 11 and 12, we will discuss how the entire end-to-end pipeline produces such "combined" saved models.

Checking Your Preprocessing Results in Your Pipeline

Implementing the data preprocessing with TFT and the integrating the preprocessing in our pipeline gives us an additional benefit. We can generate statistics from the preprocessed data and check whether they still conform with our requirements to train a machine learning model. An example for this use case is the conversion of text to tokens. If a text contains a lot of new vocabulary, the unknown tokens will be converted to so-called *UNK* or *unknown* tokens. If a certain amount of our tokens are simply unknown, it is often difficult for the machine learning model to effectively generalize from the data, and therefore, the model accuracy will be affected. In our pipelines, we can now check the preprocessing step results by generating statistics (shown in Chapter 4) after the preprocessing step.

The Difference Between tf.data and tf.transform

There is often confusion between *tf.data* and *tf.transform*. *tf.data* is a TensorFlow API for building efficient input pipelines for model training with TensorFlow. The goal of the library is to utilize hardware resources optimally, such as host CPU and RAM, for the data ingestion and preprocessing that happens during training. *tf.transform*, on the other hand, is used to express preprocessing that should happen both in training and inference time. The library makes it possible to perform a full-pass analysis of the input data (e.g., to compute vocabulary or statistics used for data normalization), and this analysis is executed ahead of the training.

Data Preprocessing with TFT

The library for preprocessing data within the TensorFlow ecosystem is TFT. Like TFDV, it is part of the TFX project.

TFT processes the data that we ingested into our pipeline with the earlier generated dataset schema, and it outputs two artifacts:

- Preprocessed training and evaluation datasets in the TFRecord format. The produced datasets can be consumed downstream in the `Trainer` component of our pipeline.
- Exported preprocessing graph (with assets), which will be used when we'll export our machine learning model.

The key to TFT is the `preprocessing_fn` function, as shown in Figure 5-4. The function defines all transformations we want to apply to the *raw* data. When we execute the `Transform` component, the `preprocessing_fn` function will receive the raw data, apply the transformation, and return the processed data. The data is provided as TensorFlow Tensors or SparseTensors (depending on the feature). All transformations applied to the tensors have to be TensorFlow operations. This allows TFT to effectively distribute the preprocessing steps.

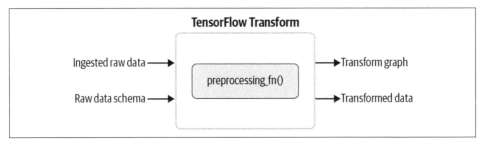

Figure 5-4. Overview of TFT

TFT Functions

TFT functions that perform elaborate processing steps behind the scenes like `tft.compute_and_apply_vocabulary` can be spotted by the prefix *tft*. It is common practice to map TFT to the abbreviation *tft* in the Python namespace. Normal TensorFlow operations will be loaded with the common prefix *tf*, as in `tf.reshape`.

TensorFlow Transform also provides useful functions (e.g., `tft.bucketize`, `tft.com pute_and_apply_vocabulary`, or `tft.scale_to_z_score`). When these functions are applied to a dataset feature, they will perform the required pass over the data and then apply the obtained boundaries to the data. For example, `tft.com` pute_and_apply_vocabulary will generate the vocabulary set of a corpus, apply the created token-to-index mapping to the feature, and return the index value. The function can limit the number of vocab tokens to the top n of the most relevant tokens. In the following sections, we will be highlighting some of the most useful TFT operations.

Installation

When we installed the tfx package as introduced in Chapter 2, TFT was installed as a dependency. If we would like to use TFT as a standalone package, we can install the PyPI package with:

```
$ pip install tensorflow-transform
```

After installing tfx or tensorflow-transform, we can integrate our preprocessing steps into our machine learning pipelines. Let's walk through a couple use cases.

Preprocessing Strategies

As we discussed previously, the applied transformations are defined in a function called preprocessing_fn(). The function will then be consumed by our Transform pipeline component or by our standalone setup of TFT. Here is an example of a preprocessing function that we will discuss in detail in the following sections:

```
def preprocessing_fn(inputs):
    x = inputs['x']
    x_normalized = tft.scale_to_0_1(x)
    return {
        'x_xf': x_normalized
    }
```

The function receives a batch of inputs as a Python dictionary. The key is the name of the feature and the values representing the raw data before the preprocessing are applied. First, TFT will perform an analysis step, as shown in Figure 5-5. In the case of our little demo example, it will determine the minimum and maximum values of our feature through a full pass over the data. This step can happen in a distributed fashion thanks to the execution of the preprocessing steps on Apache Beam.

In the second pass over the data, the determined values (in our case, the min and max of the feature column) are being used to scale our feature x between 0 and 1, as shown in Figure 5-6.

TFT also generates a graph for the prediction with the preserved minimum and maximum values. This will guarantee a consistent execution.

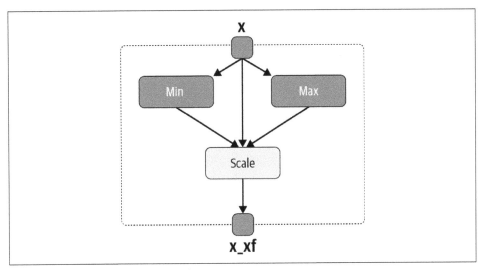

Figure 5-5. Analysis step during the TFT execution

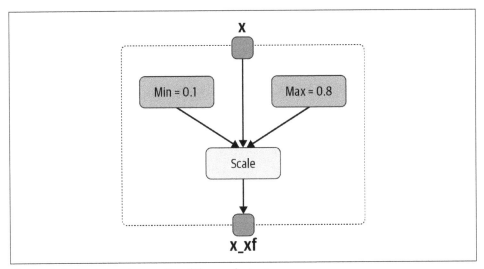

Figure 5-6. Applying the results of the analysis step

preprocessing_fn()

Please note that TFT will build a graph out of the `preprocess ing_fn()` function and it will run in its own session. It is expected that the function returns a dictionary with the transformed features as values of the Python dictionary.

Best Practices

During our work with TFT, we have learned a good number of lessons. Here are some of them:

Feature names matter
> The naming of the output features of the preprocessing is important. As you will see in the following TFT implementations, we reuse the name of the input feature and append _xf. Also, the names of the input nodes of the TensorFlow models need to match the names of the output features from the `preprocess ing_fn` function.

Consider the data types
> TFT limits the data types of the output features. It exports all preprocessed features as either `tf.string`, `tf.float32`, or `tf.int64` values. This is important in case your model can't consume these data types. Some models from TensorFlow Hub require inputs to be presented as `tf.int32` values (e.g., BERT models). We can avoid that situation if we cast the inputs to the correct data types inside our models or if we convert the data types in the estimator input functions.

Preprocessing happens in batches
> When you write preprocessing functions, you might think of it as processing one data row at a time. In fact, TFT performs the operations in batches. This is why we will need to reshape the output of the `preprocessing_fn()` function to a Tensor or SparseTensor when we use it in the context of our `Transform` component.

Remember, no eager execution
> The functions inside of the `preprocessing_fn()` function need to be represented by TensorFlow ops. If you want to lower an input string, you couldn't use `lower()`. You have to use the TensorFlow operation `tf.strings.lower()` to perform the same procedure in a graph mode. Eager execution isn't supported; all operations rely on pure TensorFlow graph operations.

`tf.function` can be used in `preprocessing_fn()` functions, but with restrictions: You can only use a `tf.function` that accepts Tensors (i.e., `lower()` wouldn't work since it doesn't work on a tensor). You can't call a TFT analyzer (or a mapper that relies on an analyzer, such as `tft.scale_to_z_score`).

TFT Functions

TFT provides a variety of functions to facilitate efficient feature engineering. The list of provided functions is extensive and constantly growing. This is why we don't claim to present a complete list of supported functions, but we want to highlight useful operations in relation to vocabulary generation, normalization, and bucketization:

`tft.scale_to_z_score()`

> If you want to normalize a feature with a mean of 0 and standard deviation of 1, you can use this useful TFT function.

`tft.bucketize()`

> This useful function lets you bucketize a feature into bins. It returns a bin or bucket index. You can specify the argument `num_buckets` to set the number of buckets. TFT will then divide the equal-sized buckets.

`tft.pca()`

> This function lets you compute the *principal component analysis* (PCA) for a given feature. PCA is a common technique to reduce dimensionality by linearly projecting the data down to the subspace that best preserves the variance of the data. It requires the argument `output_dim` to set the dimensionality of your PCA representation.

`tft.compute_and_apply_vocabulary()`

> This is one of the most amazing TFT functions. It computes all unique values of a feature column and then maps the most frequent values to an index. This index mapping is then used to convert the feature to a numerical representation. The function generates all assets for your graph behind the scenes. We can configure *most frequent* in two ways: either by defining the *n* highest-ranked unique items with `top_k` or by using the `frequency_threshold` above each element for consideration in the vocabulary.

`tft.apply_saved_model()`

> This function lets you apply entire TensorFlow models on a feature. We can load a saved model with a given `tag` and `signature_name` and then the `inputs` will be passed to the model. The predictions from the model execution will then be returned.

Text data for natural language problems

If you are working on natural language processing problems and you would like to utilize TFT for your corpus preprocessing to turn your documents into numerical representations, TFT has a good number of functions at your disposal. Besides the introduced function `tft.compute_and_apply_vocabulary()`, you could also use the following TFT functions.

`tft.ngrams()`

> This will generate *n-grams*. It takes a SparseTensor of string values as inputs. For example, if you want to generate one-grams and bi-grams for the list `['Tom', 'and', 'Jerry', 'are', 'friends'])`, the function returns `[b'Tom', b'Tom and', b'and', b'and Jerry', b'Jerry', b'Jerry are', b'are', b'are`

friends', b'friends']. Besides the sparse input tensor, the function takes two additional arguments: ngram_range and separator. ngram_range sets the range of n-grams. If your n-grams should contain one-grams and bi-grams, set the ngram_range to (1, 2). The separator allows us to set the joining string or character. In our example, we set the separator to " ".

tft.bag_of_words()
: This function uses tft.ngrams and generates a bag-of-words vector with a row for each unique n-gram. The original order of the n-grams may not be preserved if, for example, the tokens repeat within an input.

tft.tfidf()
: A frequently used concept in natural language processing is TFIDF, or term frequency inverse document frequency. It generates two outputs: a vector with the token indices and a vector representing their TFIDF weights. The function expects a sparse input vector representing the token indices (the result of the tft.compute_and_apply_vocabulary() function). The dimensionality of these vectors is set by the vocab_size input argument. The weight for every token index is calculated by the document frequency of the token in a document times the inverse document frequency. This computation is often resource intensive. Therefore, distributing the computation with TFT is of great advantage.

TensorFlow Text (*https://oreil.ly/ZV9iE*) also lets you use all available functions from the TensorFlow Text library. The library provides extensive TensorFlow support for text normalization, text tokenization, n-gram computation, and modern language models like BERT.

Image data for computer vision problems

If you are working on computer vision models, TFT can preprocess the image datasets for you. TensorFlow provides various image preprocessing operations with the tf.images (*https://oreil.ly/PAQUO*) and the tf.io APIs (*https://oreil.ly/tWuFW*).

tf.io provides useful functions to open images as part of a model graph (e.g., tf.io.decode_jpeg and tf.io.decode_png). tf.images provides functions to crop or resize images, convert color schemes, adjust the images (e.g., contrast, hue, or brightness), or perform image transformations like image flipping, transposing, etc.

In Chapter 3, we discussed strategies to ingest images into our pipelines. In TFT, we can now read the encoded images from TFRecord files and, for example, resize them to a fixed size or reduce color images to grayscale images. Here is an implementation example of such a preprocessing_fn function:

```
def process_image(raw_image):
    raw_image = tf.reshape(raw_image, [-1])
    img_rgb = tf.io.decode_jpeg(raw_image, channels=3)  ❶
```

```
img_gray = tf.image.rgb_to_grayscale(img_rgb) ❷
img = tf.image.convert_image_dtype(img, tf.float32)
resized_img = tf.image.resize_with_pad( ❸
    img,
    target_height=300,
    target_width=300
)
img_grayscale = tf.image.rgb_to_grayscale(resized_img) ❹
return tf.reshape(img_grayscale, [-1, 300, 300, 1])
```

❶ Decode the JPEG image format.

❷ Convert the loaded RGB image to grayscale.

❸ Resize the image to 300 × 300 pixels.

❹ Convert the image to grayscale.

One note regarding the `tf.reshape()` operation as part of the `return` statement: TFT might process inputs in batches. Since the batch size is handled by TFT (and Apache Beam), we need to reshape the output of our function to handle any batch size. Therefore, we are setting the first dimension of our return tensor to *-1*. The remaining dimensions represent our images. We are resizing them to 300 × 300 pixels and reducing the RGB channels to a grayscale channel.

Standalone Execution of TFT

After we have defined our `preprocessing_fn` function, we need to focus on how to execute the `Transform` function. For the execution, we have two options. We can either execute the preprocessing transformations in a standalone setup or as part of our machine learning pipeline in the form of a TFX component. Both types of executions can be performed on a local Apache Beam setup or on Google Cloud's Dataflow service. In this section, we will discuss the standalone executions of TFT. This would be the recommended situation if you would like to preprocess data effectively outside of pipelines. If you are interested in how to integrate TFT into your pipelines, feel free to jump to "Integrate TFT into Your Machine Learning Pipeline" on page 75.

Apache Beam provides a depth of functionality that is outside the scope of this book. It deserves its own publication. However, we want to walk you through the "Hello World" example of preprocessing with Apache Beam.

In our example, we would like to apply the normalization preprocessing function that we introduced earlier on our tiny raw dataset, shown in the following source code:

```
raw_data = [
    {'x':   1.20},
    {'x':   2.99},
```

```
    {'x': 100.00}
]
```

First, we need to define a data schema. We can generate a schema from a feature specification, as shown in the following source code. Our tiny dataset only contains one feature named x. We define the feature with the `tf.float32` data type:

```
import tensorflow as tf
from tensorflow_transform.tf_metadata import dataset_metadata
from tensorflow_transform.tf_metadata import schema_utils

raw_data_metadata = dataset_metadata.DatasetMetadata(
    schema_utils.schema_from_feature_spec({
        'x': tf.io.FixedLenFeature([], tf.float32),
    }))
```

With the dataset loaded and the data schema generated, we can now execute the preprocessing function `preprocessing_fn`, which we defined earlier. TFT provides bindings for the execution on Apache Beam with the function `AnalyzeAndTransform Dataset`. This function is performing the two-step process we discussed earlier: first analyze the dataset and then transform it. The execution is performed through the Python context manager `tft_beam.Context`, which allows us to set, for example, the desired batch size. However, we recommend using the default batch size because it is more performant in common use cases. The following example shows the usage of the AnalyzeAndTransformDataset function:

```
import tempfile
import tensorflow_transform.beam.impl as tft_beam

with beam.Pipeline() as pipeline:
    with tft_beam.Context(temp_dir=tempfile.mkdtemp()):

        tfrecord_file = "/your/tf_records_file.tfrecord"
        raw_data = (
            pipeline | beam.io.ReadFromTFRecord(tfrecord_file))

        transformed_dataset, transform_fn = (
            (raw_data, raw_data_metadata) | tft_beam.AnalyzeAndTransformDataset(
                preprocessing_fn))
```

The syntax of the Apache Beam function calls is a bit different from usual Python calls. In the earlier example, we apply the `preprocessing_fn` function with the Apache Beam function `AnalyzeAndTransformDataset()` and provide the two arguments with our data `raw_data` and our defined metadata schema `raw_data_meta data`. `AnalyzeAndTransformDataset()` then returns two artifacts: the preprocessed dataset and a function, here named `transform_fn`, representing the transform operations applied to our dataset.

If we test our "Hello World" example, execute the preprocessing steps, and print the results, we will see the tiny processed dataset:

```
transformed_data, transformed_metadata = transformed_dataset
print(transformed_data)
[
    {'x_xf': 0.0},
    {'x_xf': 0.018117407},
    {'x_xf': 1.0}
]
```

In our "Hello World" example, we completely ignored the fact that the data isn't available as a Python dictionary, which often needs to be read from a disk. Apache Beam provides functions to handle file ingestions effectively (e.g., with `beam.io.Read FromText()` or `beam.io.ReadFromTFRecord()`) in the context of building TensorFlow models.

As you can see, defining Apache Beam executions can get complex quickly, and we understand that data scientists and machine learning engineers aren't in the business of writing execution instructions from scratch. This is why TFX is so handy. It abstracts all the instructions under the hood and lets the data scientist focus on their problem-specific setups like defining the `preprocessing_fn()` function. In the next section, we will take a closer look into the `Transform` setup for our example project.

Integrate TFT into Your Machine Learning Pipeline

In the final section of this chapter, we discuss how to apply TFT capabilities to our example project. In Chapter 4, we investigated the dataset and determined which features are categorical or numerical, which features should be bucketized, and which feature we want to embed from string representation to a vector representation. This information is crucial for defining our feature engineering.

In the following code, we define our features. For simpler processing later on, we group the input feature names in dictionaries representing each transform output data type: one-hot encoded features, bucketized features, and raw string representations:

```
import tensorflow as tf
import tensorflow_transform as tft

LABEL_KEY = "consumer_disputed"

# Feature name, feature dimensionality.
ONE_HOT_FEATURES = {
    "product": 11,
    "sub_product": 45,
    "company_response": 5,
    "state": 60,
    "issue": 90
```

```
    }

    # Feature name, bucket count.
    BUCKET_FEATURES = {
        "zip_code": 10
    }

    # Feature name, value is unused.
    TEXT_FEATURES = {
        "consumer_complaint_narrative": None
    }
```

Before we can loop over these input feature dictionaries, let's define a few helper functions to transform the data efficiently. It is a good practice to rename the features by appending a suffix to the feature name (e.g., _xf). The suffix will help distinguish whether errors are originating from input or output features and prevent us from accidentally using a nontransformed feature in our actual model:

```
    def transformed_name(key):
        return key + '_xf'
```

Some of our features are of a sparse nature, but TFT expects the transformation outputs to be dense. We can use the following helper function to convert sparse to dense features and to fill the missing values with a default value:

```
    def fill_in_missing(x):
        default_value = '' if x.dtype == tf.string or to_string else 0
        if type(x) == tf.SparseTensor:
            x = tf.sparse.to_dense(
                tf.SparseTensor(x.indices, x.values, [x.dense_shape[0], 1]),
                                default_value)
        return tf.squeeze(x, axis=1)
```

In our model, we represent most input features as one-hot encoded vectors. The following helper function converts a given index to a one-hot encoded representation and returns the vector:

```
    def convert_num_to_one_hot(label_tensor, num_labels=2):
        one_hot_tensor = tf.one_hot(label_tensor, num_labels)
        return tf.reshape(one_hot_tensor, [-1, num_labels])
```

Before we can process our features, we need one more helper function to convert zip codes represented as strings to float values. Our dataset lists zip codes as follows:

```
    zip codes
    97XXX
    98XXX
```

To bucketize records with missing zip codes correctly, we replaced the placeholders with zeros and bucketized the resulting floats into 10 buckets:

```
    def convert_zip_code(zip_code):
        if zip_code == '':
```

```
        zip_code = "00000"
    zip_code = tf.strings.regex_replace(zip_code, r'X{0,5}', "0")
    zip_code = tf.strings.to_number(zip_code, out_type=tf.float32)
    return zip_code
```

With all the helper functions in place, we can now loop over each feature column and transform it depending on the type. For example, for our features to be converted to one-hot features, we convert the category names to an index with `tft.com pute_and_apply_vocabulary()` and then convert the index to a one-hot vector representation with our helper function `convert_num_to_one_hot()`. Since we are using `tft.compute_and_apply_vocabulary()`, TensorFlow Transform will first loop over all categories and then determine a complete category to index mapping. This mapping will then be applied during our evaluation and serving phase of the model:

```
def preprocessing_fn(inputs):
    outputs = {}
    for key in ONE_HOT_FEATURES.keys():
        dim = ONE_HOT_FEATURES[key]
        index = tft.compute_and_apply_vocabulary(
            fill_in_missing(inputs[key]), top_k=dim + 1)
        outputs[transformed_name(key)] = convert_num_to_one_hot(
            index, num_labels=dim + 1)
    ...
    return outputs
```

Our processing of the bucket features is very similar. We decided to bucketize the zipcodes because one-hot encoded zip codes seemed too sparse. Each feature is bucketized into, in our case, 10 buckets, and we encode the index of the bucket as one-hot vectors:

```
    for key, bucket_count in BUCKET_FEATURES.items():
        temp_feature = tft.bucketize(
                convert_zip_code(fill_in_missing(inputs[key])),
                bucket_count,
                always_return_num_quantiles=False)
        outputs[transformed_name(key)] = convert_num_to_one_hot(
            temp_feature,
            num_labels=bucket_count + 1)
```

Our text input features as well as our label column don't require any transformations; therefore, we simply convert them to dense features in case a feature might be sparse:

```
    for key in TEXT_FEATURES.keys():
        outputs[transformed_name(key)] = \
            fill_in_missing(inputs[key])

    outputs[transformed_name(LABEL_KEY)] = fill_in_missing(inputs[LABEL_KEY])
```

Why We Didn't Embed the Text Features to Vectors

You might wonder why we haven't embedded our text features into a fixed vector as part of our transform step. This is certainly possible. But we decided to load the TensorFlow Hub model as a part of the model instead of the preprocessing. The key reason for that decision was that we could make the embeddings trainable and refine the vector representations during our training phase. Therefore, they cannot be hard-coded into the preprocessing step and represented as a fixed graph during the training phase.

If we use the `Transform` component from TFX in our pipeline, it expects the transformation code to be provided in a separate Python file. The name of the module file can be set by the user (e.g., in our case `module.py`), but the entry point `preprocessing_fn()` needs to be contained in the module file and the function can't be renamed:

```
transform = Transform(
    examples=example_gen.outputs['examples'],
    schema=schema_gen.outputs['schema'],
    module_file=os.path.abspath("module.py"))
context.run(transform)
```

When we execute the `Transform` component, TFX will apply the transformations defined in our `module.py` module file to the loaded input data, which was converted to TFRecord data structures during the data ingestion step. The component will then output our transformed data, a transform graph, and the required metadata.

The transformed data and the transform graph can be consumed during our next step, the `Trainer` component. Check out "Running the Trainer Component" on page 88 for how to consume the outputs of our `Transform` component. The following chapter also highlights how the generated transform graph can be combined with the trained model to export a saved model. More details can be found in Example 6-2.

Summary

In this chapter, we discussed how to effectively preprocess data in our machine learning pipelines with TFT. We introduced how to write `preprocessing_fn` functions, provided an overview of some available functions provided by TFT, and discussed how to integrate the preprocessing steps into the TFX pipeline. Now that the data has been preprocessed, it is time to train our model.

Model Training

Now that the data preprocessing step is complete and the data has been transformed into the format that our model requires, the next step in our pipeline is to train the model with the freshly transformed data.

As we discussed in Chapter 1, we won't cover the process of choosing your model architecture. We assume that you have a separate experimentation process that took place before you even picked up this book and that you already know the type of model you wish to train. We discuss how to track this experimentation process in Chapter 15 because it helps with creating a full audit trail for the model. However, we don't cover any of the theoretical background you'll need to understand the model training process. If you would like to learn more about this, we strongly recommend the O'Reilly publication *Hands-On Machine Learning with Scikit-Learn, Keras, and TensorFlow*, 2nd edition.

In this chapter, we cover the model training process as part of a machine learning pipeline, including how it is automated in a TFX pipeline. We also include some details of distribution strategies available in TensorFlow and how to tune hyperparameters in a pipeline. This chapter is more specific to TFX pipelines than most of the others because we don't cover training as a standalone process.

As shown in Figure 6-1, by this point data has been ingested, validated, and preprocessed. This ensures that all the data needed by the model is present and that it has been reproducibly transformed into the features that the model requires. All of this is necessary because we don't want the pipeline to fail at our next step. We want to ensure that the training proceeds smoothly because it is often the most time-consuming part of the entire pipeline.

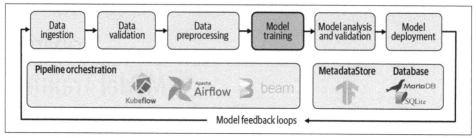

Figure 6-1. Model training as part of ML pipelines

One very important feature of training a model in a TFX pipeline is that the data pre-processing steps that we discussed in Chapter 5 are saved along with the trained model weights. This is incredibly useful once our model is deployed to production because it means that the preprocessing steps will always produce the features the model is expecting. Without this feature, it would be possible to update the data pre-processing steps without updating the model, and then the model would fail in production or the predictions would be based on the wrong data. Because we export the preprocessing steps and the model as one graph, we eliminate this potential source of error.

In the next two sections, we'll take a detailed look at the steps required to train a tf.Keras model as part of a TFX pipeline.[1]

Defining the Model for Our Example Project

Even though the model architecture is already defined, some extra code is necessary here. We need to make it possible to automate the model training part of the pipeline. In this section, we will briefly describe the model we use throughout this chapter.

The model for our example project is a hypothetical implementation, and we could probably optimize the model architecture. However, it showcases some common ingredients of many deep learning models:

- Transfer learning from a pretrained model
- Dense layers
- Concatenation layers

As we discussed in Chapter 1, the model in our example project uses data from the US Consumer Finance Protection Bureau to predict whether a consumer disputed a

---

1 We use a Keras model in our example project, but TFX also works perfectly with an Estimator model. Examples can be found in the TFX documentation (*https://oreil.ly/KIDko*).

complaint about a financial product. The features in our model include the financial product, the company's response, the US state, and the consumer complaint narrative. Our model is inspired by the Wide and Deep model architecture (*https://oreil.ly/9sXHU*), with the addition of the Universal Sentence Encoder (*https://oreil.ly/7BFZP*) from TensorFlow Hub (*https://oreil.ly/0OJZ_*) to encode the free-text feature (the consumer complaint narrative).

You can see a visual representation of our model architecture in Figure 6-2, with the text feature (narrative_xf) taking the "deep" route and the other features taking the "wide" route.

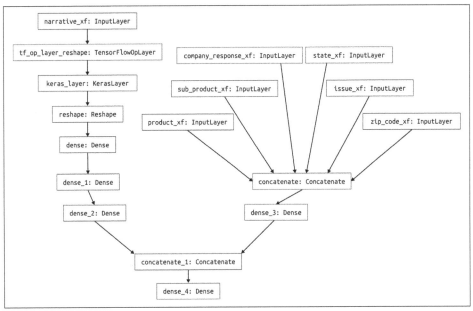

Figure 6-2. Model architecture for our example project

Example 6-1 shows the full model architecture definition. Because we want to export the model with our preprocessing steps, we need to guarantee that the model input names match the transformed feature names from preprocessing_fn(), which we discussed in Chapter 5. In our example model, we reuse the transformed_name() function described in Chapter 5 to add the suffix _xf to our features.

Example 6-1. Defining our model architecture

```
import tensorflow as tf
import tensorflow_hub as hub

def transformed_name(key):
    return key + '_xf'
```

```
def get_model():

    # One-hot categorical features
    input_features = []
    for key, dim in ONE_HOT_FEATURES.items(): ❶
        input_features.append(
            tf.keras.Input(shape=(dim + 1,),
                           name=transformed_name(key)))

    # Adding bucketized features
    for key, dim in BUCKET_FEATURES.items():
        input_features.append(
            tf.keras.Input(shape=(dim + 1,),
                           name=transformed_name(key)))

    # Adding text input features
    input_texts = []
    for key in TEXT_FEATURES.keys():
        input_texts.append(
            tf.keras.Input(shape=(1,),
                           name=transformed_name(key),
                           dtype=tf.string))

    inputs = input_features + input_texts

    # Embed text features
    MODULE_URL = "https://tfhub.dev/google/universal-sentence-encoder/4"
    embed = hub.KerasLayer(MODULE_URL) ❷
    reshaped_narrative = tf.reshape(input_texts[0], [-1]) ❸
    embed_narrative = embed(reshaped_narrative)
    deep_ff = tf.keras.layers.Reshape((512, ), input_shape=(1, 512))(embed_narrative)

    deep = tf.keras.layers.Dense(256, activation='relu')(deep_ff)
    deep = tf.keras.layers.Dense(64, activation='relu')(deep)
    deep = tf.keras.layers.Dense(16, activation='relu')(deep)

    wide_ff = tf.keras.layers.concatenate(input_features)
    wide = tf.keras.layers.Dense(16, activation='relu')(wide_ff)

    both = tf.keras.layers.concatenate([deep, wide])

    output = tf.keras.layers.Dense(1, activation='sigmoid')(both)
    keras_model = tf.keras.models.Model(inputs, output) ❹

    keras_model.compile(optimizer=tf.keras.optimizers.Adam(learning_rate=0.001),
                        loss='binary_crossentropy',
                        metrics=[
                            tf.keras.metrics.BinaryAccuracy(),
                            tf.keras.metrics.TruePositives()
                        ])
    return keras_model
```

❶ Loop over the features and create an input for each feature.

❷ Load the `tf.hub` module of the Universal Sentence Encoder model.

❸ Keras inputs are two-dimensional, but the encoder expects one-dimensional inputs.

❹ Assemble the model graph with the functional API.

Now that we have defined our model, let's move on to describe the process to integrate it into a TFX pipeline.

The TFX Trainer Component

The TFX `Trainer` component handles the training step in our pipeline. In this section, we will first describe how to train the Keras model from the example project in a one-off training run. At the end of the section, we will add some considerations for other training situations and for `Estimator` models.

All the steps we will describe may seem lengthy and unnecessary compared to the normal Keras training code. But the key point here is that the `Trainer` component will produce a model that will be put into production, where it will transform new data and use the model to make predictions. Because the `Transform` steps are included in this model, the data preprocessing steps will always match what the model is expecting. This removes a huge potential source of errors when our model is deployed.

In our example project, the `Trainer` component requires the following inputs:

- The previously generated data schema, generated by the data validation step discussed in Chapter 4
- The transformed data and its preprocessing graph, as discussed in Chapter 5
- Training parameters (e.g., the number of training steps)
- A module file containing a `run_fn()` function, which defines the training process

In the next section, we will discuss the setup of the `run_fn` function. We also will cover how to train a machine learning model in our pipeline and export it to the next pipeline step that we will discuss in Chapter 7.

run_fn() Function

The `Trainer` component will look for a `run_fn()` function in our module file and use the function as an entry point to execute the training process. The module file needs to be accessible to the `Trainer` component. If you run the component in an interactive context, you can simply define the absolute path to the module file and pass it to the component. If you run your pipelines in production, please check Chapter 11 or Chapter 12 for details on how to provide the module file.

The `run_fn()` function is a generic entry point to the training steps and not `tf.Keras` specific. It carries out the following steps:

- Loading the training and validation data (or the data generator)
- Defining the model architecture and compiling the model
- Training the model
- Exporting the model to be evaluated in the next pipeline step

The `run_fn` for our example project performs these four steps as shown in Example 6-2.

Example 6-2. run_fn() function of our example pipeline

```
def run_fn(fn_args):

    tf_transform_output = tft.TFTransformOutput(fn_args.transform_output)
    train_dataset = input_fn(fn_args.train_files, tf_transform_output) ❶
    eval_dataset = input_fn(fn_args.eval_files, tf_transform_output)

    model = get_model() ❷
    model.fit(
        train_dataset,
        steps_per_epoch=fn_args.train_steps,
        validation_data=eval_dataset,
        validation_steps=fn_args.eval_steps) ❸

    signatures = {
        'serving_default':
            _get_serve_tf_examples_fn(
                model,
                tf_transform_output).get_concrete_function(
                    tf.TensorSpec(
                        shape=[None],
                        dtype=tf.string,
                        name='examples')
                )
    } ❹
    model.save(fn_args.serving_model_dir,
            save_format='tf', signatures=signatures)
```

❶ Call the `input_fn` to get data generators.

❷ Call the `get_model` function to get the compiled Keras model.

❸ Train the model using the number of training and evaluation steps passed by the Trainer component.

❹ Define the model signature, which includes the serving function we will describe later.

This function is fairly generic and could be reused with any other `tf.Keras` model. The project-specific details are defined in helper functions like `get_model()` or `input_fn()`.

In the following sections, we want to take a closer look into how we load the data, train, and export our machine learning model inside the `run_fn()` function.

Load the data

The following lines in the `run_fn` load our training and evaluation data:

```
def run_fn(fn_args):
    tf_transform_output = tft.TFTransformOutput(fn_args.transform_output)
    train_dataset = input_fn(fn_args.train_files, tf_transform_output)
    eval_dataset = input_fn(fn_args.eval_files, tf_transform_output)
```

In the first line, the `run_fn` function receives a set of arguments, including the transform graph, example datasets, and training parameters through the `fn_args` object.

Data loading for model training and validation is performed in batches, and the loading is handled by the `input_fn()` function as shown in Example 6-3.

Example 6-3. Input_fn function of our example pipeline

```
LABEL_KEY = 'labels'

def _gzip_reader_fn(filenames):
    return tf.data.TFRecordDataset(filenames,
        compression_type='GZIP')

def input_fn(file_pattern,
             tf_transform_output, batch_size=32):

    transformed_feature_spec = (
        tf_transform_output.transformed_feature_spec().copy())

    dataset = tf.data.experimental.make_batched_features_dataset(
        file_pattern=file_pattern,
        batch_size=batch_size,
        features=transformed_feature_spec,
        reader=_gzip_reader_fn,
```

```
        label_key=transformed_name(LABEL_KEY)) ❶

    return dataset
```

❶ The dataset will be batched into the correct batch size.

The `input_fn` function lets us load the compressed, preprocessed datasets that were generated by the previous Transform step.[2] To do this, we need to pass the `tf_trans form_output` to the function. This gives us the data schema to load the dataset from the TFRecord data structures generated by the Transform component. By using the preprocessed datasets, we can avoid data preprocessing during training and speed up the training process.

The `input_fn` returns a generator (a `batched_features_dataset`) that will supply data to the model one batch at a time.

Compile and train the model

Now that we have defined our data-loading steps, the next step is defining our model architecture and compiling our model. In our `run_fn`, this will require a call to `get_model()`, which we have described, so it just needs a single line of code:

```
    model = get_model()
```

Next, we train our compiled `tf.Keras` model with the Keras method *fit()*:

```
    model.fit(
        train_dataset,
        steps_per_epoch=fn_args.train_steps,
        validation_data=eval_dataset,
        validation_steps=fn_args.eval_steps)
```

Training Steps Versus Epochs

The TFX `Trainer` component defines the training process by the number of training steps rather than by epochs. A *training step* is when the model is trained on a single batch of data. The benefit of using steps rather than epochs is that we can train or validate models with large datasets and only use a fraction of the data. At the same time, if you want to loop over the training dataset multiple times during training, you can increase the step size to a multiple of the available samples.

---

2 The `Trainer` component could be used without the previous `Transform` component, and we could load the raw datasets. However, in this case, we would miss out on an excellent feature of TFX, which is exporting the preprocessing and the model graphs as one SavedModel graph.

Once the model training is complete, the next step is to export the trained model. We will have a detailed discussion about exporting models for deployment in Chapter 8. In the following section, we want to highlight how the preprocessing steps can be exported with the model.

Model export

Finally, we export the model. We combine the preprocessing steps from the previous pipeline component with the trained model and save the model in TensorFlow's *SavedModel* format. We define a *model signature* based on the graph generated by the Example 6-4 function. We will describe model signatures in much more detail in "Model Signatures" on page 135 in Chapter 8.

In the `run_fn` function, we define the model signature and save the model with the following code:

```
signatures = {
    'serving_default':
        _get_serve_tf_examples_fn(
            model,
            tf_transform_output).get_concrete_function(
                tf.TensorSpec(
                    shape=[None],
                    dtype=tf.string,
                    name='examples')
            )
}
model.save(fn_args.serving_model_dir,
            save_format='tf', signatures=signatures)
```

The `run_fn` exports the `get_serve_tf_examples_fn` as part of the model signature. When a model has been exported and deployed, every prediction request will pass through the `serve_tf_examples_fn()` shown in Example 6-4. With every request, we parse the serialized `tf.Example` records and apply the preprocessing steps to the raw request data. The model then makes a prediction on the preprocessed data.

Example 6-4. Applying the preprocessing graph to model inputs

```
def get_serve_tf_examples_fn(model, tf_transform_output):

    model.tft_layer = tf_transform_output.transform_features_layer()  ❶

    @tf.function
    def serve_tf_examples_fn(serialized_tf_examples):
        feature_spec = tf_transform_output.raw_feature_spec()
        feature_spec.pop(LABEL_KEY)
        parsed_features = tf.io.parse_example(
            serialized_tf_examples, feature_spec)  ❷
```

```
        transformed_features = model.tft_layer(parsed_features)  ❸
        outputs = model(transformed_features)  ❹
        return {'outputs': outputs}

    return serve_tf_examples_fn
```

❶ Load the preprocessing graph.

❷ Parse the raw `tf.Example` records from the request.

❸ Apply the preprocessing transformation to raw data.

❹ Perform prediction with preprocessed data.

With the definition of our `run_fn()` function in place, let's discuss how we can run the `Trainer` component.

Running the Trainer Component

As shown in Example 6-5, the `Trainer` component takes the following as input:

- The Python module file, here saved as *module.py*, containing the `run_fn()`, `input_fn()`, `get_serve_tf_examples_fn()`, and other associated functions we discussed earlier
- The transformed examples generated by the Transform component
- The transform graph generated by the Transform component
- The schema generated by the data validation component
- The number of training and evaluation steps

Example 6-5. Trainer component

```
from tfx.components import Trainer
from tfx.components.base import executor_spec
from tfx.components.trainer.executor import GenericExecutor  ❶
from tfx.proto import trainer_pb2

TRAINING_STEPS = 1000
EVALUATION_STEPS = 100

trainer = Trainer(
    module_file=os.path.abspath("module.py"),
    custom_executor_spec=executor_spec.ExecutorClassSpec(GenericExecutor),  ❷
    transformed_examples=transform.outputs['transformed_examples'],
    transform_graph=transform.outputs['transform_graph'],
    schema=schema_gen.outputs['schema'],
```

```
train_args=trainer_pb2.TrainArgs(num_steps=TRAINING_STEPS),
eval_args=trainer_pb2.EvalArgs(num_steps=EVALUATION_STEPS))
```

❶ Load the GenericExecutor to override the training executor.

❷ Override the executor to load the run_fn() function.

In a notebook environment (an interactive context), we can run the Trainer component, like any previous component, with the following command:

```
context.run(trainer)
```

After the model training and exporting is completed, the component will register the path of the exported model with the metadata store. Downstream components can pick up the model for the model validation.

The Trainer component is generic and not limited to running TensorFlow models. However, the components later in the pipeline expect that the model is saved in the TensorFlow SavedModel format (*https://oreil.ly/fe6rp*). The SavedModel graph includes the Transform graph, so the data preprocessing steps are part of the model.

Overriding the Trainer Component's Executor

In our example project, we override the Trainer component's executor to enable the generic training entry point run_fn() function instead of the default trainer_fn() function, which only supports tf.Estimator models. In Chapter 12, we will introduce another Trainer executor, the ai_platform_trainer_execu tor.GenericExecutor. This executor allows you to train models on Google Cloud's AI Platform instead of inside your pipeline. This is an alternative if your model requires specific training hardware (e.g., GPUs or tensor processing units [TPUs]), which aren't available in your pipeline environment.

Other Trainer Component Considerations

In our examples so far in this chapter, we have only considered a single training run of a Keras model. But we can also use the Trainer component to fine-tune a model from a previous run or to train multiple models simultaneously, and we will describe these in "Advanced Pipeline Concepts" on page 190. We can also use it to optimize a model through hyperparameter search, and we will discuss this more in "Model Tuning" on page 95.

In this section, we will also discuss how to use the Trainer component with an Estimator model and how to load your SavedModel exported by the Trainer component outside a TFX pipeline.

Using the Trainer component with an Estimator model

Until recently, TFX supported only tf.Estimator models and the Trainer component was solely designed for Estimators. The default implementation of the Trainer component used the trainer_fn() function as an entry point to the training process, but this entry point is very tf.Estimator specific. The Trainer component expects the Estimator inputs to be defined by functions like train_input_fn(), eval_input_fn(), and serving_receiver_fn().[3]

As we discussed in "Running the Trainer Component" on page 88, the core functionality of the component can be swapped out with the generic training executor Generi cExecutor, which uses the run_fn() function as its entry point to the training process.[4] As the name of the executor implies, the training process becomes generic and not tied to tf.Estimator or tf.Keras models.

Using the SavedModel outside a pipeline

If we would like to inspect the exported SavedModel outside a TFX pipeline, we can load the model as a *concrete function*,[5] which represents the graph of a single signature:

```
model_path = trainer.outputs.model.get()[0].uri
model = tf.saved_model.load(export_dir=model_path)
predict_fn = model.signatures["serving_default"]
```

With the model loaded as a concrete function, we can now perform predictions. The exported model expects the input data to be provided in the tf.Example data structure as shown in the following example. More details around the tf.Example data structure, and how other features (like integers and floats) can be converted can be found in Example 3-1. The following code shows how to create the serialized data structure and perform a model prediction by calling the prediction_fn() function:

```
example = tf.train.Example(features=tf.train.Features(feature={
    'feature_A': _bytes_feature(feature_A_value),
    ...
})) ❶

serialized_example = example.SerializeToString()
print(predict_fn(tf.constant([serialized_example])))
```

---

3 tf.Keras models can be converted to tf.Estimator models through the tf.model_to_estimator() conversion. However, with the recent updates to TFX, this is no longer the recommended best practice.

4 If you are interested in the steps of how component executors can be developed and exchanged, we recommend the section "Reusing Existing Components" on page 208 in Chapter 10.

5 For more details on concrete functions, check out the TensorFlow documentation (*https://oreil.ly/Y8Hup*).

① The _bytes_feature helper function is defined in Example 3-1.

If you would like to inspect the progress of the model in detail during training, you can do this using TensorBoard. We will describe how to use TensorBoard in our pipeline in the next section.

Using TensorBoard in an Interactive Pipeline

TensorBoard is another wonderful tool that is part of the TensorFlow ecosystem. It has many helpful functions that we can use in our pipelines, for example, monitoring metrics while training, visualizing word embeddings in NLP problems, or viewing activations for layers in the model. A new Profiler feature (*https://oreil.ly/Tiw9Y*) lets us profile the model to understand performance bottlenecks.

An example of TensorBoard's basic visualization is shown in Figure 6-3.

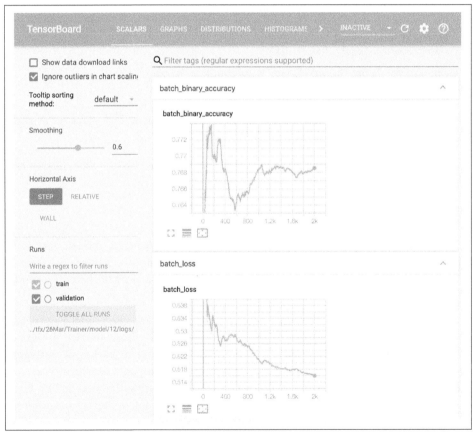

Figure 6-3. Viewing metrics while training in TensorBoard

To be able to use TensorBoard in our pipeline, we need to add callbacks in the run_fn function and log the training to a folder we specify:

```
log_dir = os.path.join(os.path.dirname(fn_args.serving_model_dir), 'logs')
tensorboard_callback = tf.keras.callbacks.TensorBoard(
    log_dir=log_dir, update_freq='batch')
```

We also need to add the callback to our model training:

```
model.fit(
    train_dataset,
    steps_per_epoch=fn_args.train_steps,
    validation_data=eval_dataset,
    validation_steps=fn_args.eval_steps,
    callbacks=[tensorboard_callback])
```

Then, to view TensorBoard in a notebook, we get the location of the model training logs and pass it to TensorBoard:

```
model_dir = trainer.outputs['output'].get()[0].uri

%load_ext tensorboard
%tensorboard --logdir {model_dir}
```

We can also use TensorBoard outside a notebook by running:

```
tensorboard --logdir path/to/logs
```

Then connect to *http://localhost:6006/* to view TensorBoard. This gives us a larger window to view the details.

Next, we will introduce some useful strategies for training large models on multiple GPUs.

Distribution Strategies

TensorFlow provides distribution strategies for machine learning models that can't be adequately trained on a single GPU. You might want to consider distribution strategies when you want to accelerate your training or you can't fit the entire model into a single GPU.

The strategies we describe here are abstractions to distribute the model parameters across multiple GPUs or even multiple servers. In general, there are two groups of strategies: *synchronous* and *asynchronous* training. Under the synchronous strategies, all training workers train with different slices of the training data synchronously and then aggregate the gradients from all workers before updating the model. The asynchronous strategies train models independently with the entire dataset on different workers. Each worker updates the gradients of the model asynchronously, without waiting for the other workers to finish. Typically, synchronous strategies are coordinated via all-reduce operations[6] and asynchronous strategies through a parameter server architecture.

A few synchronous and asynchronous strategies exist, and they have their benefits and drawbacks. At the time of writing this section, Keras supports the following strategies:

MirroredStrategy
This strategy is relevant for multiple GPUs on a single instance, and it follows the synchronous training pattern. The strategy *mirrors* the model and the parameters across the workers, but each worker receives a different batch of data. The MirroredStrategy is a good default strategy if you train a machine learning model on a single node with multiple GPUs and your machine learning model fits in the GPU memory.

CentralStorageStrategy
In contrast to the MirroredStrategy, the variables in this strategy aren't mirrored across all GPUs. Instead, they are stored in the CPU's memory and then copied into the assigned GPU to execute the relevant operations. In case of a single GPU operation, the CentralStorageStrategy will store the variables on the GPU, not in the CPU. CentralStorageStrategy is a good strategy for distributing your training when you train on a single node with multiple GPUs and your complete model doesn't fit in the memory of single GPU, or when the communication bandwidth between the GPUs is too limited.

MultiWorkerMirroredStrategy
This follows the design patterns of the MirroredStrategy, but it copies the variables across multiple workers (e.g., compute instances). The MultiWorkerMirroredStrategy is an option if one node isn't enough for your model training.

TPUStrategy
This strategy lets you use Google Cloud's TPUs. It follows the synchronous training pattern and basically works like MirroredStrategy except it uses TPUs instead of GPUs. It requires its own strategy since the MirroredStrategy uses GPU-specific all-reduce functions. TPUs have a huge amount of RAM available, and the cross-TPU communication is highly optimized, which is why the TPU strategy uses the mirrored approach.

ParameterServerStrategy
The ParameterServerStrategy uses multiple nodes as the central variable repository. This strategy is useful for models exceeding the available resources (e.g.,

---

6 The all-reduce operation reduces information from all the workers to a single information; in other words, it enables synchronization between all training workers.

RAM or I/O bandwidth) of a single node. The ParameterServerStrategy is your only option if you can't train on a single node and the model is exceeding the RAM or I/O limitations of a node.

OneDeviceStrategy

The whole point of the OneDeviceStrategy is to test the entire model setup before engaging in real distributed training. This strategy forces the model training to only use one device (e.g., one GPU). Once it is confirmed that the training setup is working, the strategy can be swapped.

Not All Strategies Are Available via the TFX Trainer Component

At the time of writing this section, the TFX `Trainer` component only supports the MirroredStrategy. While the different strategies can currently be used with `tf.keras`, they will be made accessible via the `Trainer` component in the second half of 2020, according to the TFX roadmap (*https://oreil.ly/I-OPN*).

Because the MirroredStrategy is supported by the TFX Trainer, we'll show an example of it here. We can apply the MirroredStrategy easily by adding a few lines before invoking our model creation and the subsequent `model.compile()` call:

```
mirrored_strategy = tf.distribute.MirroredStrategy() ❶
with mirrored_strategy.scope(): ❷
    model = get_model()
```

❶ Instance of distribution strategy.

❷ Wrap model creation and compilation with Python manager.

In this example setup, we create an instance of the MirroredStrategy. In order to apply the distribution strategy to our model, we wrap the model creation and compilation with the Python manager (in our case, it all happens inside of the `get_model()` function). This will create and compile our model under the distribution scope of our choice. The MirroredStrategy will use all available GPUs of the instance. If you want to reduce the number of GPU instances being used (e.g., in case you share instances), you can specify the GPUs to be used with the MirroredStrategy by changing the creation of the distribution strategy:

```
mirrored_strategy = tf.distribute.MirroredStrategy(devices=["/gpu:0", "/gpu:1"])
```

In this example, we specify two GPUs to be used for our training runs.

Batch Size Requirement When Using the MirroredStrategy

The MirroredStrategy expects that the batch size is proportional to the number of devices. For example, if you train with five GPUs, the batch size needs to be a multiple of the number of GPUs. Please keep this in mind when you set up your input_fn() function as described in Example 6-3.

These distribution strategies are useful for large training jobs that won't fit on the memory of a single GPU. Model tuning, which we will discuss in the next section, is a common reason for us to need these strategies.

Model Tuning

Hyperparameter tuning is an important part of achieving an accurate machine learning model. Depending on the use case, it may be something that we do during our initial experiments or it may be something we want to include in our pipeline. This is not a comprehensive introduction to model tuning, but we will give a brief overview of it here and describe how it may be included in a pipeline.

Strategies for Hyperparameter Tuning

Depending on the type of model in your pipeline, the choice of hyperparameters will be different. If your model is a deep neural network, hyperparameter tuning is especially critical to achieving good performance with neural networks. Two of the most important sets of hyperparameters to tune are those controlling the optimization and the network architecture.

For optimization, we recommend using Adam (*https://oreil.ly/dsdHb*) or NAdam (*https://oreil.ly/TjatF*) by default. The learning rate is a very important parameter to experiment with, and there are many possible options (*https://oreil.ly/MopUS*) for learning rate schedulers. We recommend using the largest batch size that fits in your GPU memory.

For very large models, we suggest the following steps:

- Tune the initial learning rate, starting with 0.1.
- Pick a number of steps to train for (as many as patience allows).
- Linearly decay the learning rate to 0 over the specified number of steps.

For smaller models, we recommend using early stopping (*https://oreil.ly/ACUIn*) to avoid overfitting. With this technique, model training is stopped when the validation loss does not improve after a user-defined number of epochs.

For the network architecture, two of the most important parameters to tune are the size and number of layers. Increasing these will improve training performance, but it may cause overfitting and will mean the model takes longer to train. You can also consider adding residual connections between the layers, particularly for deep architectures.

The most popular hyperparameter search approaches are *grid search* and *random search*. In grid search, every combination of parameters is tried exhaustively, whereas in random search, parameters are sampled from the available options and may not try every combination. Grid search can get extremely time consuming if the number of possible hyperparameters is large. After trying a range of values, you can fine-tune by taking the best-performing hyperparameters and starting a new search centered on them.

In the TensorFlow ecosystem, hyperparameter tuning is implemented using the Keras Tuner (*https://oreil.ly/N3DqZ*) and also Katib (*https://oreil.ly/rVwCk*), which provides hyperparameter tuning in Kubeflow. In addition to grid and random search, both of these packages support Bayesian search and the Hyperband algorithm (*https://oreil.ly/KzqJY*).

Hyperparameter Tuning in TFX Pipelines

In a TFX pipeline, hyperparameter tuning takes in the data from the Transform component and trains a variety of models to establish the best hyperparameters. The hyperparameters are then passed to the `Trainer` component, which then trains a final model using them.

In this case, the model definition function (the `get_model` function in our example) needs to accept the hyperparameters as an input and build the model according to the specified hyperparameters. So, for example, the number of layers needs to be defined as an input argument.

The TFX Tuner Component

The TFX Tuner component was released as we were finalizing this book. You can view the source code in the project's GitHub repo (*https://oreil.ly/uK7Z9*).

Summary

In this chapter, we described how to move our model training from a standalone script to an integrated part of our pipeline. This means that the process can be automated and triggered whenever we would like—as soon as new data arrives in the pipeline or when the previous model accuracy dips beneath a predefined level. We also described how the model and the data preprocessing steps are saved together to avoid any errors from a mismatch between the preprocessing and the training. We additionally covered strategies for distributing the model training and for tuning the hyperparameters.

Now that we have a saved model, the next step is to dive into the details of what it can do.

Model Analysis and Validation

At this point in our machine learning pipeline, we have checked the statistics of our data, we have transformed our data into the correct features, and we have trained our model. Surely now it's time to put the model into production? In our opinion, there should be two extra steps before you move on to deploy your model: analyzing your model's performance in-depth and checking that it will be an improvement on any model that's already in production. We show where these steps fit into the pipeline in Figure 7-1.

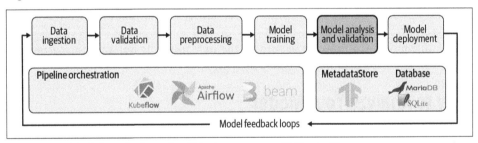

Figure 7-1. Model analysis and validation as part of ML pipelines

While we're training a model, we're monitoring its performance on an evaluation set during training, and we're also trying out a variety of hyperparameters to get peak performance. But it's common to only use one metric during training, and often this metric is accuracy.

When we're building a machine learning pipeline, we're often trying to answer a complex business question or trying to model a complex real-world system. One single metric is often not enough to tell us whether our model will answer that question. This is particularly true if our dataset is imbalanced or if some of our model's decisions have higher consequences than others.

In addition, a single metric that averages performance over an entire evaluation set can hide a lot of important details. If your model is dealing with data that is about people, does everyone who interacts with the model get the same experience? Does your model perform better for female users than male users? Are users from Japan seeing poorer results than users from the US? These differences can be both commercially damaging and cause harm to real people. If your model is doing object detection for an autonomous vehicle, does it work acceptably in all lighting conditions? Using one metric for your whole training set can hide important edge and corner cases. It's essential to be able to monitor metrics across different slices of your dataset.

It's also extremely important to monitor your metrics through time—before deployment, after deployment, and while in production. Even if your model is static, the data that comes into the pipeline will change through time, often causing a decline in performance.

In this chapter we'll introduce the next package from the TensorFlow ecosystem: TensorFlow Model Analysis (TFMA), which has all these capabilities. We'll show how you can get detailed metrics of your model's performance, slice your data to get metrics for different groups, and take a deeper dive into model fairness with Fairness Indicators and the What-If Tool. We'll then explain how you can go beyond analysis and start to explain the predictions your model is making.

We'll also describe the final step before deploying your new model: validating that the model is an improvement on any previous version. It's important that any new model deployed into production represents a step forward so that any other service depending on this model is improved in turn. If the new model is not an improvement in some way, it is not worth the effort of deploying.

How to Analyze Your Model

Our model analysis process starts with our choice of metrics. As we discussed previously, our choice is extremely important to the success of our machine learning pipeline. It's good practice to pick multiple metrics that make sense for our business problem because one single metric may hide important details. In this section, we will review some of the most important metrics for both classification and regression problems.

Classification Metrics

To calculate many classification metrics, it's necessary to first count the number of true/false positive examples and true/false negative examples in your evaluation set. Taking any one class in our labels as an example:

True positives

Training examples that belong to this class and are correctly labelled as this class by the classifier. For example, if the true label is 1, and the predicted label is 1, the example would be a true positive.

False positives

Training examples that do not belong to this class and are incorrectly labelled as this class by the classifier. For example, if the true label is 0, and the predicted label is 1, the example would be a false positive.

True negatives

Training examples that do not belong to this class and are correctly labelled as not in this class by the classifier. For example, if the true label is 0, and the predicted label is 0, the example would be a true negative.

False negatives

Training examples that belong to this class and are incorrectly labelled as not in this class by the classifier. For example, if the true label is 1, and the predicted label is 0, the example would be a false negative.

These basic metrics are all commonly shown in Table 7-1.

Table 7-1. Confusion matrix

	Predicted 1	Predicted 0
True value 1	True positives	False negatives
True value 0	False positives	True negatives

If we calculate all these metrics for the model from our example project, we get the results shown in Figure 7-2.

	Predicted Yes		Predicted No		Total	
Actual Yes	1.1%	(11)	20.8%	(208)	21.9%	(219)
Actual No	0.7%	(7)	77.4%	(774)	78.1%	(781)
Total	1.8%	(18)	98.2%	(982)		

Figure 7-2. Confusion matrix for our example project

We'll see that these counts are particularly useful when we talk about model fairness later in this chapter. There are several other metrics for comparing models that combine these counts into a single number:

Accuracy

Accuracy is defined as *(true positives + true negatives)/total examples*, or the proportion of examples that were classified correctly. This is an appropriate metric to use for a dataset where the positive and negative classes are equally balanced, but it can be misleading if the dataset is imbalanced.

Precision

Precision is defined as *true positives/(true negatives + false positives)*, or the proportion of examples predicted to be in the positive class that were classified correctly. So if a classifier has high precision, most of the examples it predicts as belonging to the positive class will indeed belong to the positive class.

Recall

Recall is defined as *true positives/(true positives + false negatives)*, or the proportion of examples where the ground truth is positive that the classifier correctly identified. So if a classifier has high recall, it will correctly identify most of the examples that are truly in the positive class.

Another way to generate a single number that describes a model's performance is the AUC (area under the curve). The "curve" here is the receiver operating characteristic (ROC), which plots the true positive rate (TPR) against the false positive rate (FPR).

The TPR is another name for *recall*, and it is defined as:

$$\text{true positive rate} = \frac{\text{true positives}}{\text{true positives } + \text{ false negatives}}$$

The FPR is defined as:

$$\text{false positive rate} = \frac{\text{false positives}}{\text{false positives } + \text{ true negatives}}$$

The ROC is generated by calculating the TPR and FPR at all classification thresholds. The *classification threshold* is the probability cutoff for assigning examples to the positive or negative class, usually 0.5. Figure 7-3 shows the ROC and the AUC for our example project. For a random predictor, the ROC would be a straight line from the origin to [1,1] that follows the *x* axis. As the ROC moves further away from the *x* axis toward the upper left of the plot, the model improves and the AUC increases. AUC is another useful metric that can be plotted in TFMA.

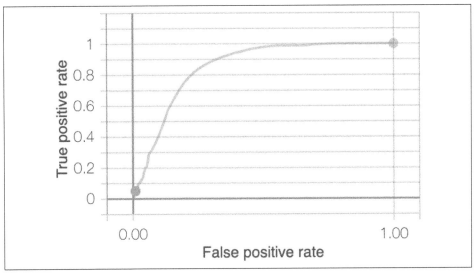

Figure 7-3. ROC for our example project

Regression Metrics

In a regression problem, the model predicts some numerical value for each training example, and this is compared with the actual value. Common regression metrics we can use in TFMA include:

Mean absolute error (MAE)
    MAE is defined as:

$$\text{MAE} = \frac{1}{n}\Sigma \, |y - \hat{y}|$$

where n is the number of training examples, y is the true value, and $\hat{y}$ is the predicted value. For each training example, the absolute difference is calculated between the predicted value and the true value. In other words, the MAE is the average error produced by the model.

Mean absolute percentage error (MAPE)
    MAPE is defined as:

$$\text{MAPE} = \frac{1}{n}\Sigma \, \left| \frac{y - \hat{y}}{y} \right| \times 100 \, \%$$

As the name implies, this metric gives the percentage error for all examples. This is particularly useful for spotting when the model makes systematic errors.

Mean squared error (MSE)

MSE is defined as:

$$MSE = \frac{1}{n} \Sigma \, (y - \hat{y})^2$$

This is similar to the MAE, except the $y - \hat{y}$ term is squared. This makes the effect of outliers on the overall error much greater.

Once you have chosen the metrics that are appropriate for your business problem, the next step is to include them in your machine learning pipeline. You can do this using TFMA, which we will describe in the next section.

TensorFlow Model Analysis

TFMA gives us an easy way to get more detailed metrics than just those used during model training. It lets us visualize metrics as time series across model versions, and it gives us the ability to view metrics on slices of a dataset. It also scales easily to large evaluation sets thanks to Apache Beam.

In a TFX pipeline, TFMA calculates metrics based on the saved model that is exported by the `Trainer` component, which is exactly the one that will be deployed. Thus, it avoids any confusion between different model versions. During model training, if you are using TensorBoard you will only get approximate metrics extrapolated from measurements on minibatches, but TFMA calculates metrics over the whole evaluation set. This is particularly relevant for large evaluation sets.

Analyzing a Single Model in TFMA

In this section, we'll look at how to use TFMA as a standalone package. TFMA is installed as follows:

```
$ pip install tensorflow-model-analysis
```

It takes a saved model and an evaluation dataset as input. In this example, we'll assume a Keras model is saved in `SavedModel` format and an evaluation dataset is available in the TFRecord file format.

First, the `SavedModel` must be converted to an `EvalSharedModel`:

```
import tensorflow_model_analysis as tfma

eval_shared_model = tfma.default_eval_shared_model(
    eval_saved_model_path=_MODEL_DIR,
    tags=[tf.saved_model.SERVING])
```

Next, we provide an `EvalConfig`. In this step, we tell TFMA what our label is, provide any specifications for slicing the model by one of the features, and stipulate all the metrics we want TFMA to calculate and display:

```
eval_config=tfma.EvalConfig(
    model_specs=[tfma.ModelSpec(label_key='consumer_disputed')],
    slicing_specs=[tfma.SlicingSpec()],
    metrics_specs=[
        tfma.MetricsSpec(metrics=[
            tfma.MetricConfig(class_name='BinaryAccuracy'),
            tfma.MetricConfig(class_name='ExampleCount'),
            tfma.MetricConfig(class_name='FalsePositives'),
            tfma.MetricConfig(class_name='TruePositives'),
            tfma.MetricConfig(class_name='FalseNegatives'),
            tfma.MetricConfig(class_name='TrueNegatives')
        ])
    ]
)
```

Analyzing TFLite Models

We can also analyze TFLite models in TFMA. In this case, the model type must be passed to the `ModelSpec`:

```
eval_config = tfma.EvalConfig(
    model_specs=[tfma.ModelSpec(label_key='my_label',
                                model_type=tfma.TF_LITE)],
    ...
)
```

We discuss TFLite in more detail in "TFLite" on page 178.

Then, run the model analysis step:

```
eval_result = tfma.run_model_analysis(
    eval_shared_model=eval_shared_model,
    eval_config=eval_config,
    data_location=_EVAL_DATA_FILE,
    output_path=_EVAL_RESULT_LOCATION,
    file_format='tfrecords')
```

And view the results in a Jupyter Notebook:

```
tfma.view.render_slicing_metrics(eval_result)
```

Even though we want to view the overall metrics, we still call `render_slicing_met rics`. The slice in this context is the *overall slice*, which is the entire dataset. The result is shown in Figure 7-4.

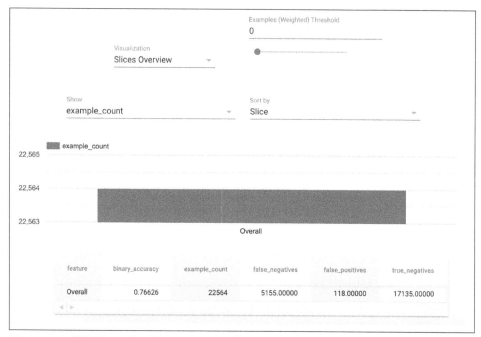

Figure 7-4. TFMA notebook visualization for overall metrics

Using TFMA in a Jupyter Notebook

TFMA works as previously described in a Google Colab notebook. But a few extra steps are required to view the visualizations in a standalone Jupyter Notebook. Install and enable the TFMA notebook extension with:

```
$ jupyter nbextension enable --py widgetsnbextension
$ jupyter nbextension install --py \
    --symlink tensorflow_model_analysis
$ jupyter nbextension enable --py tensorflow_model_analysis
```

Append the flag `--sys_prefix` to each of these commands if you are running them in a Python virtual environment. The `widgetsn bextension`, `ipywidgets`, and `jupyter_nbextensions_configura tor` packages may also require installation or upgrading.

At the time of writing, TFMA visualizations are not available in Jupyter Lab, only in Jupyter Notebook.

All the metrics we described in "How to Analyze Your Model" on page 100 can be displayed in TFMA by providing them in the `metrics_specs` argument to the `EvalConfig`:

```
metrics_specs=[
    tfma.MetricsSpec(metrics=[
        tfma.MetricConfig(class_name='BinaryAccuracy'),
        tfma.MetricConfig(class_name='AUC'),
        tfma.MetricConfig(class_name='ExampleCount'),
        tfma.MetricConfig(class_name='Precision'),
        tfma.MetricConfig(class_name='Recall')
    ])
]
```

The results are shown in Figure 7-5.

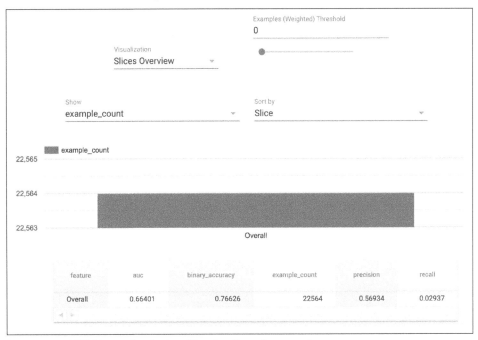

Figure 7-5. TFMA notebook visualization for other metrics

Analyzing Multiple Models in TFMA

We can also use TFMA to compare our metrics across multiple models. For example, these may be the same model trained on different datasets, or two models with different hyperparameters trained on the same dataset.

For the models we compare, we first need to generate an `eval_result` similar to the preceding code examples. We need to ensure we specify an `output_path` location to save the models. We use the same `EvalConfig` for both models so that we can calculate the same metrics:

```
eval_shared_model_2 = tfma.default_eval_shared_model(
    eval_saved_model_path=_EVAL_MODEL_DIR, tags=[tf.saved_model.SERVING])

eval_result_2 = tfma.run_model_analysis(
    eval_shared_model=eval_shared_model_2,
    eval_config=eval_config,
    data_location=_EVAL_DATA_FILE,
    output_path=_EVAL_RESULT_LOCATION_2,
    file_format='tfrecords')
```

Then, we load them using the following code:

```
eval_results_from_disk = tfma.load_eval_results(
    [_EVAL_RESULT_LOCATION, _EVAL_RESULT_LOCATION_2],
    tfma.constants.MODEL_CENTRIC_MODE)
```

And we can visualize them using:

```
tfma.view.render_time_series(eval_results_from_disk, slices[0])
```

The result is shown in Figure 7-6.

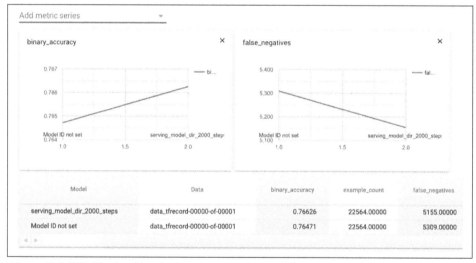

Figure 7-6. TFMA visualization comparing two models

The key thing to note here is that for both classification and regression models in TFMA it is possible to view many metrics at once, rather than being restricted to one or two during training. This helps to prevent surprising behavior once the model is deployed.

We can also slice the evaluation data based on features of the dataset, for example, to get the accuracy by product in our demo project. We'll describe how to do this in the following section.

Model Analysis for Fairness

All the data that we use to train a model is biased in some way: the real world is an incredibly complex place, and it's impossible to take a sample of data that adequately captures all this complexity. In Chapter 4, we looked at bias in data on the way into our pipeline, and in this chapter we'll look at whether the model's predictions are fair.

Fairness and Bias

The terms "fairness" and "bias" are often used interchangeably to refer to whether different groups of people experience different performance from a machine learning model. Here, we'll use the term "fairness" to avoid confusion with data bias, which we discussed in Chapter 4.

To analyze whether our model is fair, we need to identify when some groups of people get a different experience than others in a problematic way. For example, a group of people could be people who don't pay back loans. If our model is trying to predict who should be extended credit, this group of people should have a different experience than others. An example of the type of problem we want to avoid is when the only people who are incorrectly turned down for loans are of a certain race.

A high-profile example of groups getting different experiences from a model is the COMPAS algorithm that predicts recidivism risk. As reported by Propublica (*https://oreil.ly/mIw7t*), the algorithm's error rate was roughly the same for black and white defendants. However, it was especially likely to incorrectly predict that black defendants would be future criminals, at roughly twice the rate of the same incorrect prediction for white defendants.

We should try to recognize such problems before our models are deployed to production. To start with, it's useful to define numerically what we mean by *fairness*. Here are several example methods for classification problems:

Demographic parity
Decisions are made by the model at the same rate for all groups. For example, men and women would be approved for a loan at the same rate.

Equal opportunity
The error rate in the opportunity-giving class is the same for all groups. Depending on how the problem is set up, this can be the positive class or the negative class. For example, of the people who can pay back a loan, men and women would be approved for a loan at the same rate.

Equal accuracy

> Some metrics such as accuracy, precision, or AUC are equal for all groups. For example, a facial recognition system should be as accurate for dark-skinned women as it is for light-skinned men.

Equal accuracy can sometimes be misleading, as in the preceding COMPAS example. In that example, the accuracy was equal for both groups, but the consequences were much higher for one group. It's important to consider the directions of errors that have the highest consequences for your model.

Definitions of Fairness

There is no one definition of fairness that is appropriate for all machine learning projects. You will need to explore what is best for your specific business problem, taking into account potential harms and benefits to the users of your model. More guidance is provided in the book *Fairness in Machine Learning* (*https://fair mlbook.org*) by Solon Barocas et al., this article (*https://oreil.ly/GlgnV*) by Martin Wattenberg et al. from Google, and the Fairness Indicators documentation (*https://oreil.ly/O237L*) by Ben Hutchinson et al.

The groups we're referring to can be different types of customers, product users from different countries, or people of different gender and ethnicity. In US law, there is the concept of *protected groups*, where individuals are protected from discrimination based on the groups of gender, race, age, disability, color, creed, national origin, religion, and genetic information. And these groups intersect: you may need to check that your model does not discriminate against multiple combinations of groups.

Groups are A Simplification

Groups of people are never clean-cut in the real world. Everyone has their own complex story: someone may have changed their religion or their gender during their lifetime. Someone may belong to multiple races or multiple nationalities. Look for these edge cases and give people ways to tell you if they have a poor experience with your model.

Even if you are not using these groups as features in your model, this does not mean that your model is fair. Many other features, such as location, might be strongly correlated with one of these protected groups. For example, if you use a US zip code as a feature, this is highly correlated with race. You can check for these problems by slicing your data for one of the protected groups, as we describe in the following section, even if it is not a feature that you have used to train your model.

Fairness is not an easy topic to deal with, and it leads us into many ethical questions that may be complex or controversial. However, there are several projects that can help us analyze our models from a fairness perspective, and we'll describe how you can use them in the next few sections. This kind of analysis can give you an ethical and a commercial advantage by giving everyone a consistent experience. It may even be a chance to correct underlying unfairness in the system that you are modeling—for example, analyzing a recruiting tool (*https://oreil.ly/0ihec*) at Amazon revealed an underlying disadvantage experienced by female candidates.

In the next sections, we will describe how to use three projects for evaluating fairness in TensorFlow: TFMA, Fairness Indicators, and the What-If Tool.

Slicing Model Predictions in TFMA

The first step in evaluating your machine learning model for fairness is slicing your model's predictions by the groups you are interested in—for example, gender, race, or country. These slices can be generated by TFMA or the Fairness Indicators tools.

To slice data in TFMA, a slicing column must be provided as a `SliceSpec`. In this example, we'll slice on the *Product* feature:

```
slices = [tfma.slicer.SingleSliceSpec(),
          tfma.slicer.SingleSliceSpec(columns=['Product'])]
```

`SingleSliceSpec` with no specified arguments returns the entire dataset.

Next, run the model analysis step with the slices specified:

```
eval_result = tfma.run_model_analysis(
    eval_shared_model=eval_shared_model,
    eval_config=eval_config_viz,
    data_location=_EVAL_DATA_FILE,
    output_path=_EVAL_RESULT_LOCATION,
    file_format='tfrecords',
    slice_spec = slices)
```

And view the results, as shown in Figure 7-7:

```
tfma.view.render_slicing_metrics(eval_result, slicing_spec=slices[1])
```

If we want to consider Demographic parity, as defined previously, then we need to check whether the same proportion of people in each group are in the positive class. We can check this by looking at the TPR and the TNR for each group.

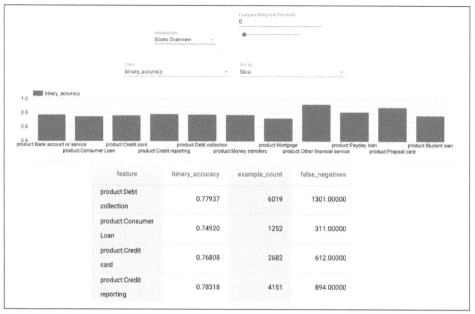

Figure 7-7. TFMA slicing visualization

Consider Which Class Is Beneficial

We're assuming that there is some choice made by the model that is beneficial to a person, and we're assuming that this is the positive class. If the positive class is not beneficial and the negative class is harmful to a person, we should consider the true negative rate and the false positive rate instead.

For equal opportunity, we can check the FPR for each group. For more details on this, the Fairness Indicators project has useful advice (*https://oreil.ly/s8Do7*).

Checking Decision Thresholds with Fairness Indicators

Fairness Indicators is another extremely useful tool for model analysis. It has some overlapping capabilities with TFMA, but one particularly useful feature of it is the ability to view metrics sliced on features at a variety of decision thresholds. As we discussed previously, the decision threshold is the probability score at which we draw the boundary between classes for a classification model. This lets us check if our model is fair to groups at different decision thresholds.

There are several ways to access the Fairness Indicators tool, but the simplest way to use it as a standalone library is via TensorBoard. We also mention how to load it as part of a TFX pipeline in "Evaluator Component" on page 125. We install the Tensor-Board Fairness Indicators plug-in via:

```
$ pip install tensorboard_plugin_fairness_indicators
```

Next, we use TFMA to evaluate the model and ask it to calculate metrics for a set of decision thresholds we supply. This is supplied to TFMA in the `metrics_spec` argument for the `EvalConfig`, along with any other metrics we wish to calculate:

```
eval_config=tfma.EvalConfig(
    model_specs=[tfma.ModelSpec(label_key='consumer_disputed')],
    slicing_specs=[tfma.SlicingSpec(),
                   tfma.SlicingSpec(feature_keys=['product'])],
    metrics_specs=[
        tfma.MetricsSpec(metrics=[
            tfma.MetricConfig(class_name='FairnessIndicators',
                              config='{"thresholds":[0.25, 0.5, 0.75]}')
        ])
    ]
)
```

Then run the model analysis step as before via `tfma.run_model_analysis`.

Next, write the TFMA evaluation result to a log directory so that it can be picked up by TensorBoard:

```
from tensorboard_plugin_fairness_indicators import summary_v2

writer = tf.summary.create_file_writer('./fairness_indicator_logs')
with writer.as_default():
    summary_v2.FairnessIndicators('./eval_result_fairness', step=1)
writer.close()
```

And load the result in TensorBoard to a Jupyter Notebook:

```
%load_ext tensorboard
%tensorboard --logdir=./fairness_indicator_logs
```

The Fairness Indicators tool highlights variations from the overall metric value, as shown in Figure 7-8.

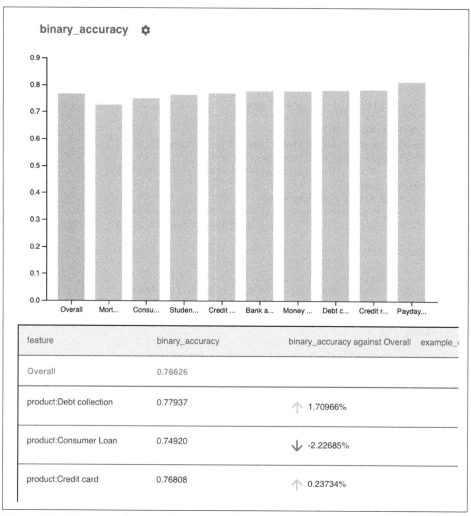

Figure 7-8. Fairness Indicators slicing visualization

And for our example project, Figure 7-9 shows more extreme differences between groups when the decision threshold is reduced to 0.25.

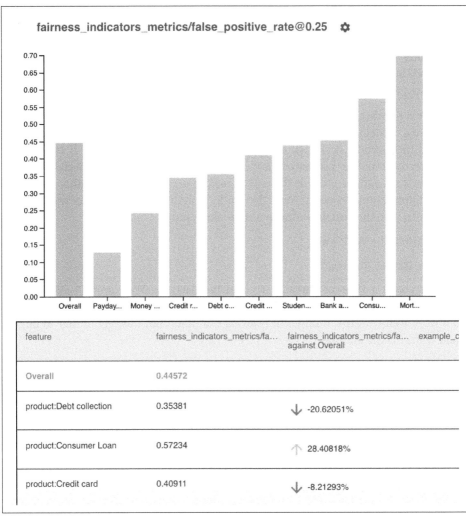

Figure 7-9. Fairness Indicators threshold visualization

In addition to exploring fairness considerations in the overall model, we might want to look at individual data points to see how individual users are affected by our model. Fortunately, there is another tool in the TensorFlow ecosystem to help us with this: the What-If Tool.

Going Deeper with the What-If Tool

After looking at slices of our dataset with TFMA and Fairness Indicators, we can go into greater detail using another project from Google: the What-If Tool (*https:// oreil.ly/NJThO*) (WIT). This lets us generate some very useful visualizations and also investigate individual data points.

There are a number of ways to use the WIT with your model and data. It can be used to analyze a model that has already been deployed with TensorFlow Serving via TensorBoard (*https://oreil.ly/sZP5l*), or a model that is running on GCP. It can also be used directly with an Estimator model. But for our example project, the most straightforward way to use it is to write a *custom prediction function* that takes in a list of training examples and returns the model's predictions for these examples. This way, we can load the visualizations in a standalone Jupyter Notebook.

We can install the WIT with:

```
$ pip install witwidget
```

Next, we create a `TFRecordDataset` to load the data file. We sample 1,000 training examples and convert it to a list of `TFExamples`. The visualizations in the What-If Tool work well with this number of training examples, but they get harder to understand with a larger sample:

```
eval_data = tf.data.TFRecordDataset(_EVAL_DATA_FILE)
subset = eval_data.take(1000)
eval_examples = [tf.train.Example.FromString(d.numpy()) for d in subset]
```

Next, we load the model and define a prediction function that takes in the list of `TFExamples` and returns the model's predictions:

```
model = tf.saved_model.load(export_dir=_MODEL_DIR)
predict_fn = model.signatures['serving_default']

def predict(test_examples):
    test_examples = tf.constant([example.SerializeToString() for example in examples])
    preds = predict_fn(examples=test_examples)
    return preds['outputs'].numpy()
```

Then we configure the WIT using:

```
from witwidget.notebook.visualization import WitConfigBuilder

config_builder = WitConfigBuilder(eval_examples).set_custom_predict_fn(predict)
```

And we can view it in a notebook using:

```
from witwidget.notebook.visualization import WitWidget

WitWidget(config_builder)
```

This will give us the visualization in Figure 7-10.

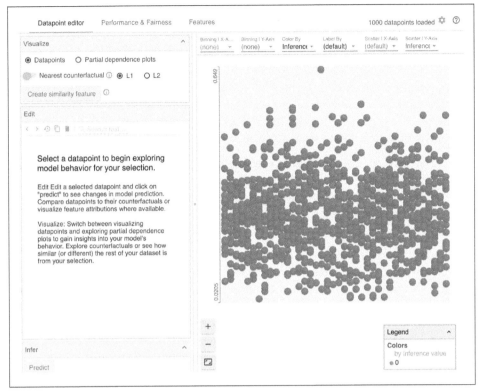

Figure 7-10. WIT front page

Using the WIT in a Jupyter Notebook

As with TFMA, a few extra steps are required to run the WIT in a standalone notebook. Install and enable the WIT notebook extension with:

```
$ jupyter nbextension install --py --symlink \
    --sys-prefix witwidget
```

```
$ jupyter nbextension enable witwidget --py --sys-prefix
```

Append the flag `--sys_prefix` to each of these commands if you are running them in a Python virtual environment.

There are many functions included in the WIT, and we will describe some of the most useful here. Full documentation is provided at the WIT project home page (*https://oreil.ly/cyTDR*).

The WIT provides *counterfactuals*, which for any individual training example show its nearest neighbor from a different classification. All the features are as similar as possible, but the model's prediction for the counterfactual is the other class. This helps us see how each feature impacts the model's prediction for the particular training example. If we see that changing a demographic feature (race, gender, etc.) changes the model's prediction to the other class, this is a warning sign that the model may not be fair to different groups.

We can explore this feature further by editing a selected example in the browser. Then we can rerun the inference and see what effect this has on the predictions made for the specific example. This can be used to explore demographic features for fairness or any other features to see what happens if they are changed.

Counterfactuals can also be used as explanations for the model's behavior. But note that there may be many possible counterfactuals for each data point that are close to being the nearest neighbor and also that there are likely to be complex interactions between features. So counterfactuals themselves should not be presented as if they completely explain the model's behavior.

Another particularly useful feature of the WIT is partial dependence plots (PDPs). These show us how each feature impacts the predictions of the model, for example, whether an increase in a numeric feature changes the class prediction probability. The PDP shows us the shape of this dependence: whether it is linear, monotonic, or more complex. PDPs can also be generated for categorical features, as shown in Figure 7-11. Again, if the model's predictions show a dependence on a demographic feature, this may be a warning that your model's predictions are unfair.

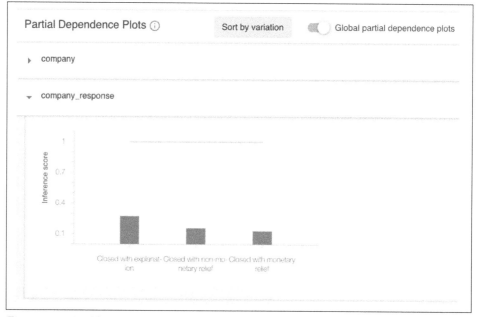

Figure 7-11. WIT PDPs

A more advanced feature, for which we won't dive into detail here, is to optimize decision thresholds for fairness strategies. This is provided as a page in the WIT, and it's possible to automatically set decision thresholds based on a chosen strategy, as shown in Figure 7-12.

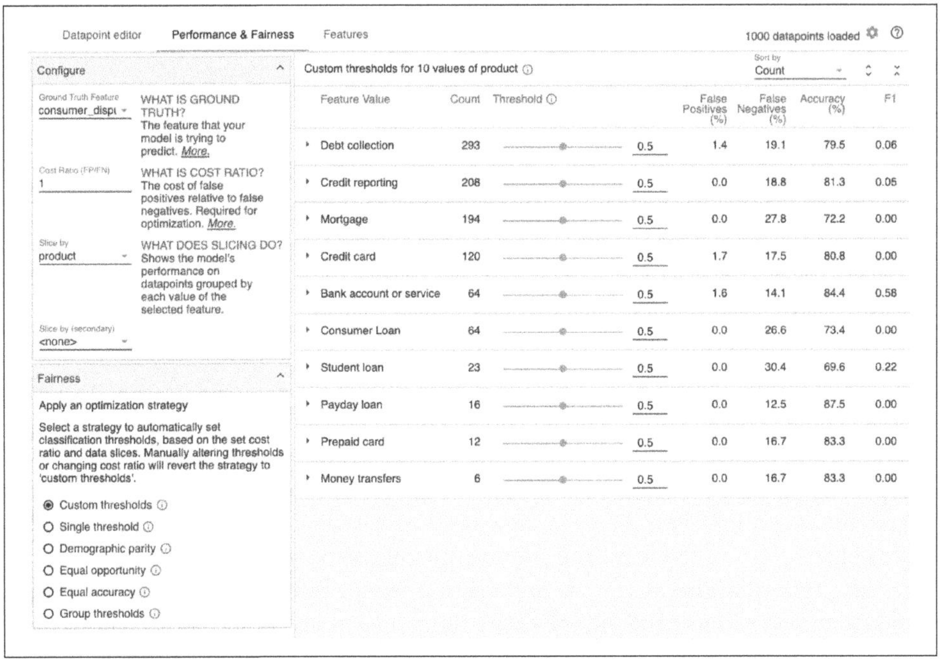

Figure 7-12. WIT decision thresholds

All of the tools we describe in this section on model fairness can also be used to interrogate any model even if it does not have the potential to harm users. They can be used to get a much better understanding of a model's behavior before it is deployed and can help avoid surprises when it reaches the real world. This is an area of active research, and new tools are released frequently. One interesting development is *constrained optimization* for model fairness, in which instead of just optimizing for one metric, models can be optimized by taking into consideration other constraints, such as equal accuracy. An experimental library (*https://oreil.ly/WkYyi*) exists for this in TensorFlow.

Model Explainability

Discussing fairness and using the WIT naturally leads us to discussing how we can not only describe the performance of our model but also explain what is going on inside it. We mentioned this briefly in the previous section on fairness, but we'll expand on it a little more here.

Model *explainability* seeks to explain why the predictions made by a model turn out that way. This is in contrast to *analysis*, which describes the model's performance with respect to various metrics. Explainability for machine learning is a big topic, with a lot of active research on the subject happening right now. It isn't something we can automate as part of our pipeline because, by definition, the explanations need to be shown to people. We will just give you a brief overview, and for more details we recommend the ebook *Interpretable Machine Learning* by Christoph Molnar (*https:// oreil.ly/fGtve*) and this whitepaper (*https://oreil.ly/3CLTk*) from Google Cloud.

There are a few possible reasons for seeking to explain your model's predictions:

- Helping a data scientist debug problems with their model
- Building trust in the model
- Auditing models
- Explaining model predictions to users

The techniques we discuss further on are helpful in all these use cases.

Predictions from simpler models are much easier to explain than predictions from complex models. Linear regression, logistic regression, and single decision trees are relatively easy to interpret. We can view the weights for each feature and know the exact contribution of the feature. For these models, looking at the entire model provides an explanation because their architecture makes them interpretable by design, so that a human can understand the entire thing. For example, the coefficients from a linear regression model give an explanation that is understandable with no further processing required.

It is more difficult to explain random forests and other ensemble models, and deep neural networks are the hardest of all to explain. This is due to the enormous number of parameters and connections in a neural network, which results in extremely complex interactions between features. If your model's predictions have high consequences and you require explanations, we recommend you choose models that are easier to explain. You can find more details on how and when to use explanations in the paper "Explainable Machine Learning in Deployment" (*https://arxiv.org/pdf/ 1909.06342.pdf*) by Umang Bhatt et al.

Local and Global Explanations

We can divide ML explainability methods into two broad groups: local and global explanations. *Local explanations* seek to explain why a model made a particular prediction for one single data point. *Global explanations* seek to explain how a model works overall, measured using a large set of data points. We will introduce techniques for both of these in the next section.

In the next section, we will introduce some techniques for generating explanations from your model.

Generating Explanations with the WIT

In "Going Deeper with the What-If Tool" on page 116, we described how we could use the WIT to help with our model fairness questions. But the WIT is also useful for explaining our models—in particular, using counterfactuals and PDPs, as we noted. Counterfactuals provide us with local explanations, but PDPs can provide either local or global explanations. We showed an example of global PDPs previously in Figure 7-11, and now we'll consider local PDPs, as shown in Figure 7-13.

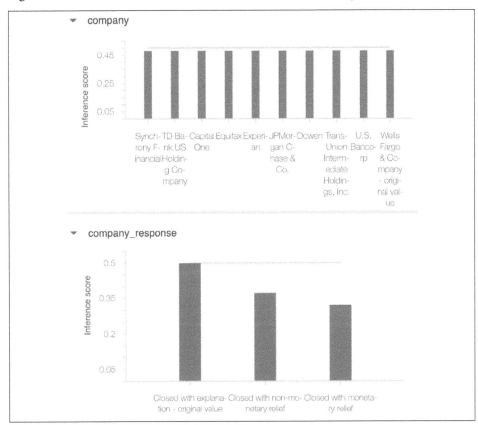

Figure 7-13. WIT local PDPs

PDPs show the change in prediction results (the *inference score*) for different valid values of a feature. There is no change in the inference score across the company feature, showing that the predictions for this data point don't depend on the value of this feature. But for the company_response feature, there is a change in the inference score, which shows that the model prediction has some dependence on the value of the feature.

Assumptions with PDPs

PDPs contain an important assumption: all features are independent of each other. For most datasets, especially those that are complex enough to need a neural network model to make accurate predictions, this is not a good assumption. These plots should be approached with caution: they can give you an indication of what your model is doing, but they do not give you a complete explanation.

If your model is deployed using Google Cloud's AI Platform, you can see *feature attributions* (*https://oreil.ly/ePiEi*) in the WIT. For a single data example, feature attributions provide positive or negative scores for each feature for each feature, which indicate the effect and magnitude of the feature's contributions to a model's prediction. They can also be aggregated to provide global explanations of the feature's importance in your model. The feature attributions are based on *Shapley values*, which are described in the following section. Shapley values do not assume that your features are independent, so unlike PDPs, they are useful if your features are correlated with each other. At the time of writing, feature attributions were only available for models trained using TensorFlow 1.x.

Other Explainability Techniques

LIME (*https://oreil.ly/SrlWc*), or local interpretable model-agnostic explanations, is another method for producing local explanations. It treats a model as a black box and generates new data points around the point that we would like to get an explanation for. LIME then obtains predictions from the model for these new data points and trains a simple model using these points. The weights for this simple model give us the explanations.

The SHAP (*https://oreil.ly/3S01U*), or Shapley Additive Explanations, library provides both global and local explanations using Shapley values. These are computationally expensive to calculate, so the SHAP library contains implementations that speed up calculations or calculate approximations for boosted trees and deep neural networks. This library is a great way to show a feature's importance for your models.

Shapley Values

Shapley values are useful for both local and global explanations. This concept is an algorithm borrowed from game theory that distributes gains and losses across each

---

player in a cooperative game for some outcome of the game. In a machine learning context, each feature is a "player," and the Shapley values can be obtained as follows:

1. Get all the possible subsets of features that don't contain feature F.
2. Compute the effect on the model's predictions of adding F to all the subsets.
3. Combine these effects to get the importance of feature F.

These are all relative to some *baseline*. For our example project, we could pose this as "how much was a prediction driven by the fact that the `company_response` was `Closed with explanation` instead of `Closed with monetary relief`." The value `Closed with monetary relief` is our baseline.

We would also like to mention model cards (*https://oreil.ly/VWcwS*), a framework for reporting on machine learning models. These are a formal way of sharing facts and limitations about machine learning models. We include these here because even though they don't explain why the model makes its predictions, they are extremely valuable for building trust in a model. A model card should include the following pieces of information:

- Benchmarked performance of the model on public datasets, including performance sliced across demographic features
- Limitations of the model, for example, disclosing if a decrease in image quality would produce a less accurate result from an image classification model
- Any trade-offs made by the model, for example, explaining if a larger image would require longer processing time

Model cards are extremely useful for communicating about models in high-stakes situations, and they encourage data scientists and machine learning engineers to document the use cases and limitations of the models they build.

Limitations of Explanations

We recommend that you proceed with caution when tackling model explainability. These techniques may give you a warm and happy feeling that you understand what your model is doing, but it may actually be doing something very complex that is impossible to explain. This is especially the case with deep learning models.

It just isn't feasible to represent all the complexity of the millions of weights that make up a deep neural network in a way that is human readable. In situations where model decisions have high real-world consequences, we recommend building the simplest models possible with features that are easy to explain.

Analysis and Validation in TFX

Up to this point in this chapter, we've focused on model analysis with a human in the loop. These tools are extremely useful for monitoring our models and checking that they are behaving in the way we want. But in an automated machine learning pipeline, we want the pipeline to run smoothly and alert us to problems. There are several components in TFX that handle this part of the pipeline: the Resolver, the Evaluator, and the Pusher. Together, these components check the model's performance on an evaluation dataset and send it to a serving location if it improves the previous model.

TFX uses the concept of *blessing* to describe the gating process for deciding whether or not to deploy a model for serving. If a model improves the previous model, based on a threshold we define, it is blessed and can move forward to the next step.

ResolverNode

A Resolver component is required if we want to compare a new model against a previous model. ResolverNodes are generic components that query the metadata store. In this case, we use the latest_blessed_model_resolver. It checks for the last blessed model and returns it as a baseline so it can be passed on to the Evaluator component with the new candidate model. The Resolver is not needed if we don't want to validate our model against a threshold of some metric, but we highly recommend this step. If you don't validate the new model, it will automatically get pushed to the serving directory, even if its performance is worse than that of the previous model. On the first run of the Evaluator when there is no blessed model, the Evaluator automatically blesses the model.

In an interactive context, we can run the Resolver component as follows:

```
from tfx.components import ResolverNode
from tfx.dsl.experimental import latest_blessed_model_resolver
from tfx.types import Channel
from tfx.types.standard_artifacts import Model
from tfx.types.standard_artifacts import ModelBlessing

model_resolver = ResolverNode(
    instance_name='latest_blessed_model_resolver',
    resolver_class=latest_blessed_model_resolver.LatestBlessedModelResolver,
    model=Channel(type=Model),
    model_blessing=Channel(type=ModelBlessing)
)
context.run(model_resolver)
```

Evaluator Component

The Evaluator component uses the TFMA library to evaluate a model's predictions on a validation dataset. It takes as input data from the ExampleGen component, the trained model from the Trainer component, and an EvalConfig for TFMA (the same as when using TFMA as a standalone library).

First, we define the EvalConfig:

```
import tensorflow_model_analysis as tfma

eval_config=tfma.EvalConfig(
    model_specs=[tfma.ModelSpec(label_key='consumer_disputed')],
    slicing_specs=[tfma.SlicingSpec(),
                    tfma.SlicingSpec(feature_keys=['product'])],
    metrics_specs=[
        tfma.MetricsSpec(metrics=[
            tfma.MetricConfig(class_name='BinaryAccuracy'),
            tfma.MetricConfig(class_name='ExampleCount'),
            tfma.MetricConfig(class_name='AUC')
        ])
    ]
)
```

Then we run the Evaluator component:

```
from tfx.components import Evaluator

evaluator = Evaluator(
    examples=example_gen.outputs['examples'],
    model=trainer.outputs['model'],
    baseline_model=model_resolver.outputs['model'],
    eval_config=eval_config
)
context.run(evaluator)
```

We can also show the TFMA visualization with:

```
eval_result = evaluator.outputs['evaluation'].get()[0].uri
tfma_result = tfma.load_eval_result(eval_result)
```

And we can load Fairness Indicators with:

```
tfma.addons.fairness.view.widget_view.render_fairness_indicator(tfma_result)
```

Validation in the Evaluator Component

The Evaluator component also carries out validation, in which it checks whether the candidate model we have just trained is an improvement on a baseline model (such as the model that is currently in production). It obtains predictions from both models on an evaluation dataset and compares a performance metric (e.g., model accuracy) from both models. If the new model is an improvement on the previous model, the new model receives a "blessing" artifact. Currently it is only possible to calculate the metric on the whole evaluation set, not on slices.

To carry out validation, we need to set a threshold in the `EvalConfig`:

```
eval_config=tfma.EvalConfig(
    model_specs=[tfma.ModelSpec(label_key='consumer_disputed')],
    slicing_specs=[tfma.SlicingSpec(),
                  tfma.SlicingSpec(feature_keys=['product'])],
    metrics_specs=[
        tfma.MetricsSpec(
            metrics=[
                tfma.MetricConfig(class_name='BinaryAccuracy'),
                tfma.MetricConfig(class_name='ExampleCount'),
                tfma.MetricConfig(class_name='AUC')
            ],
            thresholds={
                'AUC':
                    tfma.config.MetricThreshold(
                        value_threshold=tfma.GenericValueThreshold(
                            lower_bound={'value': 0.65}),
                        change_threshold=tfma.GenericChangeThreshold(
                            direction=tfma.MetricDirection.HIGHER_IS_BETTER,
                            absolute={'value': 0.01}
                        )
                    )
            }
        )
    ]
)
```

In this example, we state that the AUC must be over 0.65, and we want the model to be validated if its AUC is at least 0.01 higher than that of the baseline model. Any other metric can be added in place of AUC, but note that the metric you add must also be included in the list of `metrics` in the `MetricsSpec`.

We can check the results with:

```
eval_result = evaluator.outputs['evaluation'].get()[0].uri
print(tfma.load_validation_result(eval_result))
```

If the validation check passes, it will return the following result:

```
validation_ok: true
```

TFX Pusher Component

The Pusher component is a small but important part of our pipeline. It takes as input a saved model, the output of the `Evaluator` component, and a file path for the location our models will be stored for serving. It then checks whether the `Evaluator` has blessed the model (i.e., the model is an improvement on the previous version, and it is above any thresholds we have set). If it has been blessed, the `Pusher` pushes the model to the serving file path.

The `Pusher` component is provided with the model `Evaluator` outputs and the serving destination:

```
from tfx.components import Pusher
from tfx.proto import pusher_pb2

_serving_model_dir = "serving_model_dir"

pusher = Pusher(
    model=trainer.outputs['model'],
    model_blessing=evaluator.outputs['blessing'],
    push_destination=pusher_pb2.PushDestination(
        filesystem=pusher_pb2.PushDestination.Filesystem(
            base_directory=_serving_model_dir)))
context.run(pusher)
```

Once the new model has been pushed to the serving directory, it can then be picked up by TensorFlow Serving—see the next chapter for more details on this.

Summary

In this chapter, we saw how to analyze a model's performance in much greater detail than during model training, and we started thinking about how to make a model's performance fair. We also discussed the process for checking that a model's performance is an improvement on the previously deployed model. We also introduced explainability for machine learning and gave a brief overview of some of the techniques in this area.

We must advise caution here, though: just because you've analyzed your model's performance in detail with Fairness Indicators, this doesn't guarantee that your model is fair or ethically sound. It's important to keep monitoring your model once it is in production and provide ways for your users to let you know if they feel that the model's predictions are unjust. This is especially important when the stakes are high and the model's decisions have the potential to cause large real-world impacts to users.

Now that our model has been analyzed and validated, it's time to move on to the crucial next step in the pipeline: serving the model! The next two chapters will tell you all you need to know about this important step.

Model Deployment with TensorFlow Serving

The deployment of your machine learning model is the last step before others can use your model and make predictions with it. Unfortunately, the deployment of machine learning models falls into a gray zone in today's thinking of the division of labor in the digital world. It isn't just a DevOps task since it requires some knowledge of the model architecture and its hardware requirements. At the same time, deploying machine learning models is a bit outside the comfort zone of machine learning engineers and data scientists. They know their models inside out but tend to struggle with the deployment of machine learning models. In this and the following chapter, we want to bridge the gap between the worlds and guide data scientists and DevOps engineers through the steps to deploy machine learning models. Figure 8-1 shows the position of the deployment step in a machine learning pipeline.

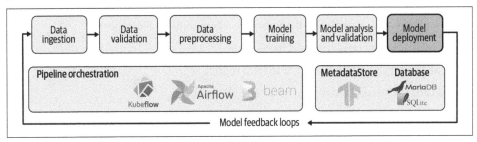

Figure 8-1. Model deployments as part of ML pipelines

Machine learning models can be deployed in three main ways: with a model server, in a user's browser, or on an edge device. The most common way today to deploy a machine learning model is with a model server, which we will focus on in this chapter. The client that requests a prediction submits the input data to the model server and in return receives a prediction. This requires that the client can connect with the model server.

There are situations when you don't want to submit the input data to a model server (e.g., when the input data is sensitive, or when there are privacy concerns). In these situations, you can deploy the machine learning model to a user's browser. For example, if you want to determine whether an image contains sensitive information, you could classify the sensitivity level of the image before it is uploaded to a cloud server.

However, there is also a third type of model deployment: deploying to edge devices. There are situations that don't allow you to connect to a model server to make predictions (i.e., remote sensors or IoT devices). The number of applications being deployed to edge devices is increasing, making it a valid option for model deployments. In Chapter 10, we discuss how TensorFlow models can be converted to TFLite models, which can be executed on edge devices.

In this chapter, we highlight TensorFlow's Serving module, a simple and consistent way of deploying TensorFlow models through a model server. We will introduce its setup and discuss efficient deployment options. This is not the only way of deploying deep learning models; there are a few alternative options, which we discuss toward the end of this chapter.

Let's start the chapter with how you shouldn't set up a model server before we take a deep dive into TensorFlow Serving.

A Simple Model Server

Most introductions to deploying machine learning models follow roughly the same workflow:

- Create a web app with Python (i.e., with web frameworks like Flask or Django).
- Create an API endpoint in the web app, as we show in Example 8-1.
- Load the model structure and its weights.
- Call the predict method on the loaded model.
- Return the prediction results as an HTTP request.

Example 8-1. Example setup of a Flask endpoint to infer model predictions

```
import json
from flask import Flask, request
from tensorflow.keras.models import load_model
from utils import preprocess ❶

model = load_model('model.h5') ❷
app = Flask(__name__)

@app.route('/classify', methods=['POST'])
def classify():
    complaint_data = request.form["complaint_data"]
    preprocessed_complaint_data = preprocess(complaint_data)
    prediction = model.predict([preprocessed_complaint_data]) ❸
    return json.dumps({"score": prediction}) ❹
```

❶ Preprocessing to convert data structure.

❷ Load your trained model.

❸ Perform the prediction.

❹ Return the prediction in an HTTP response.

This setup is a quick and easy implementation, perfect for demonstration projects. However, we do not recommend using Example 8-1 to deploy machine learning models to production endpoints.

Next, let's discuss why we don't recommend deploying machine learning models with such a setup. The reason is our benchmark for our proposed deployment solution.

The Downside of Model Deployments with Python-Based APIs

While the Example 8-1 implementation can be sufficient for demonstration purposes, such deployments often face challenges. The challenges start with proper separation between the API and the data science code, a consistent API structure and the resulting inconsistent model versioning, and inefficient model inferences. We will take a closer look at these challenges in the following sections.

Lack of Code Separation

In Example 8-1, we assumed that the trained model was being deployed with the same API code base that it was also living in. This means that there would be no separation between the API code and the machine learning model, which can be problematic when data scientists want to update a model and such an update requires coordination with the API team. Such coordination also requires that the API and data science teams work in sync to avoid unnecessary delays on the model deployments.

An intertwined API and data science code base also creates ambiguity around API ownership.

The lack of code separation also requires that the model has to be loaded in the same programming language as the API code. This mixing of backend and data science code can ultimately prevent your API team from upgrading your API backend. However, it also provides a good separation of responsibilities: the data scientists can focus on model training and the DevOps colleagues can focus on the deployment of the trained models.

We highlight how you can separate your models from your API code effectively and simplify your deployment workflows in "TensorFlow Serving".

Lack of Model Version Control

Example 8-1 doesn't make any provision for different model versions. If you wanted to add a new version, you would have to create a new endpoint (or add some branching logic to the existing endpoint). This requires extra attention to keep all endpoints structurally the same, and it requires a lot of boilerplate code.

The lack of model version control also requires the API and the data science teams to coordinate which version is the default version and how to phase in new models.

Inefficient Model Inference

For any request to your prediction endpoint written in the Flask setup as shown in Example 8-1, a full round trip is performed. This means each request is preprocessed and inferred individually. The key reason why we argue that such a setup is only for demonstration purposes is that it is highly inefficient. During the training of your model, you will probably use a batching technique that allows you to compute multiple samples at the same time and then apply the gradient change for your batch to your network's weights. You can apply the same technique when you want the model to make predictions. A model server can gather all requests during an acceptable timeframe or until the batch is full and ask the model for its predictions. This is an especially effective method when the inference runs on GPUs.

In "Batching Inference Requests" on page 156, we introduce how you can easily set up such a batching behavior for your model server.

TensorFlow Serving

As you have seen in the earlier chapters of this book, TensorFlow comes with a fantastic ecosystem of extensions and tools. One of the earlier open source extensions was TensorFlow Serving. It allows you to deploy any TensorFlow graph, and you can make predictions from the graph through its standardized endpoints. As we discuss in a moment, TensorFlow Serving handles the model and version management for you, lets you serve models based on policies, and allows you to load your models from various sources. At the same time, it is focused on high-performance throughput for low-latency predictions. TensorFlow Serving is used internally at Google and has been adopted by a good number of corporations and startups.[1]

TensorFlow Architecture Overview

TensorFlow Serving provides you the functionality to load models from a given source (e.g., AWS S3 buckets) and notifies the *loader* if the source has changed. As Figure 8-2 shows, everything behind the scenes of TensorFlow Serving is controlled by a model manager, which manages when to update the models and which model is used for the predictions. The rules for the inference determination are set by the policy which is managed by the model manager. Depending on your configuration, you can, for example, load one model at a time and have the model update automatically once the source module detects a newer version.

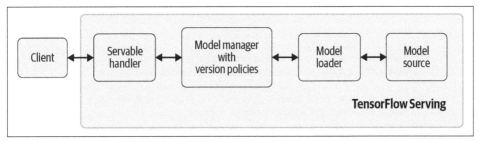

Figure 8-2. Overview of the TensorFlow Serving architecture

---

1 For application use cases, visit TensorFlow (*https://oreil.ly/qCY6J*).

Exporting Models for TensorFlow Serving

Before we dive into the TensorFlow Serving configurations, let's discuss how you can export your machine learning models so that they can be used by TensorFlow Serving.

Depending on your type of TensorFlow model, the export steps are slightly different. The exported models have the same file structure as we see in Example 8-2. For Keras models, you can use:

```
saved_model_path = model.save(file path="./saved_models", save_format="tf")
```

 Add a Timestamp to Your Export Path

It is recommended to add the timestamp of the export time to the export path for the Keras model when you are manually saving the model. Unlike the save method of tf.Estimator, model.save() doesn't create the timestamped path automatically. You can create the file path easily with the following Python code:

```
import time

ts = int(time.time())
file path = "./saved_models/{}".format(ts)
saved_model_path = model.save(file path=file path,
                              save_format="tf")
```

For TensorFlow Estimator models, you need to first declare a receiver function:

```
import tensorflow as tf

def serving_input_receiver_fn():
    # an example input feature
    input_feature = tf.compat.v1.placeholder(
        dtype=tf.string, shape=[None, 1], name="input")

    fn = tf.estimator.export.build_raw_serving_input_receiver_fn(
        features={"input_feature": input_feature})
    return fn
```

Export the Estimator model with the export_saved_model method of the Estimator:

```
estimator = tf.estimator.Estimator(model_fn, "model", params={})
estimator.export_saved_model(
    export_dir_base="saved_models/",
    serving_input_receiver_fn=serving_input_receiver_fn)
```

Both export methods produce output which looks similar to the following example:

```
...
INFO:tensorflow:Signatures INCLUDED in export for Classify: None
INFO:tensorflow:Signatures INCLUDED in export for Regress: None
```

```
INFO:tensorflow:Signatures INCLUDED in export for Predict: ['serving_default']
INFO:tensorflow:Signatures INCLUDED in export for Train: None
INFO:tensorflow:Signatures INCLUDED in export for Eval: None
INFO:tensorflow:No assets to save.
INFO:tensorflow:No assets to write.
INFO:tensorflow:SavedModel written to: saved_models/1555875926/saved_model.pb
Model exported to:  b'saved_models/1555875926'
```

In our model export examples, we specified the folder *saved_models/* as the model destination. For every exported model, TensorFlow creates a directory with the timestamp of the export as its folder name:

Example 8-2. Folder and file structure of exported models

```
$ tree saved_models/
saved_models/
└── 1555875926
    ├── assets
    │   └── saved_model.json
    ├── saved_model.pb
    └── variables
        ├── checkpoint
        ├── variables.data-00000-of-00001
        └── variables.index
```

```
3 directories, 5 files
```

The folder contains the following files and subdirectories:

saved_model.pb
> The binary protocol buffer file contains the exported model graph structure as a `MetaGraphDef` object.

variables
> The folder contains the binary files with the exported variable values and checkpoints corresponding to the exported model graph.

assets
> This folder is created when additional files are needed to load the exported model. The additional file can include vocabularies, which saw in Chapter 5.

Model Signatures

Model signatures identify the model graph's inputs and outputs as well as the *method* of the graph signature. The definition of the input and output signatures allows us to map serving inputs to a given graph node for the inference. These mappings are useful if we want to update the model without changing the requests to the model server.

In addition, the *method* of the model defines an expected pattern of inputs and outputs. At the moment, there are three supported signature types: predict, classify, or regress. We will take a closer look at the details in the following section.

Signature Methods

The most flexible signature method is *predict*. If we don't specify a different signature method, TensorFlow will use *predict* as the default method. Example 8-3 shows an example signature for the method *predict*. In the example, we are mapping the key inputs to the graph node with the name *sentence*. The prediction from the model is the output of the graph node *y*, which we are mapping to the output key scores.

The *predict* method allows you to define additional output nodes. It is useful to add more inference outputs when you want to capture the output of an attention layer for visualizations or to debug a network node.

Example 8-3. Example model prediction signature

```
signature_def: {
  key   : "prediction_signature"
  value: {
    inputs: {
      key   : "inputs"
      value: {
        name: "sentence:0"
        dtype: DT_STRING
        tensor_shape: ...
      },
      ...
    }
    outputs: {
      key   : "scores"
      value: {
        name: "y:0"
        dtype: ...
        tensor_shape: ...
      }
    }
    method_name: "tensorflow/serving/predict"
  }
}
```

Another signature method is *classify*. The method expects one input with the name *inputs* and provides two output tensors, *classes* and *scores*. At least one of the output tensors needs to be defined. In our example shown in Example 8-4, a classification model takes the input sentence and outputs the predicted classes together with the corresponding scores.

Example 8-4. Example model classification signature

```
signature_def: {
  key  : "classification_signature"
  value: {
    inputs: {
      key  : "inputs"
      value: {
        name: "sentence:0"
        dtype: DT_STRING
        tensor_shape: ...
      }
    }
    outputs: {
      key  : "classes"
      value: {
        name: "y_classes:0"
        dtype: DT_UINT16
        tensor_shape: ...
      }
    }
    outputs: {
      key  : "scores"
      value: {
        name: "y:0"
        dtype: DT_FLOAT
        tensor_shape: ...
      }
    }
    method_name: "tensorflow/serving/classify"
  }
}
```

The third available signature method is *regress*. This method takes only one input named *inputs* and provides only output with the name *outputs*. This signature method is designed for regression models. Example 8-5 shows an example of a *regress* signature.

Example 8-5. Example model regression signature

```
signature_def: {
  key  : "regression_signature"
  value: {
    inputs: {
      key  : "inputs"
      value: {
        name: "input_tensor_0"
        dtype: ...
        tensor_shape: ...
      }
    }
```

```
    outputs: {
      key  : "outputs"
      value: {
        name: "y_outputs_0"
        dtype: DT_FLOAT
        tensor_shape: ...
      }
    }
    method_name: "tensorflow/serving/regress"
  }
}
```

In "URL structure" on page 148, we will see the signature methods again when we define the URL structure for our model endpoints.

Inspecting Exported Models

After all the talk about exporting your model and the corresponding model signatures, let's discuss how you can inspect the exported models before deploying them with TensorFlow Serving.

You can install the TensorFlow Serving Python API with the following `pip` command:

```
$ pip install tensorflow-serving-api
```

After the installation, you have access to a useful command-line tool called SavedModel Command Line Interface (CLI). This tool lets you:

Inspect the signatures of exported models
> This is very useful primarily when you don't export the model yourself, and you want to learn about the inputs and outputs of the model graph.

Test the exported models
> The CLI tools let you infer the model without deploying it with TensorFlow Serving. This is extremely useful when you want to test your model input data.

We'll cover both use cases in the following two sections.

Inspecting the Model

`saved_model_cli` helps you understand the model dependencies without inspecting the original graph code.

If you don't know the available tag-sets,[2] you can inspect the model with:

---

2 Model *tag sets* are used to identify MetaGraphs for loading. A model could be exported with a graph specified for training and serving. Both MetaGraphs can be provided through different model tags.

```
$ saved_model_cli show --dir saved_models/
The given SavedModel contains the following tag-sets:
serve
```

If your model contains different graphs for different environments (e.g., a graph for a CPU or GPU inference), you will see multiple tags. If your model contains multiple tags, you need to specify a tag to inspect the details of the model.

Once you know the `tag_set` you want to inspect, add it as an argument, and `saved_model_cli` will provide you the available model signatures. Our demo model has only one signature, which is called `serving_default`:

```
$ saved_model_cli show --dir saved_models/ --tag_set serve
The given SavedModel 'MetaGraphDef' contains 'SignatureDefs' with the
following keys:
SignatureDef key: "serving_default"
```

With the `tag_set` and `signature_def` information, you can now inspect the model's inputs and outputs. To obtain the detailed information, add the `signature_def` to the CLI arguments.

The following example signature is taken from our model that was produced by our demonstration pipeline. In Example 6-4, we defined our signature function, which takes serialized `tf.Example` records as inputs and provides the prediction through the output Tensor *outputs*, as shown in the following model signature:

```
$ saved_model_cli show --dir saved_models/ \
        --tag_set serve --signature_def serving_default
The given SavedModel SignatureDef contains the following input(s):
  inputs['examples'] tensor_info:
      dtype: DT_STRING
      shape: (-1)
      name: serving_default_examples:0
The given SavedModel SignatureDef contains the following output(s):
  outputs['outputs'] tensor_info:
      dtype: DT_FLOAT
      shape: (-1, 1)
      name: StatefulPartitionedCall_1:0
Method name is: tensorflow/serving/predict
```

If you want to see all signatures regardless of the `tag_set` and `signature_def`, you can use the `--all` argument:

```
$ saved_model_cli show --dir saved_models/ --all
...
```

After we investigated the model's signature, we can now test the model inference before we deploy the machine learning model.

Testing the Model

`saved_model_cli` also lets you test the export model with sample input data.

You have three different ways to submit the sample input data for the model test inference:

`--inputs`
> The argument points at a NumPy file containing the input data formatted as NumPy `ndarray`.

`--input_exprs`
> The argument allows you to define a Python expression to specify the input data. You can use NumPy functionality in your expressions.

`--input_examples`
> The argument is expecting the input data formatted as a `tf.Example` data structure (see Chapter 4).

For testing the model, you can specify exactly one of the input arguments. Furthermore, `saved_model_cli` provides three optional arguments:

`--outdir`
> `saved_model_cli` will write any graph output to `stdout`. If you would rather write the output to a file, you can specify the target directory with `--outdir`.

`--overwrite`
> If you opt for writing the output to a file, you can specify with `--overwrite` that the files can be overwritten.

`--tf_debug`
> If you want to further inspect the model, you can step through the model graph with the TensorFlow Debugger (TFDBG).

```
$ saved_model_cli run --dir saved_models/ \
                      --tag_set serve \
                      --signature_def x1_x2_to_y \
                      --input_examples 'examples=[{"company": "HSBC", ...}]'
```

After all the introduction of how to export and inspect models, let's dive into the TensorFlow Serving installation, setup, and operation.

Setting Up TensorFlow Serving

There are two easy ways to get TensorFlow Serving installed on your serving instances. You can either run TensorFlow Serving on Docker or, if you run an Ubuntu OS on your serving instances, you can install the Ubuntu package.

Docker Installation

The easiest way of installing TensorFlow Serving is to download the prebuilt Docker image.[3] As you have seen in Chapter 2, you can obtain the image by running:

```
$ docker pull tensorflow/serving
```

If you are running the Docker container on an instance with GPUs available, you will need to download the latest build with GPU support.

```
$ docker pull tensorflow/serving:latest-gpu
```

The Docker image with GPU support requires Nvidia's Docker support for GPUs. The installation steps can be found on the company's website (*https://oreil.ly/7N5uv*).

Native Ubuntu Installation

If you want to run TensorFlow Serving without the overhead of running Docker, you can install Linux binary packages available for Ubuntu distributions.

The installation steps are similar to other nonstandard Ubuntu packages. First, you need to add a new package source to the distribution's source list or add a new list file to the sources.list.d directory by executing the following in your Linux terminal:

```
$ echo "deb [arch=amd64] http://storage.googleapis.com/tensorflow-serving-apt \
    stable tensorflow-model-server tensorflow-model-server-universal" \
    | sudo tee /etc/apt/sources.list.d/tensorflow-serving.list
```

Before updating your package registry, you should add the packages' public key to your distribution's key chain:

```
$ curl https://storage.googleapis.com/tensorflow-serving-apt/\
tensorflow-serving.release.pub.gpg | sudo apt-key add -
```

After updating your package registry, you can install TensorFlow Serving on your Ubuntu operating system:

```
$ apt-get update
$ apt-get install tensorflow-model-server
```

---

3 If you haven't installed or used Docker before, check out our brief introduction in Appendix A.

Two Ubuntu Packages for TensorFlow Serving

Google provides two Ubuntu packages for TensorFlow Serving! The earlier referenced `tensorflow-model-server` package is the preferred package, and it comes with specific CPU optimizations precompiled (e.g., AVX instructions).

At the time of writing this chapter, a second package with the name `tensorflow-model-server-universal` is also provided. It doesn't contain the precompiled optimizations and can, therefore, be run on old hardware (e.g., CPUs without the AVX instruction set).

Building TensorFlow Serving from Source

It is recommended to run TensorFlow Serving with the prebuilt Docker image or Ubuntu packages. In some situations, you have to compile TensorFlow Serving, for example when you want to optimize the model serving for your underlying hardware. At the moment, you can only build TensorFlow Serving for Linux operating systems, and the build tool `bazel` is required. You can find detailed instructions in the Tensor-Flow Serving documentation (*https://oreil.ly/tUJTw*).

Optimize Your TensorFlow Serving Instances

If you build TensorFlow Serving from scratch, we highly recommend compiling the Serving version for the specific TensorFlow version of your models and available hardware of your serving instances.

Configuring a TensorFlow Server

Out of the box, TensorFlow Serving can run in two different modes. First, you can specify a model, and have TensorFlow Serving always provide the latest model. Alternatively, you can specify a configuration file with all models and versions that you want to load, and have TensorFlow Serving load all the named models.

Single Model Configuration

If you want to run TensorFlow Serving by loading a single model and switching to newer model versions when they are available, the single model configuration is preferred.

If you run TensorFlow Serving in a Docker environment, you can run the `tensor flow\serving` image with the following command:

```
$ docker run -p 8500:8500 \   ❶
            -p 8501:8501 \
            --mount type=bind,source=/tmp/models,target=/models/my_model \   ❷
```

```
    -e MODEL_NAME=my_model \ ❸
    -e MODEL_BASE_PATH=/models/my_model \
    -t tensorflow/serving ❹
```

❶ Specify the default ports.

❷ Mount the model directory.

❸ Specify your model.

❹ Specify the docker image.

By default, TensorFlow Serving is configured to create a representational state transfer (REST) and Google Remote Procedure Calls (gRPC) endpoint. By specifying both ports, 8500 and 8501, we expose the REST and gRPC capabilities.[4] The docker run command creates a mount between a folder on the host (source) and the container (target) filesystem. In Chapter 2, we discussed how to pass environment variables to the docker container. To run the server in a single model configuration, you need to specify the model name MODEL_NAME.

If you want to run the Docker image prebuilt for GPU images, you need to swap out the name of the docker image to the latest GPU build with:

```
$ docker run ...
          -t tensorflow/serving:latest-gpu
```

If you have decided to run TensorFlow Serving without the Docker container, you can run it with the command:

```
$ tensorflow_model_server --port=8500 \
                          --rest_api_port=8501 \
                          --model_name=my_model \
                          --model_base_path=/models/my_model
```

In both scenarios, you should see output on your terminal that is similar to the following:

```
2019-04-26 03:51:20.304826: I
tensorflow_serving/model_servers/
server.cc:82]
  Building single TensorFlow model file config:
  model_name: my_model model_base_path: /models/my_model
2019-04-26 03:51:20: I tensorflow_serving/model_servers/server_core.cc:461]
  Adding/updating models.
2019-04-26 03:51:20: I
tensorflow_serving/model_servers/
server_core.cc:558]
```

---

4 For a more detailed introduction to REST and gRPC, please check "REST Versus gRPC" on page 147.

```
(Re-)adding model: my_model
...
2019-04-26 03:51:34.507436: I tensorflow_serving/core/loader_harness.cc:86]
    Successfully loaded servable version {name: my_model version: 1556250435}
2019-04-26 03:51:34.516601: I tensorflow_serving/model_servers/server.cc:313]
    Running gRPC ModelServer at 0.0.0.0:8500 ...
[warn] getaddrinfo: address family for nodename not supported
[evhttp_server.cc : 237] RAW: Entering the event loop ...
2019-04-26 03:51:34.520287: I tensorflow_serving/model_servers/server.cc:333]
    Exporting HTTP/REST API at:localhost:8501 ...
```

From the server output, you can see that the server loaded our model my_model successfully, and that created two endpoints: one REST and one gRPC endpoint.

TensorFlow Serving makes the deployment of machine learning models extremely easy. One great advantage of serving models with TensorFlow Serving is the *hot swap* capability. If a new model is uploaded, the server's model manager will detect the new version, unload the existing model, and load the newer model for inferencing.

Let's say you update the model and export the new model version to the mounted folder on the host machine (if you are running with the docker setup) and no configuration change is required. The model manager will detect the newer model and reload the endpoints. It will notify you about the unloading of the older model and the loading of the newer model. In your terminal, you should find messages like:

```
2019-04-30 00:21:56.486988: I tensorflow_serving/core/basic_manager.cc:739]
    Successfully reserved resources to load servable
    {name: my_model version: 1556583584}
2019-04-30 00:21:56.487043: I tensorflow_serving/core/loader_harness.cc:66]
    Approving load for servable version {name: my_model version: 1556583584}
2019-04-30 00:21:56.487071: I tensorflow_serving/core/loader_harness.cc:74]
    Loading servable version {name: my_model version: 1556583584}
...
2019-04-30 00:22:08.839375: I tensorflow_serving/core/loader_harness.cc:119]
    Unloading servable version {name: my_model version: 1556583236}
2019-04-30 00:22:10.292695: I ./tensorflow_serving/core/simple_loader.h:294]
    Calling MallocExtension_ReleaseToSystem() after servable unload with 1262338988
2019-04-30 00:22:10.292771: I tensorflow_serving/core/loader_harness.cc:127]
    Done unloading servable version {name: my_model version: 1556583236}
```

By default, TensorFlow Serving will load the model with the highest version number. If you use the export methods shown earlier in this chapter, all models will be exported in folders with the epoch timestamp as the folder name. Therefore, newer models will have a higher version number than older models.

The same default model loading policy of TensorFlow Serving also allows model rollbacks. In case you want to roll back a model version, you can delete the model version from the base path. The model server will then detect the removal of the version with the next polling of the filesystem,[5] unload the deleted model, and load the most recent, existing model version.

Multiple Model Configuration

You can also configure TensorFlow Serving to load multiple models at the same time. To do that, you need to create a configuration file to specify the models:

```
model_config_list {
  config {
    name: 'my_model'
    base_path: '/models/my_model/'
    model_platform: 'tensorflow'
  }
  config {
    name: 'another_model'
    base_path: '/models/another_model/'
    model_platform: 'tensorflow'
  }
}
```

The configuration file contains one or more `config` dictionaries, all listed below a `model_config_list` key.

In your Docker configuration, you can mount the configuration file and load the model server with the configuration file instead of a single model:

```
$ docker run -p 8500:8500 \
           -p 8501:8501 \
           --mount type=bind,source=/tmp/models,target=/models/my_model \
           --mount type=bind,source=/tmp/model_config,\
           target=/models/model_config \ ❶
           -e MODEL_NAME=my_model \
           -t tensorflow/serving \
           --model_config_file=/models/model_config ❷
```

❶ Mount the configuration file.

❷ Specify the model configuration file.

If you use TensorFlow Serving outside of a Docker container, you can point the model server to the configuration file with the argument `model_config_file`, which loads and the configuration from the file:

---

5 The loading and unloading of models only works if the `file_system_poll_wait_seconds` is configured to be greater than 0. The default configuration is 2s.

```
$ tensorflow_model_server --port=8500 \
                          --rest_api_port=8501 \
                          --model_config_file=/models/model_config
```

Configure Specific Model Versions

There are situations when you want to load not just the latest model version, but either all or specific model versions. For example, you may want to do model A/B testing, as we will discuss in "Model A/B Testing with TensorFlow Serving" on page 152, or provide a stable and a development model version. TensorFlow Serving, by default, always loads the latest model version. If you want to load a set of available model versions, you can extend the model configuration file with:

```
...
config {
  name: 'another_model'
  base_path: '/models/another_model/'
  model_version_policy: {all: {}}
}
...
```

If you want to specify specific model versions, you can define them as well:

```
...
config {
  name: 'another_model'
  base_path: '/models/another_model/'
  model_version_policy {
    specific {
      versions: 1556250435
      versions: 1556251435
    }
  }
}
...
```

You can even give the model version labels. The labels can be extremely handy later when you want to make predictions from the models. At the time of writing, version labels were only available through TensorFlow Serving's gRPC endpoints:

```
...
model_version_policy {
  specific {
    versions: 1556250435
    versions: 1556251435
  }
}
version_labels {
  key: 'stable'
  value: 1556250435
}
version_labels {
  key: 'testing'
  value: 1556251435
}
...
```

With the model version now configured, we can use those endpoints for the versions to run our model A/B test. If you are interested in how to infer these model versions, we recommend "Model A/B Testing with TensorFlow Serving" on page 152 for an example of a simple implementation.

Starting with TensorFlow Serving 2.3, the *version_label* functionality will be available for REST endpoints in addition to the existing gRPC functionality of TensorFlow Serving.

REST Versus gRPC

In "Single Model Configuration" on page 142, we discussed how TensorFlow Serving allows two different API types: REST and gRPC. Both protocols have their advantages and disadvantages, and we would like to take a moment to introduce both before we dive into how you can communicate with these endpoints.

REST

REST is a communication "protocol" used by today's web services. It isn't a formal protocol, but more a communication style that defines how clients communicate with web services. REST clients communicate with the server using the standard HTTP methods like GET, POST, DELETE, etc. The payloads of the requests are often encoded as XML or JSON data formats.

gRPC

gRPC is a remote procedure protocol developed by Google. While gRPC supports different data formats, the standard data format used with gRPC is protocol buffer, which we used throughout this book. gRPC provides low-latency communication and smaller payloads if protocol buffers are used. gRPC was designed with APIs in mind. The downside is that the payloads are in a binary format, which can make a quick inspection difficult.

Which Protocol to Use?

On the one hand, it looks very convenient to communicate with the model server over REST. The endpoints are easy to infer, the payloads can be easily inspected, and the endpoints can be tested with curl requests or browser tools. REST libraries are widely available for all sorts of clients and often are already available on the client system (i.e., a mobile application).

On the other hand, gRPC APIs have a higher burden of entry initially. gRPC libraries often need to be installed on the client side. However, they can lead to significant performance improvements depending on the data structures required for the model inference. If your model experiences many requests, the reduced payload size due to the protocol buffer serialization can be beneficial.

Internally, TensorFlow Serving converts JSON data structures submitted via REST to tf.Example data structures, and this can lead to slower performance. Therefore, you might see better performance with gRPC requests if the conversion requires many type conversions (i.e., if you submit a large array with float values).

Making Predictions from the Model Server

Until now, we have entirely focused on the model server setup. In this section, we want to demonstrate how a client (e.g., a web app), can interact with the model server. All code examples concerning REST or gRPC requests are executed on the client side.

Getting Model Predictions via REST

To call the model server over REST, you'll need a Python library to facilitate the communication for you. The standard library these days is `requests`. Install the library:

```
$ pip install requests
```

The following example showcases an example POST request.

```
import requests

url = "http://some-domain.abc"
payload = {"key_1": "value_1"}
r = requests.post(url, json=payload)  ❶
print(r.json())  ❷
# {'data': ...}
```

❶ Submit the request.

❷ View the HTTP response.

URL structure

The URL for your HTTP request to the model server contains information about which model and which version you would like to infer:

```
http://{HOST}:{PORT}/v1/models/{MODEL_NAME}:{VERB}
```

HOST
> The host is the IP address or domain name of your model server. If you run your model server on the same machine where you run your client code, you can set the host to `localhost`.

PORT
> You'll need to specify the port in your request URL. The standard port for the REST API is 8501. If this conflicts with other services in your service ecosystem,

you can change the port in your server arguments during the startup of the server.

MODEL_NAME

The model name needs to match the name of your model when you either set up your model configuration or started up the model server.

VERB

The type of model is specified through the verb in the URL. You have three options: `predict`, `classify`, or `regress`. The verb corresponds to the signature methods of the endpoint.

MODEL_VERSION

If you want to make predictions from a specific model version, you'll need to extend the URL with the model version identifier:

```
http://{HOST}:{PORT}/v1/models/{MODEL_NAME}[/versions/${MODEL_VERSION}]:{VERB}
```

Payloads

With the URL in place, let's discuss the request payloads. TensorFlow Serving expects the input data as a JSON data structure, as shown in the following example:

```
{
  "signature_name": <string>,
  "instances": <value>
}
```

The `signature_name` is not required. If it isn't specified, the model server will infer the model graph signed with the default `serving` label.

The input data is expected either as a list of objects or as a list of input values. To submit multiple data samples, you can submit them as a list under the `instances` key.

If you want to submit one data example for the inference, you can use `inputs` and list all input values as a list. One of the keys, `instances` and `inputs`, has to be present, but never both at the same time:

```
{
  "signature_name": <string>,
  "inputs": <value>
}
```

Example 8-6 shows an example of how to request a model prediction from our TensorFlow Serving endpoint. We only submit one data example for the inference in our example, but we could easily submit a list of data inputs representing multiple requests.

Example 8-6. Example model prediction request with a Python client

```
import requests

def get_rest_request(text, model_name="my_model"):
    url = "http://localhost:8501/v1/models/{}:predict".format(model_name) ❶
    payload = {"instances": [text]} ❷
    response = requests.post(url=url, json=payload)
    return response

rs_rest = get_rest_request(text="classify my text")
rs_rest.json()
```

❶ Exchange `localhost` with an IP address if the server is not running on the same machine.

❷ Add more examples to the `instance` list if you want to infer more samples.

Using TensorFlow Serving via gRPC

If you want to use the model with gRPC, the steps are slightly different from the REST API requests.

First, you establish a gRPC `channel`. The channel provides the connection to the gRPC server at a given host address and over a given port. If you require a secure connection, you need to establish a secure channel at this point. Once the channel is established, you'll create a `stub`. A `stub` is a local object which replicates the available methods from the server:

```
import grpc
from tensorflow_serving.apis import predict_pb2
from tensorflow_serving.apis import prediction_service_pb2_grpc
import tensorflow as tf

def create_grpc_stub(host, port=8500):
    hostport = "{}:{}".format(host, port)
    channel = grpc.insecure_channel(hostport)
    stub = prediction_service_pb2_grpc.PredictionServiceStub(channel)
    return stub
```

Once the gRPC stub is created, we can set the model and the signature to access predictions from the correct model and submit our data for the inference:

```
def grpc_request(stub, data_sample, model_name='my_model', \
                 signature_name='classification'):
    request = predict_pb2.PredictRequest()
    request.model_spec.name = model_name
    request.model_spec.signature_name = signature_name

    request.inputs['inputs'].CopyFrom(tf.make_tensor_proto(data_sample,
```

```
                                                   shape=[1,1])) ❶
    result_future = stub.Predict.future(request, 10) ❷
    return result_future
```

❶ `inputs` is the name of the input of our neural network.

❷ 10 is the max time in seconds before the function times out.

With the two function, now available, we can infer our example datasets with the two
function calls:

```
stub = create_grpc_stub(host, port=8500)
rs_grpc = grpc_request(stub, data)
```

Secure Connections

The `grpc` library also provides functionality to connect securely with the gRPC endpoints. The following example shows how to create a secure channel with gRPC from
the client side:

```
import grpc

cert = open(client_cert_file, 'rb').read()
key = open(client_key_file, 'rb').read()
ca_cert = open(ca_cert_file, 'rb').read() if ca_cert_file else ''
credentials = grpc.ssl_channel_credentials(
    ca_cert, key, cert
)
channel = implementations.secure_channel(hostport, credentials)
```

On the server side, TensorFlow Serving can terminate secure connections if SSL is
configured. To terminate secure connections, create an *SSL configuration file* as
shown in the following example:[6]

```
server_key:  "-----BEGIN PRIVATE KEY-----\n
             <your_ssl_key>\n
             -----END PRIVATE KEY-----"
server_cert: "-----BEGIN CERTIFICATE-----\n
             <your_ssl_cert>\n
             -----END CERTIFICATE-----"
custom_ca: ""
client_verify: false
```

Once you have created the configuration file, you can pass the file path to the Tensor-
Flow Serving argument `--ssl_config_file` during the start of TensorFlow Serving:

```
$ tensorflow_model_server --port=8500 \
                          --rest_api_port=8501 \
                          --model_name=my_model \
                          --model_base_path=/models/my_model \
                          --ssl_config_file="<path_to_config_file>"
```

---

6 The SSL configuration file is based on the SSL configuration protocol buffer, which can be found in the
   TensorFlow Serving API (*https://oreil.ly/ZAEte*).

Getting predictions from classification and regression models

If you are interested in making predictions from classification and regression models, you can use the gRPC API.

If you would like to get predictions from a classification model, you will need to swap out the following lines:

```
from tensorflow_serving.apis import predict_pb2
...
request = predict_pb2.PredictRequest()
```

with:

```
from tensorflow_serving.apis import classification_pb2
...
request = classification_pb2.ClassificationRequest()
```

If you want to get predictions from a regression model, you can use the following imports:

```
from tensorflow_serving.apis import regression_pb2
...
regression_pb2.RegressionRequest()
```

Payloads

gRPC API uses Protocol Buffers as the data structure for the API request. By using binary Protocol Buffer payloads, the API requests use less bandwidth compared to JSON payloads. Also, depending on the model input data structure, you might experience faster predictions as with REST endpoints. The performance difference is explained by the fact that the submitted JSON data will be converted to a `tf.Example` data structure. This conversion can slow down the model server inference, and you might encounter a slower inference performance than in the gRPC API case.

Your data submitted to the gRPC endpoints needs to be converted to the protocol buffer data structure. TensorFlow provides you a handy utility function to perform the conversion called `tf.make_tensor_proto`. It allows various data formats, including scalars, lists, NumPy scalars, and NumPy arrays. The function will then convert the given Python or NumPy data structures to the protocol buffer format for the inference.

Model A/B Testing with TensorFlow Serving

A/B testing is an excellent methodology to test different models in real-life situations. In this scenario, a certain percentage of clients will receive predictions from model version A and all other requests will be served by model version B.

We discussed earlier that you could configure TensorFlow Serving to load multiple model versions and then specify the model version in your REST request URL or gRPC specifications.

TensorFlow Serving doesn't support server-side A/B testing, meaning that the model server will direct all client requests to a single endpoint to two model versions. But with a little tweak to our request URL, we can provide the appropriate support for random A/B testing from the client side:[7]

```
from random import random ❶

def get_rest_url(model_name, host='localhost', port=8501,
                 verb='predict', version=None):
    url = "http://{}:{}/v1/models/{}/".format(host, port, model_name)
    if version:
        url += "versions/{}".format(version)
    url += ":{}".format(verb)
    return url


...

# Submit 10% of all requests from this client to version 1.
# 90% of the requests should go to the default models.
threshold = 0.1
version = 1 if random() < threshold else None ❷
url = get_rest_url(model_name='complaints_classification', version=version)
```

❶ The random library will help us pick a model.

❷ If version = None, TensorFlow Serving will infer with the default version.

As you can see, randomly changing the request URL for our model inference (in our REST API example), can provide you some basic A/B testing functionality. If you would like to extend these capabilities by performing the random routing of the model inference on the server side, we highly recommend routing tools like Istio (*https://istio.io*) for this purpose. Originally designed for web traffic, Istio can be used to route traffic to specific models. You can phase in models, perform A/B tests, or create policies for data routed to specific models.

When you perform A/B tests with your models, it is often useful to request information about the model from the model server. In the following section, we will explain how you can request the metadata information from TensorFlow Serving.

---

7 A/B testing isn't complete without the statistical test of the results you get from people interacting with the two models. The shown implementation just provides us the A/B testing backend.

Requesting Model Metadata from the Model Server

At the beginning of the book, we laid out the model life cycle and explained how we want to automate the machine learning life cycle. A critical component of the continuous life cycle is generating accuracy or general performance feedback about your model versions. We will take a deep dive into how to generate these feedback loops in Chapter 13, but for now, imagine that your model classifies some data (e.g., the sentiment of the text), and then asks the user to rate the prediction. The information of whether a model predicted something correctly or incorrectly is precious for improving future model versions, but it is only useful if we know which model version has performed the prediction.

The metadata provided by the model server will contain the information to annotate your feedback loops.

REST Requests for Model Metadata

Requesting model metadata is straightforward with TensorFlow Serving. TensorFlow Serving provides you an endpoint for model metadata:

```
http://{HOST}:{PORT}/v1/models/{MODEL_NAME}[/versions/{MODEL_VERSION}]/metadata
```

Similar to the REST API inference requests we discussed earlier, you have the option to specify the model version in the request URL, or if you don't specify it, the model server will provide the information about the default model.

As Example 8-7 shows, we can request model metadata with a single GET request.

Example 8-7. Example model metadata request with a python client

```python
import requests

def metadata_rest_request(model_name, host="localhost",
                          port=8501, version=None):
    url = "http://{}:{}/v1/models/{}/".format(host, port, model_name)
    if version:
        url += "versions/{}".format(version)
    url += "/metadata"  ❶
    response = requests.get(url=url)  ❷
    return response
```

❶ Append /metadata for model information.

❷ Perform a GET request.

The model server will return the model specifications as a model_spec dictionary and the model definitions as a metadata dictionary:

```
{
  "model_spec": {
    "name": "complaints_classification",
    "signature_name": "",
    "version": "1556583584"
  },
  "metadata": {
    "signature_def": {
      "signature_def": {
        "classification": {
          "inputs": {
            "inputs": {
              "dtype": "DT_STRING",
              "tensor_shape": {
                ...
```

gRPC Requests for Model Metadata

Requesting model metadata with gRPC is almost as easy as the REST API case. In the gRPC case, you file a GetModelMetadataRequest, add the model name to the specifications, and submit the request via the GetModelMetadata method of the stub:

```
from tensorflow_serving.apis import get_model_metadata_pb2

def get_model_version(model_name, stub):
    request = get_model_metadata_pb2.GetModelMetadataRequest()
    request.model_spec.name = model_name
    request.metadata_field.append("signature_def")
    response = stub.GetModelMetadata(request, 5)
    return response.model_spec

model_name = 'complaints_classification'
stub = create_grpc_stub('localhost')
get_model_version(model_name, stub)

name: "complaints_classification"
version {
  value: 1556583584
}
```

The gRPC response contains a ModelSpec object that contains the version number of the loaded model.

More interesting is the use case of obtaining the model signature information of the loaded models. With almost the same request functions, we can determine the model's metadata. The only difference is that we don't access the model_spec attribute of the response object, but the metadata. The information needs to be serialized to be human readable; therefore, we will use SerializeToString to convert the protocol buffer information:

```
from tensorflow_serving.apis import get_model_metadata_pb2

def get_model_meta(model_name, stub):
    request = get_model_metadata_pb2.GetModelMetadataRequest()
    request.model_spec.name = model_name
    request.metadata_field.append("signature_def")
    response = stub.GetModelMetadata(request, 5)
    return response.metadata['signature_def']

model_name = 'complaints_classification'
stub = create_grpc_stub('localhost')
meta = get_model_meta(model_name, stub)

print(meta.SerializeToString().decode("utf-8", 'ignore'))
# type.googleapis.com/tensorflow.serving.SignatureDefMap
# serving_default
# complaints_classification_input
#         input_1:0
#              2@
# complaints_classification_output(
# dense_1/Sigmoid:0
#                 tensorflow/serving/predict
```

gRPC requests are more complex than REST requests; however, in applications with high performance requirements, they can provide faster prediction performances. Another way of increasing our model prediction performance is by batching our prediction requests.

Batching Inference Requests

Batching inference requests is one of the most powerful features of TensorFlow Serving. During model training, batching accelerates our training because we can parallelize the computation of our training samples. At the same time, we can also use the computation hardware efficiently if we match the memory requirements of our batches with the available memory of the GPU.

If you run TensorFlow Serving without the batching enabled, as shown in Figure 8-3, every client request is handled individually and in sequence. If you classify an image, for example, your first request will infer the model on your CPU or GPU before the second request, third request, and so on, will be classified. In this case, we underutilize the available memory of the CPU or GPU.

As shown in Figure 8-4, multiple clients can request model predictions, and the model server batches the different client requests into one "batch" to compute. Each request inferred through this batching step might take a bit longer than a single request because of the timeout or the limit of the batch. However, similar to our training phase, we can compute the batch in parallel and return the results to all clients after the completion of the batch computation. This will utilize the hardware more efficiently than single sample requests.

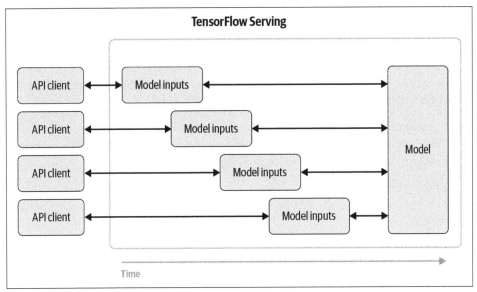

Figure 8-3. Overview of TensorFlow Serving without batching

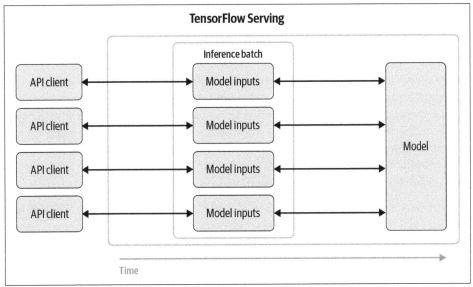

Figure 8-4. Overview of TensorFlow Serving with batching

Configuring Batch Predictions

Batching predictions needs to be enabled for TensorFlow Serving and then configured for your use case. You have five configuration options:

max_batch_size
> This parameter controls the batch size. Large batch sizes will increase the request latency and can lead to exhausting the GPU memory. Small batch sizes lose the benefit of using optimal computation resources.

batch_timeout_micros
> This parameter sets the maximum wait time for filling a batch. This parameter is handy to cap the latency for inference requests.

num_batch_threads
> The number of threads configures how many CPU or GPU cores can be used in parallel.

max_enqueued_batches
> This parameter sets the maximum number of batches queued for predictions. This configuration is beneficial to avoid an unreasonable backlog of requests. If the maximum number is reached, requests will be returned with an error instead of being queued.

pad_variable_length_inputs
> This Boolean parameter determines if input tensors with variable lengths will be padded to the same lengths for all input tensors.

As you can imagine, setting parameters for optimal batching requires some tuning and is application dependent. If you run online inferences, you should aim for limiting the latency. It is often recommended to set batch_timeout_micros initially to 0 and tune the timeout toward 10,000 microseconds. In contrast, batch requests will benefit from longer timeouts (milliseconds to a second) to constantly use the batch size for optimal performance. TensorFlow Serving will make predictions on the batch when either the max_batch_size or the timeout is reached.

Set num_batch_threads to the number of CPU cores if you configure TensorFlow Serving for CPU-based predictions. If you configure a GPU setup, tune max_batch_size to get an optimal utilization of the GPU memory. While you tune your configuration, make sure that you set max_enqueued_batches to a huge number to avoid some requests being returned early without proper inference.

You can set the parameters in a text file, as shown in the following example. In our example, we create a configuration file called *batching_parameters.txt* and add the following content:

```
max_batch_size { value: 32 }
batch_timeout_micros { value: 5000 }
pad_variable_length_inputs: true
```

If you want to enable batching, you need to pass two additional parameters to the Docker container running TensorFlow Serving. To enable batching, set `enable_batching` to true and set `batching_parameters_file` to the absolute path of the batching configuration file inside of the container. Please keep in mind that you have to mount the additional folder with the configuration file if it isn't located in the same folder as the model versions.

Here is a complete example of the `docker run` command that starts the TensorFlow Serving Docker container with batching enabled. The parameters will then be passed to the TensorFlow Serving instance:

```
docker run -p 8500:8500 \
           -p 8501:8501 \
           --mount type=bind,source=/path/to/models,target=/models/my_model \
           --mount type=bind,source=/path/to/batch_config,target=/server_config \
           -e MODEL_NAME=my_model -t tensorflow/serving \
           --enable_batching=true
           --batching_parameters_file=/server_config/batching_parameters.txt
```

As explained earlier, the configuration of the batching will require additional tuning, but the performance gains should make up for the initial setup. We highly recommend enabling this TensorFlow Serving feature. It is especially useful for inferring a large number of data samples with offline batch processes.

Other TensorFlow Serving Optimizations

TensorFlow Serving comes with a variety of additional optimization features. Additional feature flags are:

`--file_system_poll_wait_seconds=1`
   TensorFlow Serving will poll if a new model version is available. You can disable the feature by setting it to 1. If you only want to load the model once and never update it, you can set it to 0. The parameter expects an integer value. If you load models from cloud storage buckets, we highly recommend that you increase the polling time to avoid unnecessary cloud provider charges for the frequent list operations on the cloud storage bucket.

`--tensorflow_session_parallelism=0`
   TensorFlow Serving will automatically determine how many threads to use for a TensorFlow session. In case you want to set the number of a thread manually, you can overwrite it by setting this parameter to any positive integer value.

```
--tensorflow_intra_op_parallelism=0
```
This parameter sets the number of cores being used for running TensorFlow Serving. The number of available threads determines how many operations will be parallelized. If the value is 0, all available cores will be used.

```
--tensorflow_inter_op_parallelism=0
```
This parameter sets the number of available threads in a pool to execute Tensor-Flow ops. This is useful for maximizing the execution of independent operations in a TensorFlow graph. If the value is set to 0, all available cores will be used and one thread per core will be allocated.

Similar to our earlier examples, you can pass the configuration parameter to the `docker run` command, as shown in the following example:

```
docker run -p 8500:8500 \
          -p 8501:8501 \
          --mount type=bind,source=/path/to/models,target=/models/my_model \
          -e MODEL_NAME=my_model -t tensorflow/serving \
          --tensorflow_intra_op_parallelism=4 \
          --tensorflow_inter_op_parallelism=4 \
          --file_system_poll_wait_seconds=10 \
          --tensorflow_session_parallelism=2
```

The discussed configuration options can improve performance and avoid unnecessary cloud provider charges.

TensorFlow Serving Alternatives

TensorFlow Serving is a great way of deploying machine learning models. With the TensorFlow Estimators and Keras models, you should be covered for a large variety of machine learning concepts. However, if you would like to deploy a legacy model or if your machine learning framework of choice isn't TensorFlow or Keras, here are a couple of options.

BentoML

BentoML (*https://bentoml.org*) is a framework-independent library that deploys machine learning models. It supports models trained through PyTorch, scikit-learn, TensorFlow, Keras, and XGBoost. For TensorFlow models, BentoML supports the SavedModel format. BentoML supports batching requests.

Seldon

The UK startup Seldon provides a variety of open source tools to manage model life cycles, and one of their core products is Seldon Core (*https://oreil.ly/Yx_U7*). Seldon

Core provides you a toolbox to wrap your models in a Docker image, which is then deployed via Seldon in a Kubernetes cluster.

At the time of writing this chapter, Seldon supported machine learning models trained with TensorFlow, scikit-learn, XGBoost, and even R.

Seldon comes with its own ecosystem that allows building preprocessing into its own Docker images, which are deployed in conjunction with the deployment images. It also provides a routing service that allows you to perform A/B test or multiarm bandit experiments.

Seldon is highly integrated with the Kubeflow environment and, similar to TensorFlow Serving, is a way to deploy models with Kubeflow on Kubernetes.

GraphPipe

GraphPipe (*https://oreil.ly/w_U7U*) is another way of deploying TensorFlow and non-TensorFlow models. Oracle drives the open source project. It allows you to deploy not just TensorFlow (including Keras) models, but also Caffe2 models and all machine learning models that can be converted to the Open Neural Network Exchange (ONNX) format.[8] Through the ONNX format, you can deploy PyTorch models with GraphPipe.

Besides providing a model server for TensorFlow, PyTorch, etc., GraphPipe also provides client implementation for programming languages like Python, Java, and Go.

Simple TensorFlow Serving

Simple TensorFlow Serving (*https://stfs.readthedocs.io*) is a development by Dihao Chen from 4Paradigm. The library supports more than just TensorFlow models. The current list of supported model frameworks includes ONNX, scikit-learn, XGBoost, PMML, and H2O. It supports multiple models, predictions on GPUs, and client code for a variety of languages.

One significant aspect of Simple TensorFlow Serving is that it supports authentication and encrypted connections to the model server. Authentication is currently not a feature of TensorFlow Serving, and supporting SSL or Transport Layer Security (TLS) requires a custom build of TensorFlow Serving.

MLflow

MLflow (*https://mlflow.org*) supports the deployment of machine learning models, but that it is only one aspect of the tool created by DataBricks. MLflow is designed to

---

8 ONNX (*https://onnx.ai*) is a way of describing machine learning models.

manage model experiments through MLflow Tracking. The tool has a built-in model server, which provides REST API endpoints for the models managed through MLflow.

MLflow also provides interfaces to directly deploy models from MLflow to Microsoft's Azure ML platform and AWS SageMaker.

Ray Serve

The Ray Project (*https://ray.io*) provides functionality to deploy machine learning models. *Ray Serve* is framework agnostic and it supports PyTorch, TensorFlow (incl. Keras), Scikit-Learn models, or custom model predictions. The library provides capabilities to batch requests and it allows the routing of traffic between models and their versions.

Ray Serve is integrated in the *Ray Project* ecosystem and supports distributed computation setups.

Deploying with Cloud Providers

All model server solutions we have discussed up to this point have to be installed and managed by you. However, all primary cloud providers—Google Cloud, AWS, and Microsoft Azure—offer machine learning products, including the hosting of machine learning models.

In this section, we will guide you through an example deployment using Google Cloud's AI Platform. Let's start with the model deployment, and later we'll explain how you can get predictions from the deployed model from your application client.

Use Cases

Managed cloud deployments of machine learning models are a good alternative to running your model server instances if you want to deploy a model seamlessly and don't want to worry about scaling the model deployment. All cloud providers offer deployment options with the ability to scale by the number of inference requests.

However, the flexibility of your model deployment comes at a cost. Managed services provide effortless deployments, but they cost a premium. For example, two model versions running full time (requiring two computation nodes) are more expensive than a comparable compute instance that is running a TensorFlow Serving instance. Another downside of managed deployments is the limitations of the products. Some cloud providers require that you deploy via their own software development kits, and others have limits on the node size and how much memory your model can take up. These limitations can be a severe restriction for sizeable machine learning models, especially if the models contain very many layers (i.e., language models).

Example Deployment with GCP

In this section, we will walk you through one deployment with Google Cloud's AI Platform. Instead of writing configuration files and executing terminal commands, we can set up model endpoints through a web UI.

Limits of Model Size on GCP's AI Platform

GCP's endpoints are limited to model sizes up to 500 MB. However, if you deploy your endpoints via compute engines of type *N1*, the maximum model limit is increased to 2 GB. At the time of writing, this option was available as a beta feature.

Model deployment

The deployment consists of three steps:

- Make the model accessible on Google Cloud.
- Create a new model instance with Google Cloud's AI Platform.
- Create a new version with the model instance.

The deployment starts with uploading your exported TensorFlow or Keras model to a storage bucket. As shown in Figure 8-5, you will need to upload the entire exported model. Once the upload of the model is done, please copy the complete path of the storage location.

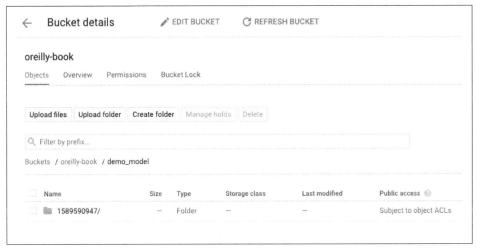

Figure 8-5. Uploading the trained model to cloud storage

Once you have uploaded your machine learning model, head over to the AI Platform of GCP to set up your machine learning model for deployment. If it is the first time that you are using the AI Platform in your GCP project, you'll need to enable the API. The automated startup process by Google Cloud can take a few minutes.

As shown in Figure 8-6, you need to give the model a unique identifier. Once you have created the identifier, selected your preferred deployment region,[9] and created an optional project description, continue with the setup by clicking Create.

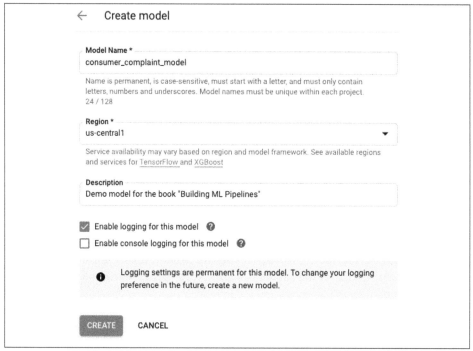

Figure 8-6. Creating a new model instance

Once the new model is registered, the model will be listed in the dashboard, as shown in Figure 8-7. You can create a new model version for the dashboard by clicking "Create version" in the overflow menu.

Figure 8-7. Creating a new model version

---

9 For the lowest prediction latencies, choose a region closest to the geographical region of the model requests.

When you create a new model version, you configure a compute instance that runs your model. Google Cloud gives you a variety of configuration options, as shown in Figure 8-8. The `version name` is important since you'll reference the `version name` later in the client setup. Please set the `Model URI` to the storage path you saved in the earlier step.

Google Cloud AI Platform supports a variety of machine learning frameworks including XGBoost, scikit-learn, and custom prediction routines.

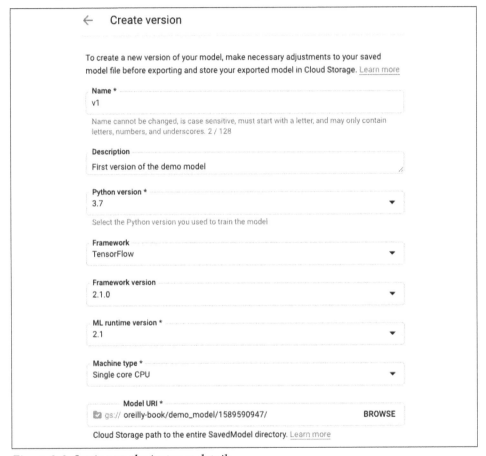

Figure 8-8. Setting up the instance details

GCP also lets you configure how your model instance scales if your model experiences a large number of inference requests. You can select between two scaling behaviors: *manual scaling* or *autoscaling*.

Manual scaling gives you the option for setting the exact number of nodes available for the predictions of your model version. In contrast, autoscaling gives you the functionality to adjust the number of instances depending on the demand for your end-point. If your nodes don't experience any requests, the number of nodes could even drop to zero. Please note that if autoscaling drops the number of nodes to zero, it will take some time to reinstantiate your model version with the next request hitting the model version endpoint. Also, if you run inference nodes in the autoscaling mode, you'll be billed in 10 min intervals.

Once the entire model version is configured, Google Cloud spins up the instances for you. If everything is ready for model predictions, you will see a green check icon next to the version name, as shown in Figure 8-9.

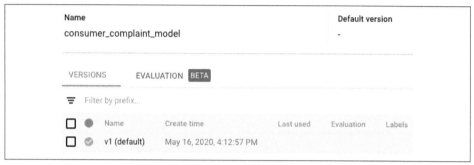

Figure 8-9. Completing the deployment with a new version available

You can run multiple model versions simultaneously. In the control panel of the model version, you can set one version as the default version, and any inference request without a version specified will be routed to the designated "default version." Just note that each model version will be hosted on an individual node and will accumulate GCP costs.

Model inference

Since TensorFlow Serving has been battle tested at Google and is used heavily internally, it is also used behind the scenes at GCP. You'll notice that the AI Platform isn't just using the same model export format as we have seen with our TensorFlow Serving instances but the payloads have the same data structure as we have seen before.

The only significant difference is the API connection. As you'll see in this section, you'll connect to the model version via the GCP API that is handling the request authentication.

To connect with the Google Cloud API, you'll need to install the library `google-api-python-client` with:

```
$ pip install google-api-python-client
```

All Google services can be connected via a service object. The helper function in the following code snippet highlights how to create the service object. The Google API client takes a `service name` and a `service version` and returns an object that provides all API functionalities via methods from the returned object:

```
import googleapiclient.discovery

def _connect_service():
    return googleapiclient.discovery.build(
        serviceName="ml", version="v1"
    )
```

Similar to our earlier REST and gRPC examples, we nest our inference data under a fixed `instances` key, which carries a list of input dictionaries. We have created a little helper function to generate the payloads. This function contains any preprocessing if you need to modify your input data before the inference:

```
def _generate_payload(sentence):
    return {"instances": [{"sentence": sentence}]}
```

With the service object created on the client side and the payload generated, it's time to request the prediction from the Google Cloud–hosted machine learning model.

The service object of the AI Platform service contains a predict method that accepts a name and a body. The name is a path string containing your GCP project name, model name, and, if you want to make predictions with a specific model version, version name. If you don't specify a version number, the default model version will be used for the model inference. The body contains the inference data structure we generated earlier:

```
project = "yourGCPProjectName"
model_name = "demo_model"
version_name = "v1"
request = service.projects().predict(
    name="projects/{}/models/{}/versions/{}".format(
        project, model_name, version_name),
    body=_generate_payload(sentence)
)
response = request.execute()
```

The Google Cloud AI Platform response contains the predict scores for the different categories similar to a REST response from a TensorFlow Serving instance:

```
{'predictions': [
    {'label': [
        0.9000182151794434,
        0.02840868942439556,
        0.009750653058290482,
        0.06182243302464485
    ]}
]}
```

The demonstrated deployment option is a quick way of deploying a machine learning model without setting up an entire deployment infrastructure. Other cloud providers like AWS or Microsoft Azure offer similar model deployment services. Depending on your deployment requirements, cloud providers can be a good alternative to self-hosted deployment options. The downsides are potentially higher costs and the lack of completely optimizing the endpoints (i.e., by providing gRPC endpoints or batching functionality, as we discussed in "Batching Inference Requests" on page 156).

Model Deployment with TFX Pipelines

In the introduction to this chapter, in Figure 8-1 we showed the deployment steps as one component of a machine learning pipeline. After discussing the inner workings of model deployments, and especially TensorFlow Serving, we want to connect the dots with our machine learning pipeline in this section.

In Figure 8-10, you can see the steps for a continuous model deployment. We assume that you have TensorFlow Serving running and configured to load models from a given file location. Furthermore, we assume that TensorFlow Serving will load the models from an external file location (i.e., a cloud storage bucket or a mounted persistent volume). Both systems, the TFX pipeline and the TensorFlow Serving instance, need to have access to the same filesystem.

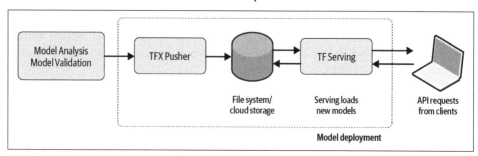

Figure 8-10. Deployment of models produced from TFX pipelines

In "TFX Pusher Component" on page 126, we discussed the Pusher component. The TFX component allows us to push validated models to a given location (e.g., a cloud storage bucket). TensorFlow Serving can pick up new model versions from the cloud storage location, unload the earlier model version, and load the latest version for the given model endpoint. This is the default model policy of TensorFlow Serving.

Due to the default model policy, we can build a simple continuous deployment setup with TFX and TensorFlow Serving fairly easily.

Summary

In this chapter, we discussed how to set up TensorFlow Serving to deploy machine learning models and why a model server is a more scalable option than deploying machine learning models through a Flask web application. We stepped through the installation and configuration steps, introduced the two main communication options, REST and gRPC, and briefly discussed the advantages and disadvantages of both communication protocols.

Furthermore, we explained some of the great benefits of TensorFlow Serving, including the batching of model requests and the ability to obtain metadata about the different model versions. We also discussed how to set up a quick A/B test setup with TensorFlow Serving.

We closed this chapter with a brief introduction of a managed cloud service, using Google Cloud AI Platform as an example. Managed cloud services provide you the ability to deploy machine learning models without managing your own server instances.

In the next chapter, we will discuss enhancing our model deployments, for example, by loading models from cloud providers or by deploying TensorFlow Serving with Kubernetes.

Advanced Model Deployments
with TensorFlow Serving

In the previous chapter, we discussed the efficient deployment of TensorFlow or Keras models with TensorFlow Serving. With the knowledge of a basic model deployment and TensorFlow Serving configuration, we now introduce advanced use cases of machine learning model deployments in this chapter. The use cases touch a variety of topics, for example, deploying model A/B testing, optimizing models for deployment and scaling, and monitoring model deployments. If you haven't had the chance to review the previous chapter, we recommend doing so because it provides the fundamentals for this chapter.

Decoupling Deployment Cycles

The basic deployments shown in Chapter 8 work well, but they have one restriction: the trained and validated model needs to be either included in the deployment container image during the build step or mounted into the container during the container runtime, as we discussed in the previous chapter. Both options require either knowledge of DevOps processes (e.g., updating Docker container images) or coordination between the data science and DevOps teams during the deployment phase of a new model version.

As we briefly mentioned in Chapter 8, TensorFlow Serving can load models from remote storage drives (e.g., AWS S3 or GCP Storage buckets). The standard loader policy of TensorFlow Serving frequently polls the model storage location, unloads the previously loaded model, and loads a newer model upon detection. Due to this behavior, we only need to deploy our model serving container once, and it continuously updates the model versions once they become available in the storage folder location.

Workflow Overview

Before we take a closer look at how to configure TensorFlow Serving to load models from remote storage locations, let's take a look at our proposed workflow.

Figure 9-1 shows the separation of workflows. The model serving container is deployed once. Data scientists can upload new versions of models to storage buckets either through the buckets' web interface or through command-line copy operations. Any changes to model versions will be discovered by the serving instances. A new build of the model server container or a redeployment of the container is not necessary.

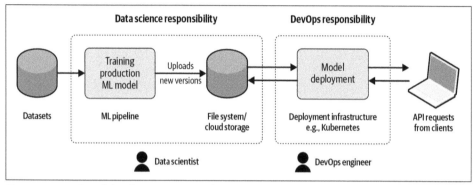

Figure 9-1. Split of the data science and DevOps deployment cycles

If your bucket folders are publicly accessible, you can serve the remote models by simply updating the model base path to the remote path:

```
docker run -p 8500:8500 \
        -p 8501:8501 \
        -e MODEL_BASE_PATH=s3://bucketname/model_path/ \  ❶
        -e MODEL_NAME=my_model \  ❷
        -t tensorflow/serving
```

❶ Remote bucket path

❷ Remaining configuration remains the same

If your models are stored in private cloud buckets, you need to configure TensorFlow Serving a bit more to provide access credentials. The setup is provider specific. We will cover two provider examples in this chapter: AWS and GCP.

Accessing private models from AWS S3

AWS authenticates users through a user-specific access key and access secret. To access private AWS S3 buckets, you need to create a user access key and secret.[1]

You can provide the AWS access key and secret as environment variables to the docker run command. This allows TensorFlow Serving to pick up the credentials and access private buckets:

```
docker run -p 8500:8500 \
          -p 8501:8501 \
          -e MODEL_BASE_PATH=s3://bucketname/model_path/ \
          -e MODEL_NAME=my_model \
          -e AWS_ACCESS_KEY_ID=XXXXX \  ❶
          -e AWS_SECRET_ACCESS_KEY=XXXXX \
          -t tensorflow/serving
```

❶ The name of the environment variables is important.

TensorFlow Serving relies on the standard AWS environment variables and its default values. You can overwrite the default values (e.g., if your bucket isn't located in the us-east-1 region or if you want to change the S3 endpoint).

You have the following configuration options:

- AWS_REGION=us-east-1

- S3_ENDPOINT=s3.us-east-1.amazonaws.com

- S3_USE_HTTPS=1

- S3_VERIFY_SSL=1

The configuration options can be added as environment variables or added to the docker run command as shown in the following example:

```
docker run -p 8500:8500 \
          -p 8501:8501 \
          -e MODEL_BASE_PATH=s3://bucketname/model_path/ \
          -e MODEL_NAME=my_model \
          -e AWS_ACCESS_KEY_ID=XXXXX \
          -e AWS_SECRET_ACCESS_KEY=XXXXX \
          -e AWS_REGION=us-west-1 \  ❶
          -t tensorflow/serving
```

❶ Additional configurations can be added through environment variables.

---

1 More details on managing AWS access keys can be found in the documentation (*https://oreil.ly/pHJ5N*).

With these few additional environment variables provided to TensorFlow Serving, you are now able to load models from remote AWS S3 buckets.

Accessing private models from GCP Buckets

GCP authenticates users through *service accounts*. To access private GCP Storage buckets, you need to create a service account file.[2]

Unlike in the case of AWS, we can't simply provide the credential as an environment variable since the GCP authentication expects a JSON file with the service account credentials. In the GCP case, we need to mount a folder on the host machine containing the credentials inside a Docker container and then define an environment variable to point TensorFlow Serving to the correct credential file.

For the following example, we assume that you have saved your newly created service account credential file under /home/*your_username*/.credentials/ on your host machine. We downloaded the service account credentials from GCP and saved the file as sa-credentials.json. You can give the credential file any name, but you need to update the environmental variable GOOGLE_APPLICATION_CREDENTIALS with the full path inside of the Docker container:

```
docker run -p 8500:8500 \
            -p 8501:8501 \
            -e MODEL_BASE_PATH=gcp://bucketname/model_path/ \
            -e MODEL_NAME=my_model \
            -v /home/your_username/.credentials/:/credentials/ ❶
            -e GOOGLE_APPLICATION_CREDENTIALS=/credentials/sa-credentials.json \ ❷
            -t tensorflow/serving
```

❶ Mount host directory with credentials.

❷ Specify path inside of the container.

With a couple steps, you have configured a remote GCP bucket as a storage location.

Optimization of Remote Model Loading

By default, TensorFlow Serving polls any model folder every two seconds for updated model versions, regardless of whether the model is stored in a local or remote location. If your model is stored in a remote location, the polling operation generates a bucket list view through your cloud provider. If you continuously update your model versions, your bucket might contain a large number of files. This results in large list-view messages and therefore consumes a small, but over time not insignificant,

---

2 More details on how to create and manage service accounts can be found in the documentation (*https://oreil.ly/pbO8q*).

amount of traffic. Your cloud provider will most likely charge for the network traffic generated by these list operations. To avoid billing surprises, we recommend reducing the polling frequency to every 120 seconds, which still provides you up to 30 potential updates per hour but generates 60 times less traffic:

```
docker run -p 8500:8500 \
    ...
    -t tensorflow/serving \
    --file_system_poll_wait_seconds=120
```

TensorFlow Serving arguments need to be added after the image specification of the docker run command. You can specify any polling wait time greater than one second. If you set the wait time to zero, TensorFlow Serving will not attempt to refresh the loaded model.

Model Optimizations for Deployments

With the increasing size of machine learning models, model optimization becomes more important to efficient deployments. Model quantization allows you to reduce the computation complexity of a model by reducing the precision of the weight's representation. Model pruning allows you to implicitly remove unnecessary weights by zeroing them out of your model network. And model distillation will force a smaller neural network to learn the objectives of a larger neural network.

All three optimization methods aim for smaller models that allow faster model inferences. In the following sections, we will explain the three optimization options further.

Quantization

The weights of a neural network are often stored as float 32-bit data types (or, as the IEEE 754 standard calls it, single-precision binary floating-point format). A floating-point number is stored as the following: 1 bit storing the sign of the number, 8 bits for the exponent, and 23 bits for the precision of the floating number.

The network weights, however, can be expressed in bfloat16 floating-point format or as 8-bit integers. As shown in Figure 9-2, we still need 1 bit to store the sign of the number. The exponent is also still represented through 8 bits when we store weights as *bfloat16* floating points because it is used by TensorFlow. However, the fraction representation is reduced from 23 bits to 7 bits. The weights can even sometimes be represented as integers using only 8 bits.

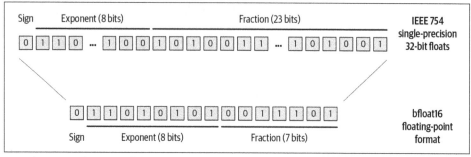

Figure 9-2. Reduction of the floating precision

By changing the network's weight representation to 16-bit floating points or integers, we can achieve the following benefits:

- The weights can be represented with fewer bytes, requiring less memory during the model inference.

- Due to the weights' reduced representation, predictions can be inferred faster.

- The quantization allows the execution of neural networks on 16-bit, or even 8-bit, embedded systems.

Current workflows for model quantization are applied after model training and are often called *post-training quantization*. Since a quantized model can be underfitted due to the lack of precision, we highly recommend analyzing and validating any model after quantization and before deployment. As an example of model quantizations, we discuss Nvidia's TensorRT library (see "Using TensorRT with TensorFlow Serving" on page 177) and TensorFlow's TFLite library (see "TFLite" on page 178).

Pruning

An alternative to reducing the precision of network weights is *model pruning*. The idea here is that a trained network can be reduced to a smaller network by removing unnecessary weights. In practice, this means that "unnecessary" weights are set to zero. By setting unnecessary weights to zero, the inference or prediction can be sped up. Also, the pruned models can be compressed to smaller models sizes since sparse weights lead to higher compression rates.

Distillation

Instead of reducing the network connections, we can also train a smaller, less complex neural network to learn trained tasks from a much more extensive network. This approach is called *distillation*. Instead of simply training a smaller machine learning model with the same objective as the bigger model, the predictions of the bigger model (the teacher neural network) influence the update of the smaller model's (the student neural network) weights, as shown in Figure 9-3. By using the predictions from the teacher and student neural networks, the student network can be *forced* to learn an objective from the teacher neural network. Ultimately, we can express the same model objective with fewer weights and with a model architecture that wouldn't have been able to learn the objective without the teacher forcing it.

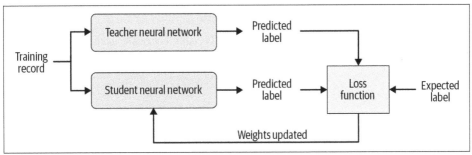

Figure 9-3. Student network learning from a teacher network

Using TensorRT with TensorFlow Serving

One option for performing quantization on a trained TensorFlow model before deploying it to production is converting the model with Nvidia's TensorRT.

If you are running computationally intensive deep learning models on an Nvidia GPU, you can use this additional way of optimizing your model server. Nvidia provides a library called TensorRT that optimizes the inference of deep learning models by reducing the precision of the numerical representations of the network weights

---

3 See TensorFlow's website for more information about optimzation methods (*https://oreil.ly/UGjss*) and an indepth pruning example (*https://oreil.ly/n9rWc*).

and biases. TensorRT supports int8 and float16 representations. The reduced precision will lower the inference latency of the model.

After your model is trained, you need to optimize the model with TensorRT's own optimizer or with `saved_model_cli`.[4] The optimized model can then be loaded into TensorFlow Serving. At the time of writing this chapter, TensorRT was limited to certain Nvidia products, including Tesla V100 and P4.

First, we'll convert our deep learning model with `saved_model_cli`:

```
$ saved_model_cli convert --dir saved_models/ \
                          --output_dir trt-savedmodel/ \
                          --tag_set serve tensorrt
```

After the conversion, you can load the model in our GPU setup of TensorFlow Serving as follows:

```
$ docker run --runtime=nvidia \
            -p 8500:8500 \
            -p 8501:8501 \
            --mount type=bind,source=/path/to/models,target=/models/my_model \
            -e MODEL_NAME=my_model \
            -t tensorflow/serving:latest-gpu
```

If you are inferring your models on Nvidia GPUs, the hardware is supported by TensorRT. Switching to TensorRT can be an excellent way to lower your inference latencies further.

TFLite

If you want to optimize your machine learning model but you're not running Nvidia GPUs, you can use TFLite to perform optimizations on your machine learning.

TFLite has traditionally been used to convert machine learning models to smaller model sizes for deployment to mobile or IoT devices. However, these models can also be used with TensorFlow Serving. So instead of deploying a machine learning model to an edge device, you can deploy a machine learning model with TensorFlow Serving that will have a low inference latency and a smaller memory footprint.

While optimizing with TFLite looks very promising, there are a few caveats: at the time of writing this section, the TensorFlow Serving support for TFLite models is only in experimental stages. And furthermore, not all TensorFlow operations can be converted to TFLite instructions. However, the number of supported operations is continuously growing.

---

4 See Nvidia's documentation about TensorRT (*https://oreil.ly/Ft8Y2*).

Steps to Optimize Your Model with TFLite

TFLite can also be used to optimize TensorFlow and Keras models. The library provides a variety of optimization options and tools. You can either convert your model through command-line tools or through the Python library.

The starting point is always a trained and exported model in the SavedModel format. In the following example, we focus on Python instructions. The conversion process consists of four steps:

1. Loading the exported saved model

2. Defining your optimization goals

3. Converting the model

4. Saving the optimized model as a TFLite model

```
import tensorflow as tf

saved_model_dir = "path_to_saved_model"
converter = tf.lite.TFLiteConverter.from_saved_model(
    saved_model_dir)

converter.optimizations = [
    tf.lite.Optimize.DEFAULT ❶
]
tflite_model = converter.convert()

with open("/tmp/model.tflite", "wb") as f:
    f.write(tflite_model)
```

❶ Set the optimization strategy.

TFLite Optimizations

TFLite provides predefined optimization objectives. By changing the optimization goal, the converter will optimize the models differently. A few options are DEFAULT, OPTIMIZE_FOR_LATENCY, and OPTIMIZE_FOR_SIZE.

In the DEFAULT mode, your model will be optimized for latency and size, whereas the other two options prefer one option over the other. You can set the convert options as follows:

```
...
converter.optimizations = [tf.lite.Optimize.OPTIMIZE_FOR_SIZE]
converter.target_spec.supported_types = [tf.lite.constants.FLOAT16]
tflite_model = converter.convert()
...
```

If your model includes a TensorFlow operation that is not supported by TFLite at the time of exporting your model, the conversion step will fail with an error message. You can enable an additional set of selected TensorFlow operations to be available for the conversion process. However, this will increase the size of your TFLite model by ca. 30 MB. The following code snippet shows how to enable the additional Tensor-Flow operations before the converter is executed:

```
...
converter.target_spec.supported_ops = [tf.lite.OpsSet.TFLITE_BUILTINS,
                                        tf.lite.OpsSet.SELECT_TF_OPS]
tflite_model = converter.convert()
...
```

If the conversion of your model still fails due to an unsupported TensorFlow operation, you can bring it to the attention of the TensorFlow community. The community is actively increasing the number of operations supported by TFLite and welcomes suggestions for future operations to be included in TFLite. TensorFlow ops can be nominated via the TFLite Op Request form (*https://oreil.ly/rPUqr*).

Serving TFLite Models with TensorFlow Serving

The latest TensorFlow Serving versions can read TFLite models without any major configuration change. You only need to start TensorFlow Serving with the enabled `use_tflite_model` flag and it will load the optimized model as shown in the following example:

```
docker run -p 8501:8501 \
            --mount type=bind,\
            source=/path/to/models,\
            target=/models/my_model \
            -e MODEL_BASE_PATH=/models \
            -e MODEL_NAME=my_model \
            -t tensorflow/serving:latest \
            --use_tflite_model=true  ❶
```

❶   Enable TFLite model loading.

TensorFlow Lite optimized models can provide you with low-latency and low-memory footprint model deployments.

Deploy Your Models to Edge Devices

After optimizing your TensorFlow or Keras model and deploying your TFLite machine learning model with TensorFlow Serving, you can also deploy the model to a variety of mobile and edge devices; for example:

- Android and iOS mobile phones
- ARM64-based computers
- Microcontrollers and other embedded devices (e.g., Raspberry Pi)
- Edge devices (e.g., IoT devices)
- Edge TPUs (e.g., Coral)

If you are interested in deployments to mobile or edge devices, we recommend the publication *Practical Deep Learning for Cloud, Mobile, and Edge* by Anirudh Koul et al. (O'Reilly) for further reading. If you are looking for materials on edge devices with a focus on TFMicro, we recommend *TinyML* by Pete Warden and Daniel Situnayake (O'Reilly).

Monitoring Your TensorFlow Serving Instances

TensorFlow Serving allows you to monitor your inference setup. For this task, TensorFlow Serving provides metric endpoints that can be consumed by Prometheus. Prometheus is a free application for real-time event logging and alerting, currently under Apache License 2.0. It is used extensively within the Kubernetes community, but it can easily be used without Kubernetes.

To track your inference metrics, you need to run TensorFlow Serving and Prometheus side by side. Prometheus can then be configured to pull metrics from TensorFlow Serving continuously. The two applications communicate via a REST endpoint, which requires that REST endpoints are enabled for TensorFlow Serving even if you are only using gRPC endpoints in your application.

Prometheus Setup

Before configuring TensorFlow Serving to provide metrics to Prometheus, we need to set up and configure our Prometheus instance. For the simplicity of this example, we are running two Docker instances (TensorFlow Serving and Prometheus) side by side, as shown in Figure 9-4. In a more elaborate setup, the applications would be Kubernetes deployments.

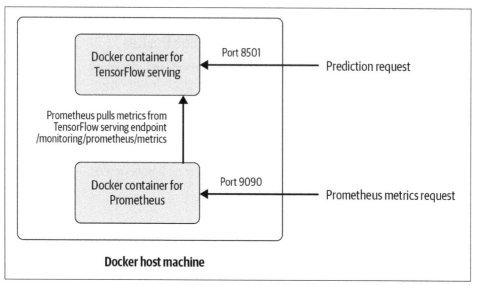

Figure 9-4. Prometheus Docker setup

We need to create a Prometheus configuration file before starting up Prometheus. For this purpose, we will create a configuration file located at */tmp/prometheus.yml* and add the following configuration details:

```
global:
  scrape_interval: 15s
  evaluation_interval: 15s
  external_labels:
    monitor: 'tf-serving-monitor'

scrape_configs:
  - job_name: 'prometheus'
    scrape_interval: 5s ❶
    metrics_path: /monitoring/prometheus/metrics ❷
    static_configs:
      - targets: ['host.docker.internal:8501'] ❸
```

❶ Interval when metrics are pulled.

❷ Metrics endpoints from TensorFlow Serving.

❸ Replace with the IP address of your application.

In our example configuration, we configured the target host to be `host.docker.internal`. We are taking advantage of Docker's domain name resolution to access the TensorFlow Serving container via the host machine. Docker automatically resolves the domain name `host.docker.internal` to the host's IP address.

Once you have created your Prometheus configuration file, you can start the Docker container, which runs the Prometheus instance:

```
$ docker run -p 9090:9090 \ ❶
            -v /tmp/prometheus.yml:/etc/prometheus/prometheus.yml \ ❷
            prom/prometheus
```

❶ Enable port 9090.

❷ Mount your configuration file.

Prometheus provides a dashboard for the metrics, which we will later access via port 9090.

TensorFlow Serving Configuration

Similar to our previous configuration for the inference batching, we need to write a small configuration file to configure the logging settings.

With a text editor of your choice, create a text file containing the following configuration (in our example, we saved the configuration file to */tmp/monitoring_config.txt*):

```
prometheus_config {
    enable: true,
    path: "/monitoring/prometheus/metrics"
}
```

In the configuration file, we are setting the URL path for the metrics data. The path needs to match the path we specified in the Prometheus configuration that we previously created (*/tmp/prometheus.yml*).

To enable the monitoring functionality, we only need to add the path of the `monitoring_config_file` and TensorFlow Serving will provide a REST endpoint with the metrics data for Prometheus:

```
$ docker run -p 8501:8501 \
            --mount type=bind,source=`pwd`,target=/models/my_model \
            --mount type=bind,source=/tmp,target=/model_config \
            tensorflow/serving \
            --monitoring_config_file=/model_config/monitoring_config.txt
```

Prometheus in Action

With the Prometheus instance running, you can now access the Prometheus dashboard to view the TensorFlow Serving metrics with the Prometheus UI, as shown in Figure 9-5.

Figure 9-5. Prometheus dashboard for TensorFlow Serving

Prometheus provides a standardized UI for common metrics. Tensorflow Serving provides a variety of metric options, including the number of session runs, the load latency, or the time to run a particular graph, as shown in Figure 9-6.

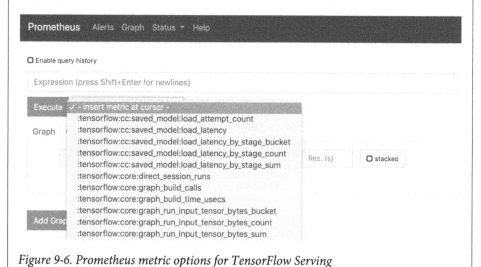

Figure 9-6. Prometheus metric options for TensorFlow Serving

Simple Scaling with TensorFlow Serving and Kubernetes

So far, we have discussed the deployment of a single TensorFlow Serving instance hosting one or more model versions. While this solution is sufficient for a good number of deployments, it isn't enough for applications experiencing a high volume of prediction requests. In these situations, your single Docker container with TensorFlow Serving needs to be replicated to reply to the additional prediction requests. The *orchestration* of the container replication is usually managed by tools like Docker Swarm or Kubernetes. While it would go beyond the scope of this publication to introduce Kubernetes in depth, we would like to provide a small glimpse of how your deployment could orchestrate through Kubernetes.

For the following example, we assume that you'll have a Kubernetes cluster running and that access to the cluster will be via kubectl. Because you can deploy TensorFlow models without building specific Docker containers, you will see that, in our example, we reused Google-provided Docker containers and configured Kubernetes to load our models from a remote storage bucket.

The first source code example highlights two aspects:

- Deploying via Kubernetes without building specific Docker containers
- Handling the Google Cloud authentication to access the remote model storage location

In the following example, we use the GCP as the cloud provider for our deployment:[5]

```
apiVersion: apps/v1
kind: Deployment
metadata:
  labels:
    app: ml-pipelines
  name: ml-pipelines
spec:
  replicas: 1 ❶
  selector:
    matchLabels:
      app: ml-pipelines
  template:
    spec:
      containers:
        - args:
            - --rest_api_port=8501
            - --model_name=my_model
```

---

5 Deployments with AWS are similar; instead of the credential file, the AWS secret and key need to be provided as environment variables.

```
          - --model_base_path=gs://your_gcp_bucket/my_model ❷
        command:
          - /usr/bin/tensorflow_model_server
        env:
          - name: GOOGLE_APPLICATION_CREDENTIALS
            value: /secret/gcp-credentials/user-gcp-sa.json ❸
        image: tensorflow/serving ❹
        name: ml-pipelines
        ports:
          - containerPort: 8501
        volumeMounts:
          - mountPath: /secret/gcp-credentials ❺
            name: gcp-credentials
      volumes:
        - name: gcp-credentials
          secret:
            secretName: gcp-credentials ❻
```

❶ Increase replicas if needed.

❷ Load model from remote location.

❸ Provide cloud credentials here for GCP.

❹ Load the prebuilt TensorFlow Serving image.

❺ Mount the service account credential file (if Kubernetes cluster is deployed through the GCP).

❻ Load credential file as a volume.

With this example, we can now deploy and scale your TensorFlow or Keras models without building custom Docker images.

You can create your service account credential file within the Kubernetes environment with the following command:

```
$ kubectl create secret generic gcp-credentials \
  --from-file=/path/to/your/user-gcp-sa.json
```

A corresponding service setup in Kubernetes for the given model deployment could look like the following configuration:

```
apiVersion: v1
kind: Service
metadata:
  name: ml-pipelines
spec:
  ports:
    - name: http
      nodePort: 30601
```

```
    port: 8501
selector:
  app: ml-pipelines
type: NodePort
```

With a few lines of YAML configuration code, you can now deploy and, most importantly, scale your machine learning deployments. For more complex scenarios like traffic routing to deployed ML models with Istio, we highly recommend a deep dive into Kubernetes and Kubeflow.

 Further Reading on Kubernetes and Kubeflow

Kubernetes and Kubeflow are amazing DevOps tools, and we couldn't provide a holistic introduction here. It requires its own publications. If you are looking for further reading on the two topics, we can recommend the following publications:

- *Kubernetes: Up and Running*, 2nd edition by Brendan Burns et al. (O'Reilly)
- *Kubeflow Operations Guide* by Josh Patterson et al. (O'Reilly)
- *Kubeflow for Machine Learning* (forthcoming) by Holden Karau et al. (O'Reilly)

Summary

In this chapter, we discussed advanced deployment scenarios, such as splitting the data science and DevOps deployment life cycles by deploying models via remote cloud storage buckets, optimizing models to reducing the prediction latency and the model memory footprint, or how to scale your deployment.

In the following chapter, we now want to combine all the individual pipeline components into a single machine learning pipeline to provide reproducible machine learning workflows.

Advanced TensorFlow Extended

With the previous two chapters on model deployments, we completed our overview of individual pipeline components. Before we take a deep dive into orchestrating these pipeline components, we want to pause and introduce advanced concepts of TFX in this chapter.

With the pipeline components we have introduced so far, we can create machine learning pipelines for most problems. However, sometimes we need to build our own TFX component or more complex pipeline graphs. Therefore, in this chapter, we will focus on how to build custom TFX components. We introduce the topic with a custom ingestion component that ingests images directly for computer vision ML pipelines. Furthermore, we will introduce advanced concepts of pipeline structures: generating two models simultaneously (e.g., for deployments with TensorFlow Serving and TFLite), as well as adding a human reviewer into the pipeline workflow.

Ongoing Developments

At the time of this writing, some of the concepts we are introducing are still under development and, therefore, might be subject to future updates. We have done our best to update code examples with changes to the TFX functionality throughout the production of this publication, and all examples work with TFX 0.22. Updates to the TFX APIs can be found in the TFX documentation (*https://oreil.ly/POS_m*).

Advanced Pipeline Concepts

In this section, we will discuss three additional concepts to advance your pipeline set-ups. So far, all the pipeline concepts we've discussed comprised linear graphs with one entry and one exit point. In Chapter 1, we discussed the fundamentals of directed acyclic graphs. As long as our pipeline graph is directed and doesn't create any circular connections, we can be creative with our setup. In the next sections, we will highlight a few concepts to increase the productivity of pipelines by:

- Training multiple models simultaneously
- Exporting models for mobile deployments
- Warm starting model training

Training Multiple Models Simultaneously

As we mentioned before, you can train multiple models simultaneously. A common use case for training multiple models from the same pipeline is when you want to train a different type of model (e.g., a more simplistic model), but you want to make sure that the trained model is getting fed with exactly the same transformed data and the exact same transform graph. Figure 10-1 shows how this setup would work.

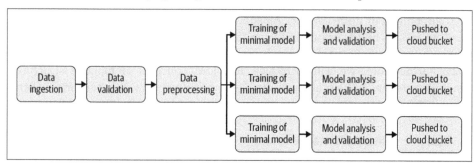

Figure 10-1. Training multiple models simultaneously

You can assemble such a graph with TFX by defining multiple `Trainer` components, as shown in the following code example:

```
def set_trainer(module_file, instance_name,
                train_steps=5000, eval_steps=100): ❶
    return Trainer(
        module_file=module_file,
        custom_executor_spec=executor_spec.ExecutorClassSpec(
            GenericExecutor),
        examples=transform.outputs['transformed_examples'],
        transform_graph=transform.outputs['transform_graph'],
        schema=schema_gen.outputs['schema'],
```

```
        train_args=trainer_pb2.TrainArgs(num_steps=train_steps),
        eval_args=trainer_pb2.EvalArgs(num_steps=eval_steps),
        instance_name=instance_name)

    prod_module_file = os.path.join(pipeline_dir, 'prod_module.py')  ❷
    trial_module_file = os.path.join(pipeline_dir, 'trial_module.py')
    ...

    trainer_prod_model = set_trainer(module_file, 'production_model')  ❸
    trainer_trial_model = set_trainer(trial_module_file, 'trial_model',
                                      train_steps=10000, eval_steps=500)
    ...
```

❶ Function to instantiate the `Trainer` efficiently.

❷ Load module for each `Trainer`.

❸ Instantiate a `Trainer` component for each graph branch.

At this step, we basically branch the graph into as many training branches as we want to run simultaneously. Each of the `Trainer` components consumes the same inputs from the ingestion, schema, and `Transform` components. The key difference between the components is that each component can run a different training setup, which is defined in the individual training module files. We have also added the arguments for the training and evaluation steps as a parameter to the function. This allows us to train two models with the same training setup (i.e., the same module file), but we can compare the models based on the different training runs.

Each instantiated training component needs to be consumed by its own `Evaluator`, as shown in the following code example. Afterward, the models can be pushed by its own `Pusher` components:

```
evaluator_prod_model = Evaluator(
    examples=example_gen.outputs['examples'],
    model=trainer_prod_model.outputs['model'],
    eval_config=eval_config_prod_model,
    instance_name='production_model')

evaluator_trial_model = Evaluator(
    examples=example_gen.outputs['examples'],
    model=trainer_trial_model.outputs['model'],
    eval_config=eval_config_trial_model,
    instance_name='trial_model')

...
```

As we have seen in this section, we can assemble fairly complex pipeline scenarios using TFX. In the following section, we will discuss how we can amend a training setup to export models for mobile deployments with TFLite.

Exporting TFLite Models

Mobile deployments have become an increasingly important platform for machine learning models. Machine learning pipelines can help with consistent exports for mobile deployments. Very few changes are required for mobile deployment compared to deployment to model servers (such as TensorFlow Serving, as discussed in Chapter 8). This helps keep the mobile and the server models updated consistently and helps the consumers of the model have a consistent experience across different devices.

TFLite Limitations

Because of hardware limitations of mobile and edge devices, TFLite doesn't support all TensorFlow operations. Therefore, not every model can be converted to a TFLite-compatible model. For more information on which TensorFlow operations are supported, visit the TFLite website (*https://oreil.ly/LbDBK*).

In the TensorFlow ecosystem, TFLite is the solution for mobile deployments. TFLite is a version of TensorFlow that can be run on edge or mobile devices. Figure 10-2 shows how the pipeline can include two training branches.

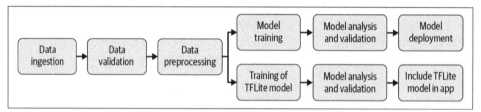

Figure 10-2. Exporting models for deployments in mobile apps

We can use the branch strategy we discussed in the previous section and amend our run_fn function of the module file to rewrite the saved models to a TFLite-compatible format.

Example 10-1 shows the additional functionality we need to add to our run_fn function.

Example 10-1. TFX Rewriter example

```
from tfx.components.trainer.executor import TrainerFnArgs
from tfx.components.trainer.rewriting import converters
from tfx.components.trainer.rewriting import rewriter
from tfx.components.trainer.rewriting import rewriter_factory

def run_fn(fn_args: TrainerFnArgs):
```

```
...
temp_saving_model_dir = os.path.join(fn_args.serving_model_dir, 'temp')
model.save(temp_saving_model_dir,
           save_format='tf',
           signatures=signatures) ❶

tfrw = rewriter_factory.create_rewriter(
    rewriter_factory.TFLITE_REWRITER,
    name='tflite_rewriter',
    enable_experimental_new_converter=True
) ❷
converters.rewrite_saved_model(temp_saving_model_dir, ❸
                               fn_args.serving_model_dir,
                               tfrw,
                               rewriter.ModelType.TFLITE_MODEL)

tf.io.gfile.rmtree(temp_saving_model_dir) ❹
```

❶ Export the model as a saved model.

❷ Instantiate the TFLite rewriter.

❸ Convert the model to TFLite format.

❹ Delete the saved model after conversion.

Instead of exporting a saved model after the training, we convert the saved model to a TFLite-compatible model and delete the saved model after exporting it. Our `Trainer` component then exports and registers the TFLite model with the metadata store. The downstream components like the `Evaluator` or the `Pusher` can then consume the TFLite-compliant model. The following example shows how we can evaluate the TFLite model, which is helpful in detecting whether the model optimizations (e.g., quantization) have led to a degradation of the model's performance:

```
eval_config = tfma.EvalConfig(
    model_specs=[tfma.ModelSpec(label_key='my_label', model_type=tfma.TF_LITE)],
    ...
)

evaluator = Evaluator(
    examples=example_gen.outputs['examples'],
    model=trainer_mobile_model.outputs['model'],
    eval_config=eval_config,
    instance_name='tflite_model')
```

With this presented pipeline setup, we can now produce models for mobile deployment automatically and push them in the artifact stores for model deployment in mobile apps. For example, a `Pusher` component could ship the produced TFLite model to a cloud bucket where a mobile developer could pick up the model and deploy it with Google's *ML Kit* (*https://oreil.ly/dw8zr*) in an iOS or Android mobile app.

Converting Models to TensorFlow.js

Since TFX version 0.22, an additional feature of the `rewriter_fac tory` is available: the conversion of preexisting TensorFlow models to TensorFlow.js models. This conversion allows the deployment of models to web browsers and Node.js runtime environments. You can use this new functionality by replacing the `rewriter_fac tory` name with `rewriter_factory.TFJS_REWRITER` and set the `rewriter.ModelType` to `rewriter.ModelType.TFJS_MODEL` in Example 10-1.

Warm Starting Model Training

In some situations, we may not want to start training a model from scratch. *Warm starting* is the process of beginning our model training from a checkpoint of a previous training run, which is particularly useful if the model is large and training is time consuming. This may also be useful in situations under the General Data Protection Regulation (GDPR), the European privacy law that states that a user of a product can withdraw their consent for the use of their data at any time. By using warm start training, we can remove only the data belonging to this particular user and fine-tune the model rather than needing to begin training again from scratch.

In a TFX pipeline, warm start training requires the `Resolver` component that we introduced in Chapter 7. The `Resolver` picks up the details of the latest trained model and passes them on to the `Trainer` component:

```
latest_model_resolver = ResolverNode(
    instance_name='latest_model_resolver',
    resolver_class=latest_artifacts_resolver.LatestArtifactsResolver,
    latest_model=Channel(type=Model))
```

The latest model is then passed to the `Trainer` using the `base_model` argument:

```
trainer = Trainer(
    module_file=trainer_file,
    transformed_examples=transform.outputs['transformed_examples'],
    custom_executor_spec=executor_spec.ExecutorClassSpec(GenericExecutor),
    schema=schema_gen.outputs['schema'],
    base_model=latest_model_resolver.outputs['latest_model'],
    transform_graph=transform.outputs['transform_graph'],
    train_args=trainer_pb2.TrainArgs(num_steps=TRAINING_STEPS),
    eval_args=trainer_pb2.EvalArgs(num_steps=EVALUATION_STEPS))
```

The pipeline then continues as normal. Next, we want to introduce another useful feature we can add to our pipeline.

Human in the Loop

As part of the advanced TFX concepts, we want to highlight an experimental component that could elevate your pipeline setup. All the pipelines we have discussed so far run automatically from start to finish, and they might deploy your machine learning model automatically. Some TFX users have expressed their concerns about the fully automated setup because they wanted a human to review the trained model after the automatic model analysis. This could be to spot check your trained model or to gain confidence in the automated pipeline setup.

In this section, we will discuss the functionality of a *human in the loop* component. In Chapter 7, we discussed that once a model passes the validation step, it is "blessed." The downstream Pusher component listens to this blessing signal to know whether to push the model or not. But such a blessing can also be generated by a human, as Figure 10-3 shows.

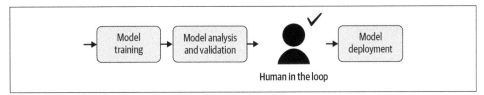

Figure 10-3. Human in the loop

Google's TFX team published a Slack notification component as an example of this custom component. The functionality we are discussing in this section could be extended and isn't limited to the Slack messenger.

The component's functionality is pretty straightforward. Once it is triggered by the orchestration tool, it submits a message to a given Slack channel with a link to the latest exported model and asks for a review by a data scientist (shown in Figure 10-4). A data scientist could now investigate the model manually with the WIT and review edge cases that aren't tested during the Evaluator step.

Figure 10-4. Slack message asking for review

Once the data scientist concludes their manual model analysis, they can respond in the Slack thread with their approval or rejection. The TFX component listens to the Slack responses and stores the decision in the metadata store. The decision can then be used by the downstream components. It is tracked in the model's audit trail. Figure 10-5 shows an example record from Kubeflow Pipeline's lineage browser. The metadata store tracks the "blessing" by the data scientist (i.e., the decision maker) and the time stamp (the Slack thread ID 1584638332.0001 identifies the timestamp as the time in Unix epoch format).

Figure 10-5. Audit trail in Kubeflow Pipelines

Slack Component Setup

For the Slack component to communicate with your Slack account, it requires a Slack *bot token*. You can request a bot token through the Slack API (*https://api.slack.com*). Once you have a token, set an environment variable in your pipeline environment with the token string as shown in the following bash command:

```
$ export SLACK_BOT_TOKEN={your_slack_bot_token}
```

The Slack component is not a standard TFX component and therefore needs to be installed separately. You can install the component by cloning the TFX repository from GitHub and then installing the component individually:

```
$ git clone https://github.com/tensorflow/tfx.git

$ cd tfx/tfx/examples/custom_components/slack
$ pip install -e .
```

Once the component package is installed in your Python environment, the component can then be found on the Python path and loaded inside your TFX scripts. An example is shown in the following Python code. Please also remember to install the Slack component in the environment where you run your TFX pipelines. For example, if you run your pipelines with Kubeflow Pipelines, you will have to create a custom Docker image for your pipeline component, which contains the source code of the Slack component (since it isn't a standard TFX component).

How to Use the Slack Component

The installed Slack component can be loaded like any other TFX component:

```
from slack_component.component import SlackComponent

slack_validator = SlackComponent(
    model=trainer.outputs['model'],
    model_blessing=model_validator.outputs['blessing'],
    slack_token=os.environ['SLACK_BOT_TOKEN'], ❶
    slack_channel_id='my-channel-id', ❷
    timeout_sec=3600,
)
```

❶ Load the Slack token from your environment.

❷ Specify the channel where the message should appear.

When executed, the component will post a message and wait up to an hour (defined by the `timeout_sec` argument) for an answer. During this time, a data scientist can evaluate the model and respond with their approval or rejection. The downstream component (e.g., a `Pusher` component) can consume the result from the Slack component, as shown in the following code example:

```
pusher = Pusher(
    model=trainer.outputs['model'],
    model_blessing=slack_validator.outputs['slack_blessing'], ❶
    push_destination=pusher_pb2.PushDestination(
        filesystem=pusher_pb2.PushDestination.Filesystem(
            base_directory=serving_model_dir)))
```

❶ Model blessing provided by the Slack component.

With a few additional steps, you can enrich your pipelines with a human audit of the machine learning models that is triggered by the pipeline itself. This opens up many more workflows for pipeline applications (e.g., auditing dataset statistics or reviewing data drift metrics).

Slack API Standards

The implementation of the Slack component relies on the *Real Time Messaging* (RTM) protocol. This protocol is deprecated and might be replaced by a new protocol standard, which would affect the component's functionality.

Custom TFX Components

In Chapter 2, we discussed the architecture of TFX components and how each component consists of three parts: the driver, executor, and publisher. In this section, we want to go a little deeper and discuss how you can build your own components. First, we discuss how to write a component from scratch, and afterward, we'll discuss how to reuse existing components and customize them for your own use cases. In general, it is always easier to change an existing component's functionality than to write a component from scratch.

To demonstrate the implementation to you, as seen in Figure 10-6, we will develop a custom component for ingesting JPEG images and its labels in the pipeline. We will load all images from a provided folder and determine the label based on the filename. In our example, we want to train a machine learning model to classify cats and dogs. The filenames of our images carry the content of the image (e.g., *dog-1.jpeg*), so we can determine the label from the filename itself. We will load each image, convert it to tf.Example data structures, and save all samples together as TFRecord files for consumption by downstream components.

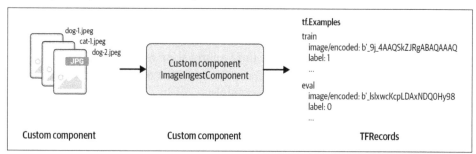

Figure 10-6. Functionality of our demo custom component

Use Cases of Custom Components

Even though we are discussing an ingestion component as an example for a custom component, you aren't limited by the architecture. Your custom component could be applied anywhere along your machine learning pipeline. The concepts discussed in the following sections provide you the highest flexibility to customize your machine learning pipelines to your needs. Some ideas for using custom components are:

- Ingesting data from your custom database
- Sending an email with the generated data statistics to the data science team
- Notifying the DevOps team if a new model was exported
- Kicking off a post-export build process for Docker containers
- Tracking additional information in your machine learning audit trail

We won't describe how to build each of these separately, but if one of these ideas is useful to you, the following sections will provide the knowledge to build your own component.

Writing a Custom Component from Scratch

If we want to write a custom component from scratch, we will need to implement a few component pieces. First, we must define the inputs and outputs of our component as a ComponentSpec. Then we can define our component executor, which defines how the input data should be processed and how the output data is generated. If the component requires inputs that aren't registered in the metadata store, we'll need to write a custom component driver. This is the case when, for example, we want to register an image path in the component and the artifact hasn't been registered in the metadata store previously.

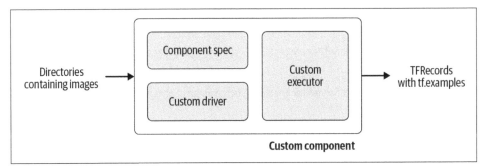

Figure 10-7. Parts of our custom component

The steps in Figure 10-7 might seem complicated, but we will discuss them each in turn in the following sections.

Try to Reuse Components

If you are thinking about altering an existing TFX component in its functionality, consider reusing existing TFX components and changing the executor instead of starting from scratch, as we will discuss in the section "Reusing Existing Components" on page 208.

Component specifications

The component specifications, or `ComponentSpec`, define how components communicate with each other. They describe three important details of each component: the component inputs, the component outputs, and potential component parameters that are required during the component execution. Components communicate through *channels*, which are inputs and outputs. These channels are types, as we will see in the following example. The component inputs define the artifacts that the component will receive from previously executed components or new artifacts like file paths. The component outputs define which artifacts will be registered with the metadata store.

The component parameters define options that are required for execution but aren't available in the metadata store. This could be the `push_destination` in the case of the `Pusher` component or the `train_args` in the `Trainer` component. The following example shows a definition of our component specifications for our image ingestion component:

```
from tfx.types.component_spec import ChannelParameter
from tfx.types.component_spec import ExecutionParameter
from tfx.types import standard_artifacts

class ImageIngestComponentSpec(types.ComponentSpec):
    """ComponentSpec for a Custom TFX Image Ingestion Component."""
    PARAMETERS = {
        'name': ExecutionParameter(type=Text),
    }
    INPUTS = {
        'input': ChannelParameter(type=standard_artifacts.ExternalArtifact),  ❶
    }
    OUTPUTS = {
        'examples': ChannelParameter(type=standard_artifacts.Examples),  ❷
    }
```

❶ Using `ExternalArtifact` to allow new input paths

❷ Exporting `Examples`

In our example implementation of `ImageIngestComponentSpec`, we are ingesting an input path through the input argument `input`. The generated TFRecord files with the converted images will be stored in the path passed to the downstream components

---

via the examples argument. In addition, we are defining a parameter for the component called name.

Component channels

In our example ComponentSpec, we introduced two types of component channels: ExternalArtifact and Examples. This is a particular pattern used for ingestion components since they are usually the first component in a pipeline and no upstream component is available from which we could have received already-processed Examples. If you develop a component further down in the pipeline, you might want to ingest Examples. Therefore the channel type needs to be standard_artifacts. Examples. But we aren't limited to only two types. TFX provides a variety of types. The following shows a small list of available types:

- ExampleStatistics
- Model
- ModelBlessing
- Bytes
- String
- Integer
- Float
- HyperParameters

With our ComponentSpec now set up, let's take a look at the component executor.

Component executors

The component executor defines the processes inside the component, including how the inputs are used to generate the component outputs. Even though we will write this basic component from scratch, we can rely on TFX classes to inherit function patterns. As part of the Executor object, TFX will be looking for a function called Do for the execution details of our component. We will implement our component functionality in this function:

```
from tfx.components.base import base_executor

class Executor(base_executor.BaseExecutor):
    """Executor for Image Ingestion Component."""

    def Do(self, input_dict: Dict[Text, List[types.Artifact]],
            output_dict: Dict[Text, List[types.Artifact]],
            exec_properties: Dict[Text, Any]) -> None:
```

...

The code snippet shows that the Do function of our Executor expects three arguments: `input_dict`, `output_dict`, and `exec_properties`. These Python dictionaries contain the artifact references that we pass to and from the component as well as the execution properties.

Artifacts Contain References

The information provided via the `input_dict` and `output_dict` contain the information stored in the metadata store. These are the references to the artifacts, not the underlying data itself. For example, our `input_dict` dictionary will contain a protocol buffer with the file location information instead of the data. This allows us to process the data efficiently with programs like Apache Beam.

To walk you through a basic implementation of a working Do method of the executor, we will reuse the implementation that we discussed in "Image Data for Computer Vision Problems" on page 41 to convert images to TFRecord data structures. An explanation of the conversion process and details around the TFRecord data structures can be found there. This code should look familiar:

```
def convert_image_to_TFExample(image_filename, tf_writer, input_base_uri):

    image_path = os.path.join(input_base_uri, image_filename) ❶

    lowered_filename = image_path.lower() ❷
    if "dog" in lowered_filename:
        label = 0
    elif "cat" in lowered_filename:
        label = 1
    else:
        raise NotImplementedError("Found unknown image")

    raw_file = tf.io.read_file(image_path) ❸

    example = tf.train.Example(features=tf.train.Features(feature={ ❹
        'image_raw': _bytes_feature(raw_file.numpy()),
        'label': _int64_feature(label)
    }))
    writer.write(example.SerializeToString()) ❺
```

❶ Assemble the complete image path.

❷ Determine the label for each image based on the file path.

❸ Read the image from a disk.

❹ Create the `TensorFlow Example` data structure.

❺ Write the `tf.Example` to TFRecord files.

With the completed generic function of reading an image file and storing it in files containing the TFRecord data structures, we can now focus on custom component-specific code.

We want our very basic component to load our images, convert them to `tf.Exam ples`, and return two image sets for training and evaluation. For the simplicity of our example, we are hardcoding the number of evaluation examples. In a production-grade component, this parameter should be dynamically set through an execution parameter in the `ComponentSpecs`. The input to our component will be the path to the folder containing all the images. The output of our component will be the path where we'll store the training and evaluation datasets. The path will contain two sub-directories (`train` and `eval`) that contain the TFRecord files:

```python
class ImageIngestExecutor(base_executor.BaseExecutor):

    def Do(self, input_dict: Dict[Text, List[types.Artifact]],
            output_dict: Dict[Text, List[types.Artifact]],
            exec_properties: Dict[Text, Any]) -> None:

        self._log_startup(input_dict, output_dict, exec_properties) ❶

        input_base_uri = artifact_utils.get_single_uri(input_dict['input']) ❷
        image_files = tf.io.gfile.listdir(input_base_uri) ❸
        random.shuffle(image_files)
        splits = get_splits(images)

        for split_name, images in splits:
            output_dir = artifact_utils.get_split_uri(
                output_dict['examples'], split_name) ❹

            tfrecord_filename = os.path.join(output_dir, 'images.tfrecord')
            options = tf.io.TFRecordOptions(compression_type=None)
            writer = tf.io.TFRecordWriter(tfrecord_filename, options=options) ❺
            for image in images:
                convert_image_to_TFExample(image, tf_writer, input_base_uri) ❻
```

❶ Log arguments.

❷ Get the folder path from the artifact.

❸ Obtain all the filenames.

❹ Set the split Uniform Resource Identifier (URI).

❺ Create a TFRecord writer instance with options.

❻ Write an image to a file containing the TFRecord data structures.

Our basic `Do` method receives `input_dict`, `output_dict`, and `exec_properties` as arguments to the method. The first argument contains the artifact references from the metadata store stored as a Python dictionary, the second argument receives the references we want to export from the component, and the last method argument contains additional execution parameters like, in our case, the component name. TFX provides the very useful `artifact_utils` function that lets us process our artifact information. For example, we can use the following code to extract the data input path:

```
artifact_utils.get_single_uri(input_dict['input'])
```

We can also set the name of the output path based on the split name:

```
artifact_utils.get_split_uri(output_dict['examples'], split_name)
```

The last mentioned function brings up a good point. For simplicity of the example, we have ignored the options to dynamically set data splits, as we discussed in Chapter 3. In fact, in our example, we are hardcoding the split names and quantity:

```
def get_splits(images: List, num_eval_samples=1000):
    """ Split the list of image filenames into train/eval lists """
    train_images = images[num_test_samples:]
    eval_images = images[:num_test_samples]
    splits = [('train', train_images), ('eval', eval_images)]
    return splits
```

Such functionality wouldn't be desirable for a component in production, but a full-blown implementation would go beyond the scope of this chapter. In the following section, we will discuss how you can reuse existing component functions and simplify your implementations. Our component in this section will have the same functionality as we discussed in Chapter 3.

Component drivers

If we would run the component with the executor that we have defined so far, we would encounter a TFX error that the input isn't registered with the metadata store and that we need to execute the previous component before running our custom component. But in our case, we don't have an upstream component since we are ingesting the data into our pipeline. The data ingestion step is the start of every pipeline. So what is going on?

As we discussed previously, components in TFX communicate with each other via the metadata store, and the components expect that the input artifacts are already registered in the metadata store. In our case, we want to ingest data from a disk, and we are reading the data for the first time in our pipeline; therefore, the data isn't passed down from a different component and we need to register the data sources in the metadata store.

Custom Drivers Are Rare

It is rare that you need to implement custom drivers. If you can reuse the input/output architecture of an existing TFX component or if the inputs are already registered with the metadata store, you won't need to write a custom driver and you can skip this step.

Similar to our custom executor, we can reuse a `BaseDriver` class provided by TFX to write a custom driver. We need to overwrite the standard behavior of the component, and we can do that by overwriting the `resolve_input_artifacts` method of the `BaseDriver`. A bare-bones driver will register our inputs, which is straightforward. We need to *unpack* the channel to obtain the `input_dict`. By looping over all the values of the `input_dict`, we can access each list of inputs. By looping again over each list, we can obtain each input and then register it at the metadata store by passing it to the function `publish_artifacts`. `publish_artifacts` will call the metadata store, publish the artifact, and set the state of the artifact as ready to be published:

```
class ImageIngestDriver(base_driver.BaseDriver):
  """Custom driver for ImageIngest."""

  def resolve_input_artifacts(
      self,
      input_channels: Dict[Text, types.Channel],
      exec_properties: Dict[Text, Any],
      driver_args: data_types.DriverArgs,
      pipeline_info: data_types.PipelineInfo) -> Dict[Text, List[types.Artifact]]:
    """Overrides BaseDriver.resolve_input_artifacts()."""
    del driver_args ❶
    del pipeline_info

    input_dict = channel_utils.unwrap_channel_dict(input_channels) ❷
    for input_list in input_dict.values():
      for single_input in input_list:
        self._metadata_handler.publish_artifacts([single_input]) ❸
        absl.logging.debug("Registered input: {}".format(single_input))
        absl.logging.debug("single_input.mlmd_artifact "
                           "{}".format(single_input.mlmd_artifact)) ❹
    return input_dict
```

❶ Delete unused arguments.

❷ Unwrap channel to obtain the input dictionary.

❸ Publish the artifact.

❹ Print artifact information.

While we loop over each input, we can print additional information:

```
print("Registered new input: {}".format(single_input))
print("Artifact URI: {}".format(single_input.uri))
print("MLMD Artifact Info: {}".format(single_input.mlmd_artifact))
```

With the custom driver now in place, we need to assemble our component.

Assembling the custom component

With our `ImageIngestComponentSpec` defined, the `ImageIngestExecutor` completed, and the `ImageIngestDriver` set up, let's tie it all together in our `ImageIngestCompo` nent. We could then, for example, load the component in a pipeline that trains image classification models.

To define the actual component, we need to define the specification, executor, and driver classes. We can do this by setting `SPEC_CLASS`, `EXECUTOR_SPEC`, and `DRIVER_CLASS`, as shown in the following example code. As the final step, we need to instantiate our `ComponentSpecs` with the component's arguments (e.g., input and output examples, and the provided name) and pass it to the instantiated `ImageIngest` `Component`.

In the unlikely case that we don't provide an output artifact, we can set our default output artifact to be of type `tf.Example`, define our hard-coded split names, and set it up as a channel:

```
from tfx.components.base import base_component
from tfx import types
from tfx.types import channel_utils

class ImageIngestComponent(base_component.BaseComponent):
    """Custom ImageIngestWorld Component."""
    SPEC_CLASS = ImageIngestComponentSpec
    EXECUTOR_SPEC = executor_spec.ExecutorClassSpec(ImageIngestExecutor)
    DRIVER_CLASS = ImageIngestDriver

    def __init__(self, input, output_data=None, name=None):
        if not output_data:
            examples_artifact = standard_artifacts.Examples()
            examples_artifact.split_names = \
                artifact_utils.encode_split_names(['train', 'eval'])

            output_data = channel_utils.as_channel([examples_artifact])

        spec = ImageIngestComponentSpec(input=input,
                                        examples=output_data,
                                        name=name)
        super(ImageIngestComponent, self).__init__(spec=spec)
```

By assembling our `ImageIngestComponent`, we have tied together the individual pieces of our basic custom component. In the next section, we will take a look at how we can execute our basic component.

Using our basic custom component

After implementing the entire basic component to ingest images and turn them into TFRecord files, we can use the component like any other component in our pipeline. The following code example shows how. Notice that it looks exactly like the setup of other ingestion components that we discussed in Chapter 3. The only difference is that we need to import our newly created component and then run the initialized component:

```
import os

from tfx.utils.dsl_utils import external_input
from tfx.orchestration.experimental.interactive.interactive_context import \
    InteractiveContext

from image_ingestion_component.component import ImageIngestComponent

context = InteractiveContext()

image_file_path = "/path/to/files"
examples = external_input(dataimage_file_path_root)
example_gen = ImageIngestComponent(input=examples,
                                   name=u'ImageIngestComponent')
context.run(example_gen)
```

The output from the component can then be consumed by downstream components like `StatisticsGen`:

```
from tfx.components import StatisticsGen

statistics_gen = StatisticsGen(examples=example_gen.outputs['examples'])
context.run(statistics_gen)

context.show(statistics_gen.outputs['statistics'])
```

Very Basic Implementation

We want to caution you that the discussed implementation only provides basic functionality and is not production ready. For details of the missing functionality, please see the following section. For a product-ready implementation, please see our updated component implementation in the next sections.

Implementation review

In the previous sections, we walked through a basic component implementation. While the component is functioning, it is missing some key functionality that we discussed in Chapter 3 (e.g., dynamic split names or split ratios)—and we would expect such functionality from our ingestion component. The basic implementation also required a lot of boiler-plate code (e.g., the setup of the component driver). The ingestion of the images should be handled efficiently and in a scalable way. We can achieve such efficient data ingestion through the Apache Beam usage under the hood of TFX components.

In the next section, we will discuss how we could simplify the implementations and adopt the patterns we discussed in Chapter 3—for example, ingesting data from Presto databases. By reusing common functionality, such as the component drivers, we can speed up implementation and reduce code bugs.

Reusing Existing Components

Instead of writing a component for TFX entirely from scratch, we can inherit an existing component and customize it by overwriting the executor functionality. As shown in Figure 10-8, this is generally the preferred approach when a component is reusing an existing component architecture. In the case of our demo component, the architecture is equivalent with a file base ingestion component (e.g., CsvExampleGen). Such components receive a directory path as a component input, load the data from the provided directory, turn the data into tf.Examples, and return the data structures in TFRecord files as output from the component.

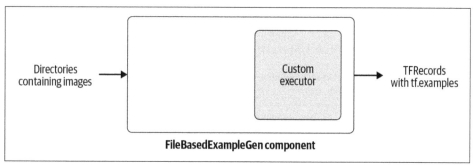

Figure 10-8. Extending existing components

As we discussed in Chapter 3, TFX provides the FileBasedExampleGen for this purpose. Since we are going to reuse an existing component, similar to our Avro and Parquet examples, we can simply focus on developing our custom executor and making it more flexible as our previous basic component. By reusing existing code infrastructure, we can also piggyback on existing Apache Beam implementations.

By reusing an existing component architecture for ingesting data into our pipelines, we can also reuse setups to ingest data efficiently with Apache Beam. TFX and Apache Beam provide classes (e.g., GetInputSourceToExamplePTransform) and function decorators (e.g., @beam.ptransform_fn) to ingest the data via Apache Beam pipelines. In our example, we use the function decorator @beam.ptransform_fn, which allows us to define Apache Beam transformation (PTransform). The decorator accepts an Apache Beam pipeline, runs a given transformation (e.g., in our case, the loading of the images and their conversion to tf.Examples), and returns the Apache Beam PCollection with the transformation results.

The conversion functionality is handled by a function very similar to our previous implementation. The updated conversion implementation has one major difference: we don't need to instantiate and use a TFRecord writer; instead, we can fully focus on loading images and converting them to tf.Examples. We don't need to implement any functions to write the tf.Examples to TFRecord data structures because we did it in our previous implementation. Instead, we return the generated tf.Examples and let the underlying TFX/Apache Beam code handle the writing of the TFRecord files. The following code example shows the updated conversion function:

```
def convert_image_to_TFExample(image_path)): ❶

    # Determine the label for each image based on the file path.
    lowered_filename = image_path.lower()
    print(lowered_filename)
    if "dog" in lowered_filename:
        label = 0
    elif "cat" in lowered_filename:
        label = 1
    else:
        raise NotImplementedError("Found unknown image")

    # Read the image.
    raw_file = tf.io.read_file(image_path)

    # Create the TensorFlow Example data structure.
    example = tf.train.Example(features=tf.train.Features(feature={
        'image_raw': _bytes_feature(raw_file.numpy()),
        'label': _int64_feature(label)
    }))
    return example ❷
```

❶ Only the file path is needed.

❷ The function returns examples instead of writing them to a disk.

With the updated conversion function in place, we can now focus on implementing the core executor functionality. Since we are customizing an existing component architecture, we can use the same arguments as we discussed in Chapter 3, such as split patterns. Our `image_to_example` function in the following code example takes four input arguments: an Apache Beam pipeline object, an `input_dict` with artifact information, a dictionary with execution properties, and split patterns for ingestion. In the function, we generate a list of available files in the given directories and pass the list of images to an Apache Beam pipeline to convert each image found in the ingestion directories to `tf.Examples`:

```python
@beam.ptransform_fn
def image_to_example(
    pipeline: beam.Pipeline,
    input_dict: Dict[Text, List[types.Artifact]],
    exec_properties: Dict[Text, Any],
    split_pattern: Text) -> beam.pvalue.PCollection:

    input_base_uri = artifact_utils.get_single_uri(input_dict['input'])
    image_pattern = os.path.join(input_base_uri, split_pattern)
    absl.logging.info(
        "Processing input image data {} "
        "to tf.Example.".format(image_pattern))

    image_files = tf.io.gfile.glob(image_pattern)  ❶
    if not image_files:
        raise RuntimeError(
            "Split pattern {} did not match any valid path."
            "".format(image_pattern))

    p_collection = (
        pipeline
        | beam.Create(image_files)  ❷
        | 'ConvertImagesToTFRecords' >> beam.Map(
            lambda image: convert_image_to_TFExample(image))  ❸
    )
    return p_collection
```

❶ Generate a list of files present in the ingestion paths.

❷ Convert the list to a Beam `PCollection`.

❸ Apply the conversion to every image.

The final step in our custom executor is to overwrite the `GetInputSourceToExampleP Transform` of the `BaseExampleGenExecutor` with our `image_to_example`:

```python
class ImageExampleGenExecutor(BaseExampleGenExecutor):

    @beam.ptransform_fn
    def image_to_example(...):
        ...
```

```
def GetInputSourceToExamplePTransform(self) -> beam.PTransform:
    return image_to_example
```

Our custom image ingestion component is now complete!

Using our custom executor

Since we are reusing an ingestion component and swapping out the processing executor, we can now follow the same patterns we discussed for the Avro ingestion in
Chapter 3 and specify a `custom_executor_spec`. By reusing the `FileBasedExample`
`Gen` component and overwriting the `executor`, we can use the entire functionality of
ingestion components that we discussed in Chapter 3, like defining the input split
patterns or the output train/eval splits. The following code snippet gives a complete
example of using our custom component:

```
from tfx.components import FileBasedExampleGen
from tfx.utils.dsl_utils import external_input

from image_ingestion_component.executor import ImageExampleGenExecutor

input_config = example_gen_pb2.Input(splits=[
    example_gen_pb2.Input.Split(name='images',
                                pattern='sub-directory/if/needed/*.jpg'),
])

output = example_gen_pb2.Output(
    split_config=example_gen_pb2.SplitConfig(splits=[
        example_gen_pb2.SplitConfig.Split(
            name='train', hash_buckets=4),
        example_gen_pb2.SplitConfig.Split(
            name='eval', hash_buckets=1)
    ])
)

example_gen = FileBasedExampleGen(
    input=external_input("/path/to/images/"),
    input_config=input_config,
    output_config=output,
    custom_executor_spec=executor_spec.ExecutorClassSpec(
        ImageExampleGenExecutor)
)
```

As we have discussed in this section, extending the component executor will always
be a simpler and faster implementation than writing a custom component from
scratch. Therefore, we recommend this process if you are able to reuse existing component architectures.

Summary

In the chapter, we expanded on the TFX concepts from previous chapters. We discussed how to write custom components in detail. Writing custom components gives us the flexibility to extend existing TFX components and tailor them for our pipeline needs. Custom components allow us to integrate more steps into our machine learning pipelines. By adding more components to our pipeline, we can guarantee that all models produced by the pipeline have gone through the same steps. Since the implementation of custom components can be complex, we reviewed a basic implementation of a component from scratch and highlighted an implementation of a new component executor by inheriting existing component functionality.

We also discussed advanced settings for a training setup, such as branching pipeline graphs to produce multiple models from the same pipeline execution. This functionality can be used to produce TFLite models for deployments in mobile apps. We also discussed warm starting the training process to continuously train machine learning models. Warm starting model training is a great way of shortening the training steps for continuously trained models.

We introduced the concept of having a human in the loop in a machine learning pipeline setup and also discussed how the experimental component can be implemented. The human in the loop concept is a way of adding an expert review as a required pipeline step before deploying models. We believe that the combination of fully automated components and a few, critical reviews by data scientists will support the adoption of machine learning pipelines.

In the next two chapters, we will take a look at how to run our TFX pipeline in the orchestration environment of your choice.

Pipelines Part 1: Apache Beam and Apache Airflow

In the previous chapters, we introduced all the necessary components to build a machine learning pipeline using TFX. In this chapter, we will put all the components together and show how to run the full pipeline with two orchestrators: Apache Beam and Apache Airflow. In Chapter 12, we will also show how to run the pipeline with Kubeflow Pipelines. All of these tools follow similar principles, but we will show how the details differ and provide example code for each.

As we discussed in Chapter 1, the pipeline orchestration tool is vital to abstract the glue code that we would otherwise need to write to automate a machine learning pipeline. As shown in Figure 11-1, the pipeline orchestrators sit underneath the components we have already mentioned in previous chapters. Without one of these orchestration tools, we would need to write code that checks when one component has finished, starts the next component, schedules runs of the pipeline, and so on. Fortunately all this code already exists in the form of these orchestrators!

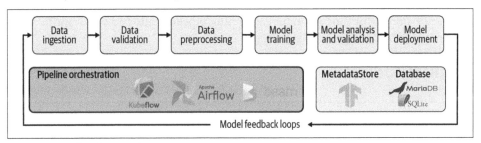

Figure 11-1. Pipeline orchestrators

We will start this chapter by discussing the use cases for the different tools. Then, we will walk through some common code that is required to move from an interactive pipeline to one that can be orchestrated by these tools. Apache Beam and Apache Airflow are simpler to set up than Kubeflow Pipelines, so we will discuss them in this chapter before moving on to the more powerful Kubeflow Pipelines in Chapter 12.

Which Orchestration Tool to Choose?

In this chapter and in Chapter 12, we discuss three orchestration tools that you could use to run your pipelines: Apache Beam, Apache Airflow, and Kubeflow Pipelines. You need to pick only one of them to run each pipeline. Before we take a deep dive into how to use all of these tools, we will describe some of the benefits and drawbacks to each of them, which will help you decide what is best for your needs.

Apache Beam

If you are using TFX for your pipeline tasks, you have already installed Apache Beam. Therefore, if you are looking for a minimal installation, reusing Beam to orchestrate is a logical choice. It is straightforward to set up, and it also allows you to use any existing distributed data processing infrastructure you might already be familiar with (e.g., Google Cloud Dataflow). You can also use Beam as an intermediate step to ensure your pipeline runs correctly before moving to Airflow or Kubeflow Pipelines.

However, Apache Beam is missing a variety of tools for scheduling your model updates or monitoring the process of a pipeline job. That's where Apache Airflow and Kubeflow Pipelines shine.

Apache Airflow

Apache Airflow is often already used in companies for data-loading tasks. Expanding an existing Apache Airflow setup to run your pipeline means you would not need to learn a new tool such as Kubeflow.

If you use Apache Airflow in combination with a production-ready database like PostgreSQL, you can take advantage of executing partial pipelines. This can save a significant amount of time if a time-consuming pipeline fails and you want to avoid rerunning all the previous pipeline steps.

Kubeflow Pipelines

If you already have experience with Kubernetes and access to a Kubernetes cluster, it makes sense to consider Kubeflow Pipelines. While the setup of Kubeflow is more complicated than the Airflow installation, it opens up a variety of new opportunities, including the ability to view TFDV and TFMA visualizations, model lineage, and the artifact collections.

Kubernetes is also an excellent infrastructure platform to deploy machine learning models. Inference routing through the Kubernetes tool Istio is currently state of the art in the field of machine learning infrastructure.

You can set up a Kubernetes cluster with a variety of cloud providers, so you are not limited to a single vendor. Kubeflow Pipelines also lets you take advantage of state-of-the-art training hardware supplied by cloud providers. You can run your pipeline efficiently and scale up and down the nodes of your cluster.

Kubeflow Pipelines on AI Platform

It's also possible to run Kubeflow Pipelines on Google's AI Platform, which is part of GCP. This takes care of much of the infrastructure for you and makes it easy to load data from Google Cloud Storage buckets. Also, the integration of Google's Dataflow simplifies the scaling of your pipelines. However, this locks you into one single cloud provider.

If you decide to go with Apache Beam or Airflow, this chapter has the information you will need. If you choose Kubeflow (either via Kubernetes or on Google Cloud's AI Platform), you will only need to read the next section of this chapter. This will show you how to convert your interactive pipeline to a script, and then you can head over to Chapter 12 afterward.

Converting Your Interactive TFX Pipeline to a Production Pipeline

Up to this point, our examples have shown how to run all the different components of a TFX pipeline in a notebook-style environment, or *interactive context*. To run the pipeline in a notebook, each component needs to be triggered manually when the previous one has finished. In order to automate our pipelines, we will need to write a Python script that will run all these components without any input from us.

Fortunately, we already have all the pieces of this script. We'll summarize all the pipeline components that we have discussed so far:

ExampleGen
    Ingests the new data from the data source we wish to use (Chapter 3)

StatisticsGen
    Calculates the summary statistics of the new data (Chapter 4)

SchemaGen
    Defines the expected features for the model, as well as their types and ranges (Chapter 4)

ExampleValidator
: Checks the data against the schema and flags any anomalies (Chapter 4)

Transform
: Preprocesses the data into the correct numerical representation that the model is expecting (Chapter 5)

Trainer
: Trains the model on the new data (Chapter 6)

Resolver
: Checks for the presence of a previously blessed model and returns it for comparison (Chapter 7)

Evaluator
: Evaluates the model's performance on an evaluation dataset and validates the model if it is an improvement on the previous version (Chapter 7)

Pusher
: Pushes the model to a serving directory if it passes the validation step (Chapter 7)

The full pipeline is shown in Example 11-1.

Example 11-1. The base pipeline

```
import tensorflow_model_analysis as tfma
from tfx.components import (CsvExampleGen, Evaluator, ExampleValidator, Pusher,
                            ResolverNode, SchemaGen, StatisticsGen, Trainer,
                            Transform)
from tfx.components.base import executor_spec
from tfx.components.trainer.executor import GenericExecutor
from tfx.dsl.experimental import latest_blessed_model_resolver
from tfx.proto import pusher_pb2, trainer_pb2
from tfx.types import Channel
from tfx.types.standard_artifacts import Model, ModelBlessing
from tfx.utils.dsl_utils import external_input


def init_components(data_dir, module_file, serving_model_dir,
                    training_steps=2000, eval_steps=200):

    examples = external_input(data_dir)
    example_gen = CsvExampleGen(...)
    statistics_gen = StatisticsGen(...)
    schema_gen = SchemaGen(...)
    example_validator = ExampleValidator(...)
    transform = Transform(...)
    trainer = Trainer(...)
    model_resolver = ResolverNode(...)
    eval_config=tfma.EvalConfig(...)
```

```
    evaluator = Evaluator(...)
    pusher = Pusher(...)

    components = [
        example_gen,
        statistics_gen,
        schema_gen,
        example_validator,
        transform,
        trainer,
        model_resolver,
        evaluator,
        pusher
    ]
    return components
```

In our example project, we have split the component instantiation from the pipeline configuration to focus on the pipeline setup for the different orchestrators.

The init_components function instantiates the components. It requires three inputs in addition to the number of training steps and evaluation steps:

data_dir
    Path where the training/eval data can be found.

module_file
    Python module required by the Transform and Trainer components. These are described in Chapters 5 and 6, respectively.

serving_model_dir
    Path where the exported model should be stored.

Besides the small tweaks to the Google Cloud setup we will discuss in Chapter 12, the component setup will be identical for each orchestrator platform. Therefore, we'll reuse the component definition across the different example setups for Apache Beam, Apache Airflow, and Kubeflow Pipelines. If you would like to use Kubeflow Pipelines, you may find Beam is useful for debugging your pipeline. But if you would like to jump straight in to Kubeflow Pipelines, turn to the next chapter!

Simple Interactive Pipeline Conversion for Beam and Airflow

If you would like to orchestrate your pipeline using Apache Beam or Airflow, you can also convert a notebook to a pipeline via the following steps. For any cells in your notebook that you don't want to export, use the %%skip_for_export Jupyter magic command at the start of each cell.

First, set the pipeline name and the orchestration tool:

```
runner_type = 'beam'  ❶
pipeline_name = 'consumer_complaints_beam'
```

❶ Alternatively, `airflow`.

Then, set all the relevant file paths:

```
notebook_file = os.path.join(os.getcwd(), notebook_filename)

# Pipeline inputs
data_dir = os.path.join(pipeline_dir, 'data')
module_file = os.path.join(pipeline_dir, 'components', 'module.py')
requirement_file = os.path.join(pipeline_dir, 'requirements.txt')

# Pipeline outputs
output_base = os.path.join(pipeline_dir, 'output', pipeline_name)
serving_model_dir = os.path.join(output_base, pipeline_name)
pipeline_root = os.path.join(output_base, 'pipeline_root')
metadata_path = os.path.join(pipeline_root, 'metadata.sqlite')
```

Next, list the components you wish to include in your pipeline:

```
components = [
    example_gen, statistics_gen, schema_gen, example_validator,
    transform, trainer, evaluator, pusher
]
```

And export the pipeline:

```
pipeline_export_file = 'consumer_complaints_beam_export.py'
context.export_to_pipeline(notebook_file path=_notebook_file,
                            export_file path=pipeline_export_file,
                            runner_type=runner_type)
```

This export command will generate a script that can be run using Beam or Airflow, depending on the `runner_type` you choose.

Introduction to Apache Beam

Because Apache Beam is running behind the scenes in many TFX components, we introduced it in Chapter 2. Various TFX components (e.g., TFDV or TensorFlow `Transform`) use Apache Beam for the abstraction of the internal data processing. But many of the same Beam functions can also be used to run your pipeline. In the next section, we'll show you how to orchestrate our example project using Beam.

Orchestrating TFX Pipelines with Apache Beam

Apache Beam is already installed as a dependency of TFX, and this makes it very easy to start using it as our pipeline orchestration tool. Beam is very simple and does not have all the functionality of Airflow or Kubeflow Pipelines, like graph visualizations, scheduled executions, etc.

Beam can also be a good way to debug your machine learning pipeline. By using Beam during your pipeline debugging and then moving to Airflow or Kubeflow Pipelines, you can rule out root causes of pipeline errors coming from the more complex Airflow or Kubeflow Pipelines setups.

In this section, we will run through how to set up and execute our example TFX pipeline with Beam. We introduced the Beam `Pipeline` function in Chapter 2. This is what we'll use together with our Example 11-1 script to run the pipeline. We will define a Beam `Pipeline` that accepts the TFX pipeline components as an argument and also connects to the SQLite database holding the ML MetadataStore:

```
import absl
from tfx.orchestration import metadata, pipeline

def init_beam_pipeline(components, pipeline_root, direct_num_workers):

    absl.logging.info("Pipeline root set to: {}".format(pipeline_root))
    beam_arg = [
        "--direct_num_workers={}".format(direct_num_workers),  ❶
        "--requirements_file={}".format(requirement_file)
    ]

    p = pipeline.Pipeline(  ❷
        pipeline_name=pipeline_name,
        pipeline_root=pipeline_root,
        components=components,
        enable_cache=False,  ❸
        metadata_connection_config=\
            metadata.sqlite_metadata_connection_config(metadata_path),
        beam_pipeline_args=beam_arg)
    return p
```

❶ Beam lets you specify the number of workers. A sensible default is half the number of CPUs (if there is more than one CPU).

❷ This is where you define your pipeline object with a configuration.

❸ We can set the cache to `True` if we would like to avoid rerunning components that have already finished. If we set this flag to `False`, everything gets recomputed every time we run the pipeline.

The Beam pipeline configuration needs to include the name of the pipeline, the path to the root of the pipeline directory, and a list of components to be executed as part of the pipeline.

Next, we will initialize the components from Example 11-1, initialize the pipeline as earlier, and run the pipeline using `BeamDagRunner().run(pipeline)`:

```
from tfx.orchestration.beam.beam_dag_runner import BeamDagRunner

components = init_components(data_dir, module_file, serving_model_dir,
                            training_steps=100, eval_steps=100)
pipeline = init_beam_pipeline(components, pipeline_root, direct_num_workers)
BeamDagRunner().run(pipeline)
```

This is a minimal setup that you can easily integrate with the rest of your infrastructure or schedule using a cron job. You can also scale up this pipeline using Apache Flink (*https://flink.apache.org*) or Spark. An example using Flink is briefly described in this TFX example (*https://oreil.ly/FYzLY*).

In the next section, we will move on to Apache Airflow, which offers many extra features when we use it to orchestrate our pipelines.

Introduction to Apache Airflow

Airflow is Apache's project for workflow automation. The project was initiated in 2016, and it has gained significant attention from large corporations and the general data science community since then. In December 2018, the project "graduated" from the Apache Incubator and became its own Apache project (*https://airflow.apache.org*).

Apache Airflow lets you represent workflow tasks through DAGs represented via Python code. Also, Airflow lets you schedule and monitor workflows. This makes it an ideal orchestration tool for our TFX pipelines.

In this section, we'll go through the basics of setting up Airflow. Then, we'll show how we can use it to run our example project.

Installation and Initial Setup

The basic setup of Apache Airflow is straightforward. If you are using Mac or Linux, define the location for the Airflow data with this command:

```
$ export AIRFLOW_HOME=~/airflow
```

Once the main data folder for Airflow is defined, you can install Airflow:

```
$ pip install apache-airflow
```

Airflow can be installed with a variety of dependencies. At the time of writing, the list of extensions is PostgreSQL support, Dask, Celery, and Kubernetes.

A complete list of Airflow extensions and how to install them can be found in the Airflow documentation (*https://oreil.ly/evVfY*).

With Airflow now installed, you need to create an initial database where all the task status information will be stored. Airflow provides you a command to initialize the Airflow database:

```
$ airflow initdb
```

If you use Airflow out of the box and haven't changed any configurations, Airflow will instantiate an SQLite database. This setup works to execute demo projects and to run smaller workflows. If you want to scale your workflow with Apache Airflow, we highly recommend a deep dive into the documentation (*https://oreil.ly/Pgc9S*).

A minimal Airflow setup consists of the Airflow scheduler, which coordinates the tasks and task dependencies, as well as a web server, which provides a UI to start, stop, and monitor the tasks.

Start the scheduler with the following command:

```
$ airflow scheduler
```

In a different terminal window, start the Airflow web server with this command:

```
$ airflow webserver -p 8081
```

The command argument -p sets the port where your web browser can access the Airflow interface. When everything is working, go to *http://127.0.0.1:8081* and you should see the interface shown in Figure 11-2.

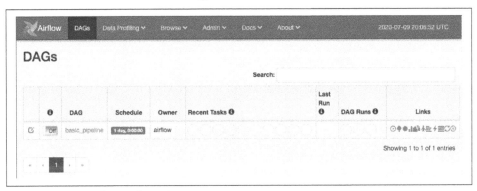

Figure 11-2. Apache Airflow UI

Airflow Configuration

The default settings of Airflow can be overwritten by changing the relevant parameters in the Airflow configuration. If you store your graph definitions in a different place than ~/airflow/dags, you may want to overwrite the default configuration by defining the new locations of the pipeline graphs in ~/airflow/airflow.cfg.

Basic Airflow Example

With the Airflow installation in place, let's take a look at how to set up a basic Airflow pipeline. In this example, we won't include any TFX components.

Workflow pipelines are defined as Python scripts, and Airflow expects the DAG definitions to be located in ~/airflow/dags. A basic pipeline consists of project-specific Airflow configurations, task definitions, and the definition of the task dependencies.

Project-specific configurations

Airflow gives you the option to configure project-specific settings, such as when to retry failed workflows or notifying a specific person if a workflow fails. The list of configuration options is extensive. We recommend you reference the Airflow documentation (*https://airflow.apache.org*) for an updated overview.

Your Airflow pipeline definitions start with importing the relevant Python modules and project configurations:

```
from airflow import DAG
from datetime import datetime, timedelta

project_cfg = {  ❶
    'owner': 'airflow',
    'email': ['your-email@example.com'],
    'email_on_failure': True,
    'start_date': datetime(2019, 8, 1),
    'retries': 1,
    'retry_delay': timedelta(hours=1),
}

dag = DAG(  ❷
    'basic_pipeline',
    default_args=project_cfg,
    schedule_interval=timedelta(days=1))
```

❶ Location to define the project configuration.

❷ The DAG object will be picked up by Airflow.

Again, Airflow provides a range of configuration options to set up DAG objects.

Task definitions

Once the DAG object is set up, we can create workflow tasks. Airflow provides task operators that execute tasks in a Bash or Python environment. Other predefined operators let you connect to cloud data storage buckets like GCP Storage or AWS S3.

A very basic example of task definitions is shown in the following:

```
from airflow.operators.python_operator import PythonOperator

def example_task(_id, **kwargs):
    print("task {}".format(_id))
    return "completed task {}".format(_id)

task_1 = PythonOperator(
    task_id='task 1',
    provide_context=True,
    python_callable=example_task,
    op_kwargs={'_id': 1},
    dag=dag,
)

task_2 = PythonOperator(
    task_id='task 2',
    provide_context=True,
    python_callable=example_task,
    op_kwargs={'_id': 2},
    dag=dag,
)
```

In a TFX pipeline, you don't need to define these tasks because the TFX library takes care of it for you. But these examples will help you understand what is going on behind the scenes.

Task dependencies

In our machine learning pipelines, tasks depend on each other. For example, our model training tasks require that data validation is performed before training starts. Airflow gives you a variety of options for declaring these dependencies.

Let's assume that our `task_2` depends on `task_1`. You could define the task dependency as follows:

```
task_1.set_downstream(task_2)
```

Airflow also offers a `bit-shift` operator to denote the task dependencies:

```
task_1 >> task_2 >> task_X
```

In the preceding example, we defined a chain of tasks. Each of the tasks will be executed if the previous task is successfully completed. If a task does not complete successfully, dependent tasks will not be executed and Airflow marks them as skipped.

Again, this will be taken care of by the TFX library in a TFX pipeline.

Putting it all together

After explaining all the individual setup steps, let's put it all together. In your DAG folder in your AIRFLOW_HOME path, usually at ~/airflow/dags, create a new file *basic_pipeline.py*:

```
from airflow import DAG
from airflow.operators.python_operator import PythonOperator
from datetime import datetime, timedelta

project_cfg = {
    'owner': 'airflow',
    'email': ['your-email@example.com'],
    'email_on_failure': True,
    'start_date': datetime(2020, 5, 13),
    'retries': 1,
    'retry_delay': timedelta(hours=1),
}

dag = DAG('basic_pipeline',
          default_args=project_cfg,
          schedule_interval=timedelta(days=1))

def example_task(_id, **kwargs):
    print("Task {}".format(_id))
    return "completed task {}".format(_id)

task_1 = PythonOperator(
    task_id='task_1',
    provide_context=True,
    python_callable=example_task,
    op_kwargs={'_id': 1},
    dag=dag,
)

task_2 = PythonOperator(
    task_id='task_2',
    provide_context=True,
    python_callable=example_task,
    op_kwargs={'_id': 2},
    dag=dag,
)

task_1 >> task_2
```

You can test the pipeline setup by executing this command in your terminal:

```
python ~/airflow/dags/basic_pipeline.py
```

Our print statement will be printed to Airflow's log files instead of the terminal. You can find the log file at:

```
~/airflow/logs/NAME OF YOUR PIPELINE/TASK NAME/EXECUTION TIME/
```

If we want to inspect the results of the first task from our basic pipeline, we have to investigate the log file:

```
$ cat ../logs/basic_pipeline/task_1/2019-09-07T19\:36\:18.027474+00\:00/1.log

...
[2019-09-07 19:36:25,165] {logging_mixin.py:95} INFO - Task 1 ❶
[2019-09-07 19:36:25,166] {python_operator.py:114} INFO - Done. Returned value was:
    completed task 1
[2019-09-07 19:36:26,112] {logging_mixin.py:95} INFO - [2019-09-07 19:36:26,112] ❷
    {local_task_job.py:105} INFO - Task exited with return code 0
```

❶ Our print statement

❷ Our return message after a successful completion

To test whether Airflow recognized the new pipeline, you can execute:

```
$ airflow list_dags

-------------------------------------------------------------------
DAGS
-------------------------------------------------------------------
basic_pipeline
```

This shows that the pipeline was recognized successfully.

Now that you have an understanding of the principles behind an Airflow pipeline, let's put it into practice with our example project.

Orchestrating TFX Pipelines with Apache Airflow

In this section, we will demonstrate how we can orchestrate TFX pipelines with Airflow. This lets us use features such as Airflow's UI and its scheduling capabilities, which are very helpful in a production setup.

Pipeline Setup

Setting up a TFX pipeline with Airflow is very similar to the BeamDagRunner setup for Beam, except that we have to configure more settings for the Airflow use case.

Instead of importing the BeamDagRunner, we will use the AirflowDAGRunner. The runner tasks an additional argument, which is the configurations of Apache Airflow (the same configurations that we discussed in "Project-specific configurations" on page 222). The `AirflowDagRunner` takes care of all the task definitions and dependencies that we described previously so that we can focus on our pipeline.

As we discussed earlier, the files for an Airflow pipeline need to be located in the *~/airflow/dags* folder. We also discussed some common configurations for Airflow, such as scheduling. We provide these for our pipeline:

```
airflow_config = {
    'schedule_interval': None,
    'start_date': datetime.datetime(2020, 4, 17),
    'pipeline_name': 'your_ml_pipeline',
}
```

Similar to the Beam example, we initialize the components and define the number of workers:

```
from tfx.orchestration import metadata, pipeline

def init_pipeline(components, pipeline_root:Text,
                  direct_num_workers:int) -> pipeline.Pipeline:

    beam_arg = [
        "--direct_num_workers={}".format(direct_num_workers),
    ]
    p = pipeline.Pipeline(pipeline_name=pipeline_name,
                          pipeline_root=pipeline_root,
                          components=components,
                          enable_cache=True,
                          metadata_connection_config=metadata.
                          sqlite_metadata_connection_config(metadata_path),
                          beam_pipeline_args=beam_arg)
    return p
```

Then, we initialize the pipeline and execute it:

```
from tfx.orchestration.airflow.airflow_dag_runner import AirflowDagRunner
from tfx.orchestration.airflow.airflow_dag_runner import AirflowPipelineConfig
from base_pipeline import init_components

components = init_components(data_dir, module_file, serving_model_dir,
                            training_steps=100, eval_steps=100)
pipeline = init_pipeline(components, pipeline_root, 0)
DAG = AirflowDagRunner(AirflowPipelineConfig(airflow_config)).run(pipeline)
```

Again, this code is very similar to the code for the Apache Beam pipeline, but instead of `BeamDagRunner`, we use `AirflowDagRunner` and `AirflowPipelineConfig`. We initialize the components using Example 11-1, and then Airflow looks for a variable named `DAG`.

In this book's GitHub repo (*https://oreil.ly/bmlp-git*), we provide a Docker container that allows you to easily try out the example pipeline using Airflow. It sets up the Airflow web server and scheduler, and moves the files to the correct locations. You can also learn more about Docker in Appendix A.

Pipeline Execution

As we discussed earlier, once we have started our Airflow web server, we can open the UI at the port we define. The view should look very similar to Figure 11-3. To run a pipeline, we need to turn the pipeline on and then trigger it using the Trigger DAG button, indicated by the Play icon.

Figure 11-3. Turning on a DAG in Airflow

The graph view in the web server UI (Figure 11-4) is useful to see the dependencies of the components and the progress of the pipeline execution.

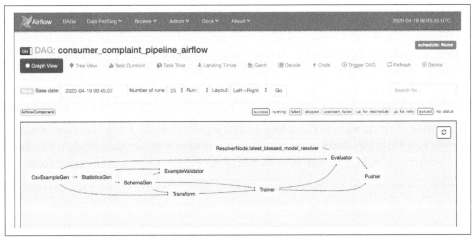

Figure 11-4. Airflow graph view

You will need to refresh the browser page to see the updated progress. As the components finish, they will acquire a green box around the edge, as shown in Figure 11-5. You can view the logs from each component by clicking on them.

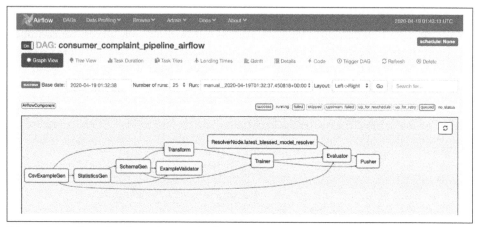

Figure 11-5. Completed pipeline in Airflow

Orchestrating pipelines with Airflow is a good choice if you want a fairly lightweight setup that includes a UI or if your company is already using Airflow. But if your company is already running Kubernetes clusters, the next chapter describes Kubeflow Pipelines, a much better orchestration tool for this situation.

Summary

In this chapter, we discussed the different options for orchestrating your machine learning pipelines. You need to choose the tool that best suits your setup and your use case. We demonstrated how to use Apache Beam to run a pipeline, then introduced Airflow and its principles, and finally showed how to run the complete pipeline with Airflow.

In the next chapter, we will show how to run pipelines using Kubeflow Pipelines and Google's AI Platform. If these do not fit your use case, you can skip straight to Chapter 13 where we will show you how to turn your pipeline into a cycle using feedback loops.

Pipelines Part 2: Kubeflow Pipelines

In Chapter 11, we discussed the orchestration of our pipelines with Apache Beam and Apache Airflow. These two orchestration tools have some great benefits: Apache Beam is simple to set up, and Apache Airflow is widely adopted for other ETL tasks.

In this chapter, we want to discuss the orchestration of our pipelines with Kubeflow Pipelines. Kubeflow Pipelines allows us to run machine learning tasks within Kubernetes clusters, which provides a highly scalable pipeline solution. As we discussed in Chapter 11 and show in Figure 12-1, our orchestration tool takes care of the coordination between the pipeline components.

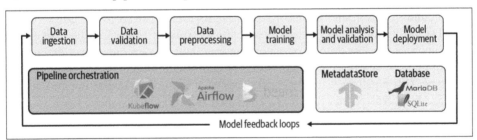

Figure 12-1. Pipeline orchestrators

The setup of Kubeflow Pipelines is more complex than the installation of Apache Airflow or Apache Beam. But, as we will discuss later in this chapter, it provides great features, including *Pipeline Lineage Browser*, *TensorBoard Integration*, and the ability to view TFDV and TFMA visualizations. Furthermore, it leverages the advantages of Kubernetes, such as autoscaling of computation pods, persistent volume, resource requests, and limits, to name just a few.

This chapter is split into two parts. In the first part, we will discuss how to set up and execute pipelines with Kubeflow Pipelines. The demonstrated setup is independent from the execution environment. It can be a cloud provider offering managed Kubernetes clusters or an on-premise Kubernetes installation.

Introduction to Kubernetes

If Kubernetes concepts and terminology are new to you, check out our appendices. Appendix A provides a brief overview of Kubernetes.

In the second part of the chapter, we will discuss how to run Kubeflow Pipelines with the Google Cloud AI Platform. This is specific to the Google Cloud environment. It takes care of much of the infrastructure and lets you use Dataflow to easily scale data tasks (e.g., the data preprocessing). We recommend this route if you would like to use Kubeflow Pipelines but do not want to spend time managing your Kubernetes infrastructure.

Introduction to Kubeflow Pipelines

Kubeflow Pipelines is a Kubernetes-based orchestration tool with machine learning in mind. While Apache Airflow was designed for ETL processes, Kubeflow Pipelines has the end-to-end execution of machine learning pipelines at its heart.

Kubeflow Pipelines provides a consistent UI to track machine learning pipeline runs, a central place to collaborate between data scientists (as we'll discuss in "Useful Features of Kubeflow Pipelines" on page 247), and a way to schedule runs for continuous model builds. In addition, Kubeflow Pipelines provides its own software development kit (SDK) to build Docker containers for pipeline runs or to orchestrate containers. The Kubeflow Pipeline domain-specific language (DSL) allows more flexibility in setting up pipeline steps but also requires more coordination between the components. We think TFX pipelines lead to a higher level of pipeline standardization and, therefore, are less error prone. If you are interested in more details about the Kubeflow Pipelines SDK, we can recommend the suggested reading in "Kubeflow Versus Kubeflow Pipelines" on page 231.

When we set up Kubeflow Pipelines, as we discuss in "Installation and Initial Setup" on page 232, Kubeflow Pipelines will install a variety of tools, including the UI, the workflow controller, a MySQL database instance, and the ML MetadataStore we discussed in "What Is ML Metadata?" on page 17.

When we run our TFX pipeline with Kubeflow Pipelines, you will notice that every component is run as its own Kubernetes pod. As shown in Figure 12-2, each component connects with the central metadata store in the cluster and can load artifacts from either a persistent storage volume of a Kubernetes cluster or from a cloud storage bucket. All the outputs of the components (e.g., data statistics from the TFDV execution or the exported models) are registered with the metadata store and stored as artifacts on a persistent volume or a cloud storage bucket.

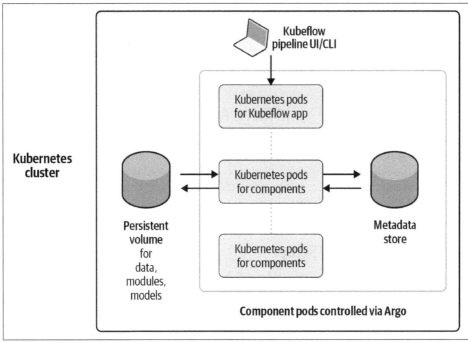

Figure 12-2. Overview of Kubeflow Pipelines

Kubeflow Versus Kubeflow Pipelines

Kubeflow and Kubeflow Pipelines are often mixed up. Kubeflow is a suite of open source projects which encompass a variety of machine learning tools, including TFJob for the training of machine models, Katib for the optimization of model hyperparameters, and KFServing for the deployment of machine learning models. Kubeflow Pipelines is another one of the projects of the Kubeflow suite, and it is focused on deploying and managing end-to-end ML workflows.

In this chapter, we will focus on the installation and the operation of Kubeflow Pipelines only. If you are interested in a deeper introduction to Kubeflow, we recommend the project's documentation (*https://oreil.ly/cxmu7*).

Furthermore, we can recommend two Kubeflow books:

- *Kubeflow Operations Guide* by Josh Patterson et al. (O'Reilly)
- *Kubeflow for Machine Learning* (forthcoming) by Holden Karau et al. (O'Reilly)

As we will demonstrate in this chapter, Kubeflow Pipelines provides a highly scalable way of running machine learning pipelines. Kubeflow Pipelines is running Argo behind the scenes to orchestrate the individual component dependencies. Due to this orchestration through Argo, our pipeline orchestration will have a different workflow, as we discussed in Chapter 11. We will take a look at the Kubeflow Pipelines orchestration workflow in "Orchestrating TFX Pipelines with Kubeflow Pipelines" on page 235.

What Is Argo?

Argo is a collection of tools for managing workflows, rollouts, and continuous delivery tasks. Initially designed to manage DevOps tasks, it is also a great manager for machine learning workflows. Argo manages all tasks as containers within the Kubernetes environment. For more information, please check out the continuously growing documentation (*https://oreil.ly/K2R5H*).

Installation and Initial Setup

Kubeflow Pipelines is executed inside a Kubernetes cluster. For this section, we will assume that you have a Kubernetes cluster created with at least 16 GB and 8 CPUs across your node pool and that you have configured kubectl to connect with your newly created Kubernetes cluster.

Create a Kubernetes Cluster

For a basic setup of a Kubernetes cluster on a local machine or a cloud provider like Google Cloud, please check out Appendix A and Appendix B. Due to the resource requirements by Kubeflow Pipelines, the Kubernetes setup with a cloud provider is preferred. Managed Kubernetes services available from cloud providers include:

1. Amazon Elastic Kubernetes Service (Amazon EKS)

2. Google Kubernetes Engine (GKE)

3. Microsoft Azure Kubernetes Service (AKS)

4. IBM's Kubernetes Service

For more details regarding Kubeflow's underlying architecture, Kubernetes, we highly recommend *Kubernetes: Up and Running* by Brendan Burns et al. (O'Reilly).

For the orchestration of our pipeline, we are installing Kubeflow Pipelines as a standalone application and without all the other tools that are part of the Kubeflow project. With the following bash commands, we can set up our standalone Kubeflow

Pipelines installation. The complete setup might take five minutes to fully spin up correctly.

```
$ export PIPELINE_VERSION=0.5.0
$ kubectl apply -k "github.com/kubeflow/pipelines/manifests/"\
    "kustomize/cluster-scoped-resources?ref=$PIPELINE_VERSION"
customresourcedefinition.apiextensions.k8s.io/
    applications.app.k8s.io created
...
clusterrolebinding.rbac.authorization.k8s.io/
    kubeflow-pipelines-cache-deployer-clusterrolebinding created

$ kubectl wait --for condition=established \
            --timeout=60s crd/applications.app.k8s.io
customresourcedefinition.apiextensions.k8s.io/
    applications.app.k8s.io condition met

$ kubectl apply -k "github.com/kubeflow/pipelines/manifests/"\
    "kustomize/env/dev?ref=$PIPELINE_VERSION"
```

You can check the progress of the installation by printing the information about the created pods:

```
$ kubectl -n kubeflow get pods
NAME                                          READY   STATUS    AGE
cache-deployer-deployment-c6896d66b-62gc5     0/1     Pending   90s
cache-server-8869f945b-4k7qk                  0/1     Pending   89s
controller-manager-5cbdfbc5bd-bnfxx           0/1     Pending   89s
...
```

After a few minutes, the status of all the pods should turn to Running. If your pipeline is experiencing any issues (e.g., not enough compute resources), the pods' status would indicate the error:

```
$ kubectl -n kubeflow get pods
NAME                                          READY   STATUS    AGE
cache-deployer-deployment-c6896d66b-62gc5     1/1     Running   4m6s
cache-server-8869f945b-4k7qk                  1/1     Running   4m6s
controller-manager-5cbdfbc5bd-bnfxx           1/1     Running   4m6s
...
```

Individual pods can be investigated with:

```
kubectl -n kubeflow describe pod <pod name>
```

Managed Kubeflow Pipelines Installations

If you would like to experiment with Kubeflow Pipelines, Google Cloud provides managed installations through the Google Cloud AI Platform. In "Pipelines Based on Google Cloud AI Platform" on page 252, we'll discuss in-depth how to run your TFX pipelines on Google Cloud's AI Platform and how to create setups on Kubeflow Pipelines from Google Cloud's Marketplace.

Accessing Your Kubeflow Pipelines Installation

If the installation completed successfully, regardless of your cloud provider or Kubernetes service, you can access the installed Kubeflow Pipelines UI by creating a port forward with Kubernetes:

```
$ kubectl port-forward -n kubeflow svc/ml-pipeline-ui 8080:80
```

With the port forward running, you can access Kubeflow Pipelines in your browser by accessing *http://localhost:8080*. For production use cases, a load balancer should be created for the Kubernetes service.

Google Cloud users can access Kubeflow Pipelines by accessing the public domain created for your Kubeflow installation. You can obtain the URL by executing:

```
$ kubectl describe configmap inverse-proxy-config -n kubeflow \
| grep googleusercontent.com
<id>-dot-<region>.pipelines.googleusercontent.com
```

You can then access the provided URL with your browser of choice. If everything works out, you will see the Kubeflow Pipelines dashboard or the landing page, as shown in Figure 12-3.

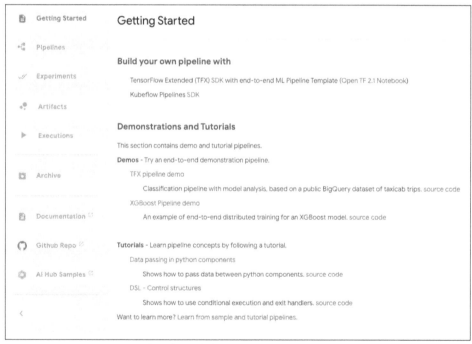

Figure 12-3. Getting started with Kubeflow Pipelines

With the Kubeflow Pipelines setup up and running, we can focus on how to run pipelines. In the next section, we will discuss the pipeline orchestration and the workflow from TFX to Kubeflow Pipelines.

Orchestrating TFX Pipelines with Kubeflow Pipelines

In earlier sections, we discussed how to set up the Kubeflow Pipelines application on Kubernetes. In this section, we will describe how to run your pipelines on the Kubeflow Pipelines setup, and we'll focus on execution only within your Kubernetes clusters. This guarantees that the pipeline execution can be performed on clusters independent from the cloud service provider. In "Pipelines Based on Google Cloud AI Platform" on page 252, we'll show how we can take advantage of a managed cloud service like GCP's Dataflow to scale your pipelines beyond your Kubernetes cluster.

Before we get into the details of how to orchestrate machine learning pipelines with Kubeflow Pipelines, we want to step back for a moment. The workflow from TFX code to your pipeline execution is a little more complex than what we discussed in Chapter 11, so we will begin with an overview of the full picture. Figure 12-4 shows the overall architecture.

As with Airflow and Beam, we still need a Python script that defines the TFX components in our pipeline. We'll reuse the Example 11-1 script from Chapter 11. In contrast to the execution of the Apache Beam or Airflow TFX runners, the Kubeflow runner won't trigger a pipeline run, but rather generates the configuration files for an execution on the Kubeflow setup.

As shown in Figure 12-4, TFX KubeflowRunner will convert our Python TFX scripts with all the component specifications to Argo instructions, which can then be executed with Kubeflow Pipelines. Argo will spin up each TFX component as its own Kubernetes pod and run the TFX Executor for the specific component in the container.

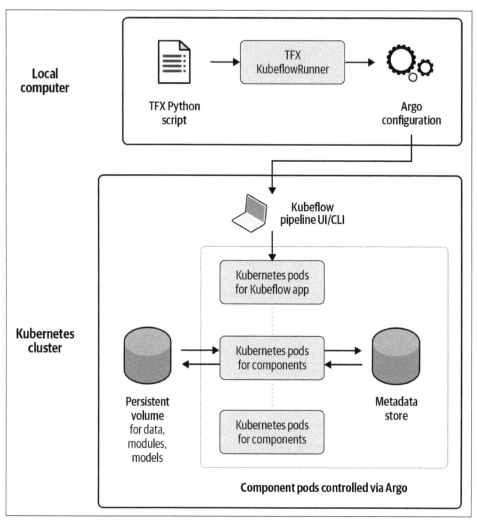

Figure 12-4. Workflow from TFX script to Kubeflow Pipelines

Custom TFX Container Images

The TFX image used for all component containers needs to include all required Python packages. The default TFX image provides a recent TensorFlow version and basic packages. If your pipeline requires additional packages, you will need to build a custom TFX container image and specify it in the `KubeflowDagRunnerConfig`. We describe how to do this in Appendix C.

All components need to read or write to a filesystem outside of the executor container itself. For example, the data ingestion component needs to read the data from a filesystem or the final model needs to be pushed by the Pusher to a particular location. It would be impractical to read and write only within the component container; therefore, we recommend storing artifacts in hard drives that can be accessed by all components (e.g., in cloud storage buckets or persistent volumes in a Kubernetes cluster). If you are interested in setting up a persistent volume, check out "Exchange Data Through Persistent Volumes" on page 319 in Appendix C.

Pipeline Setup

You can store your training data, Python module, and pipeline artifacts in a cloud storage bucket or in a persistent volume; that is up to you. Your pipeline just needs access to the files. If you choose to read or write data to and from cloud storage buckets, make sure that your TFX components have the necessary cloud credentials when running in your Kubernetes cluster.

With all files in place, and a custom TFX image for our pipeline containers (if required), we can now "assemble" the TFX Runner script to generate the Argo YAML instructions for our Kubeflow Pipelines execution.[1]

As we discussed in Chapter 11, we can reuse the init_components function to generate our components. This allows us to focus on the Kubeflow-specific configuration.

First, let's configure the file path for our Python module code required to run the Transform and Trainer components. In addition, we will set setting the folder locations for our raw training data, the pipeline artifacts, and the location where our trained model should be stored at. In the following example, we show you how to mount a persistent volume with TFX:

```
import os

pipeline_name = 'consumer_complaint_pipeline_kubeflow'

persistent_volume_claim = 'tfx-pvc'
persistent_volume = 'tfx-pv'
persistent_volume_mount = '/tfx-data'

# Pipeline inputs
data_dir = os.path.join(persistent_volume_mount, 'data')
module_file = os.path.join(persistent_volume_mount, 'components', 'module.py')

# Pipeline outputs
output_base = os.path.join(persistent_volume_mount, 'output', pipeline_name)
serving_model_dir = os.path.join(output_base, pipeline_name)
```

---

1 You can follow along with the script that generates the Argo YAML instructions in the book's GitHub repo (*https://oreil.ly/bmlp-gitkubeflowpy*).

If you decide to use a cloud storage provider, the root of the folder structure can be a bucket, as shown in the following example:

```
import os
...
bucket = 'gs://tfx-demo-pipeline'

# Pipeline inputs
data_dir = os.path.join(bucket, 'data')
module_file = os.path.join(bucket, 'components', 'module.py')
...
```

With the files paths defined, we can now configure our `KubeflowDagRunnerConfig`. Three arguments are important to configure the TFX setup in our Kubeflow Pipelines setup:

`kubeflow_metadata_config`

Kubeflow runs a MySQL database inside the Kubernetes cluster. Calling `get_default_kubeflow_metadata_config()` will return the database information provided by the Kubernetes cluster. If you want to use a managed database (e.g., AWS RDS or Google Cloud Databases), you can overwrite the connection details through the argument.

`tfx_image`

The image URI is optional. If no URI is defined, TFX will set the image corresponding to the TFX version executing the runner. In our example demonstration, we set the URI to the path of the image in the container registry (e.g., *gcr.io/oreilly-book/ml-pipelines-tfx-custom:0.22.0*).

`pipeline_operator_funcs`

This argument accesses a list of configuration information that is needed to run TFX inside Kubeflow Pipelines (e.g., the service name and port of the gRPC server). Since this information can be provided through the Kubernetes Config-Map,[2] the `get_default_pipeline_operator_funcs` function will read the ConfigMap and provide the details to the `pipeline_operator_funcs` argument. In our example project, we will be manually mounting a persistent volume with our project data; therefore, we need to append the list with this information:

```
from kfp import onprem
from tfx.orchestration.kubeflow import kubeflow_dag_runner

...
PROJECT_ID = 'oreilly-book'
IMAGE_NAME = 'ml-pipelines-tfx-custom'
TFX_VERSION = '0.22.0'
```

---

2 For more information on Kubernetes ConfigMaps, check out "Some Kubernetes Definitions" on page 303.

```
metadata_config = \
    kubeflow_dag_runner.get_default_kubeflow_metadata_config() ❶
pipeline_operator_funcs = \
    kubeflow_dag_runner.get_default_pipeline_operator_funcs() ❷
pipeline_operator_funcs.append( ❸
    onprem.mount_pvc(persistent_volume_claim,
                     persistent_volume,
                     persistent_volume_mount))
runner_config = kubeflow_dag_runner.KubeflowDagRunnerConfig(
    kubeflow_metadata_config=metadata_config,
    tfx_image="gcr.io/{}/{}:{}".format(
        PROJECT_ID, IMAGE_NAME, TFX_VERSION), ❹
    pipeline_operator_funcs=pipeline_operator_funcs
)
```

❶ Obtain the default metadata configuration.

❷ Obtain the default OpFunc functions.

❸ Mount volumes by adding them to the OpFunc functions.

❹ Add a custom TFX image if required.

OpFunc Functions

OpFunc functions allow us to set cluster-specific details, which are important for the execution of our pipeline. These functions allow us to interact with the underlying digital subscriber line (DSL) objects in Kubeflow Pipelines. The OpFunc functions take the Kubeflow Pipelines DSL object *dsl.ContainerOp* as an input, apply the additional functionality, and return the same object.

Two common use cases for adding OpFunc functions to your `pipeline_opera` `tor_funcs` are requesting a memory minimum or specifying GPUs for the container execution. But OpFunc functions also allow setting cloud-provider-specific credentials or requesting TPUs (in the case of Google Cloud).

Let's look at the two most common use cases of OpFunc functions: setting the minimum memory limit to run your TFX component containers and requesting GPUs for executing all the TFX components. The following example sets the minimum memory resources required to run each component container to 4 GB:

```
def request_min_4G_memory():
    def _set_memory_spec(container_op):
        container_op.set_memory_request('4G')
    return _set_memory_spec
...
pipeline_operator_funcs.append(request_min_4G_memory())
```

The function receives the `container_op` object, sets the limit, and returns the function itself.

We can request a GPU for the execution of our TFX component containers in the same way, as shown in the following example. If you require GPUs for your container execution, your pipeline will only run if GPUs are available and fully configured in your Kubernetes cluster:[3].]

```
def request_gpu():
    def _set_gpu_limit(container_op):
        container_op.set_gpu_limit('1')
    return _set_gpu_limit
...
pipeline_op_funcs.append(request_gpu())
```

The Kubeflow Pipelines SDK provides common OpFunc functions for each major cloud provider. The following example shows how to add AWS credentials to TFX component containers:

```
from kfp import aws
...
pipeline_op_funcs.append(
    aws.use_aws_secret()
)
```

The function `use_aws_secret()` assumes that the *AWS_ACCESS_KEY_ID* and *AWS_SECRET_ACCESS_KEY* are registered as base64-encoded Kubernetes secrets.[4] The equivalent function for Google Cloud credentials is called `use_gcp_secrets()`.

With the `runner_config` in place, we can now initialize the components and execute the `KubeflowDagRunner`. But instead of kicking off a pipeline run, the runner will output the Argo configuration, which we will upload in Kubeflow Pipelines in the next section:

```
from tfx.orchestration.kubeflow import kubeflow_dag_runner
from pipelines.base_pipeline import init_components, init_pipeline ❶

components = init_components(data_dir, module_file, serving_model_dir,
                            training_steps=50000, eval_steps=15000)
p = init_pipeline(components, output_base, direct_num_workers=0)

output_filename = "{}.yaml".format(pipeline_name)
kubeflow_dag_runner.KubeflowDagRunner(config=runner_config,
```

---

3 Visit Nvidia (*https://oreil.ly/HGj50*) for more on installing their latest drivers for Kubernetes clusters

4 Check the documentation (*https://oreil.ly/AxcHf*) for information on Kubernetes secrets and how to set them up.

```
                              output_dir=output_dir, ❷
                              output_filename=output_filename).run(p)
```

❶ Reuse the base modules for the components.

❷ Optional Argument.

The arguments `output_dir` and `output_filename` are optional. If not provided, the
Argo configuration will be provided as a compressed *tar.gz* file in the same directory
from which we executed the following python script. For better visibility, we configured the output format to be YAML, and we set a specific output path.

After running the following command, you will find the Argo configuration *con-
sumer_complaint_pipeline_kubeflow.yaml* in the directory *pipelines/kubeflow_pipe-
lines/argo_pipeline_files/*:

```
$ python pipelines/kubeflow_pipelines/pipeline_kubeflow.py
```

Executing the Pipeline

Now it is time to access your Kubeflow Pipelines dashboard. If you want to create a
new pipeline, click "Upload pipeline" for uploading, as shown in Figure 12-5. Alternatively, you can select an existing pipeline and upload a new version.

Figure 12-5. Overview of loaded pipelines

Select the Argo configuration, as shown in Figure 12-6.

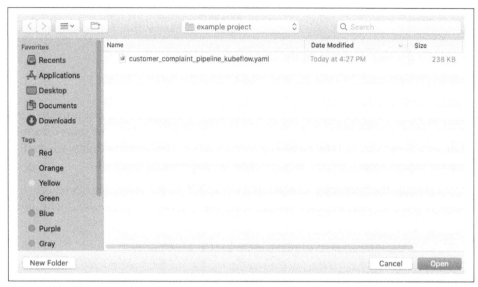

Figure 12-6. Selecting your generated Argo configuration file

Kubeflow Pipelines will now visualize your component dependencies. If you want to kick off a new run of your pipeline, select "Create run" as shown in Figure 12-7.

You can now configure your pipeline run. Pipelines can be run once or on a reoccurring basis (e.g., with a cron job). Kubeflow Pipelines also allows you to group your pipeline runs in *experiments*.

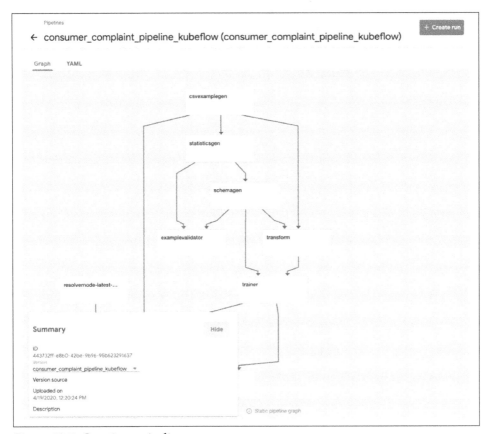

Figure 12-7. Creating a pipeline run

Once you hit Start, as shown in Figure 12-8, Kubeflow Pipelines with the help of Argo will kick into action and spin up a pod for each container, depending on your direct component graph. When all conditions for a component are met, a pod for a component will be spun up and run the component's executor.

If you want to see the execution details of a run in progress, you can click the "Run name," as shown in Figure 12-9.

Figure 12-8. Defined pipeline run details

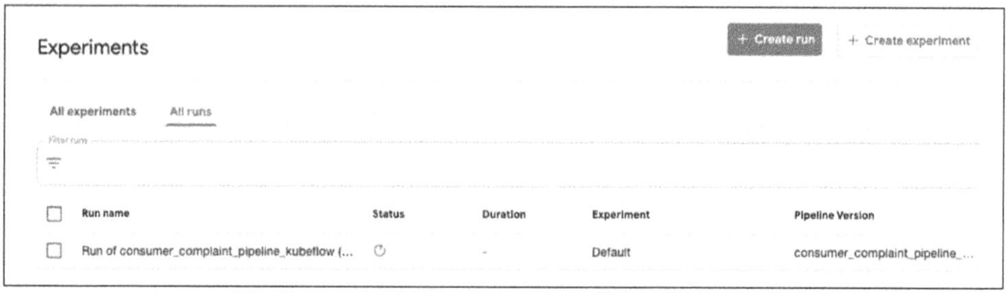

Figure 12-9. Pipeline run in progress

You can now inspect the components during or after their execution. For example, you can check the log files from a particular component if the component failed. Figure 12-10 shows an example where the Transform component is missing a Python library. Missing libraries can be provided by adding them to a custom TFX container image as discussed in Appendix C.

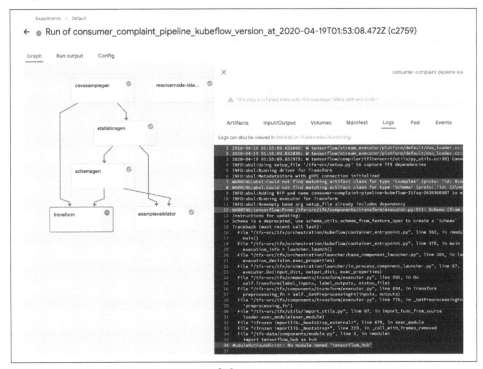

Figure 12-10. Inspecting a component failure

A successful pipeline run is shown in Figure 12-11. After a run completes, you can find the validated and exported machine learning model in the filesystem location set in the Pusher component. In our example case, we pushed the model to the path */tfx-data/output/consumer_complaint_pipeline_kubeflow/* on the persistent volume.

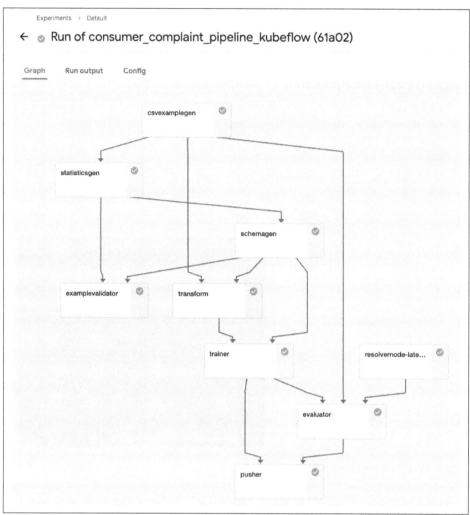

Figure 12-11. Successful pipeline run

You can also inspect the status of your pipeline with kubectl. Since every component runs as its own pod, all pods with the pipeline name in the name prefix should be in the state Completed:

```
$ kubectl -n kubeflow get pods
NAME                                                      READY   STATUS      AGE
cache-deployer-deployment-c6896d66b-gmkqf                 1/1     Running     28m
cache-server-8869f945b-lb8tb                              1/1     Running     28m
consumer-complaint-pipeline-kubeflow-nmvzb-1111865054     0/2     Completed   10m
consumer-complaint-pipeline-kubeflow-nmvzb-1148904497     0/2     Completed   3m38s
consumer-complaint-pipeline-kubeflow-nmvzb-1170114787     0/2     Completed   9m
consumer-complaint-pipeline-kubeflow-nmvzb-1528408999     0/2     Completed   5m43s
consumer-complaint-pipeline-kubeflow-nmvzb-2236032954     0/2     Completed   13m
consumer-complaint-pipeline-kubeflow-nmvzb-2253512504     0/2     Completed   13m
consumer-complaint-pipeline-kubeflow-nmvzb-2453066854     0/2     Completed   10m
consumer-complaint-pipeline-kubeflow-nmvzb-2732473209     0/2     Completed   11m
consumer-complaint-pipeline-kubeflow-nmvzb-997527881      0/2     Completed   10m
...
```

You can also investigate the logs of a specific component through kubectl by executing the following command. Logs for specific components can be retrieved through the corresponding pod:

```
$ kubectl logs -n kubeflow podname
```

TFX CLI

Alternative to the UI-based pipeline creation process, you can also create pipelines and kick off pipeline runs programmatically through the TFX CLI. You can find details on how to set up the TFX CLI and how to deploy machine learning pipelines without a UI in "TFX Command-Line Interface" on page 320 of Appendix C.

Useful Features of Kubeflow Pipelines

In the following sections, we want to highlight useful features of Kubeflow Pipelines.

Restart failed pipelines

The execution of pipeline runs can take a while, sometimes a matter of hours. TFX stores the state of each component in the ML MetadataStore, and it is possible for Kubeflow Pipelines to track the successfully completed component tasks of a pipeline run. Therefore, it offers the functionality to restart failed pipeline runs from the component of the last failure. This will avoid rerunning successfully completed components and, therefore, save time during the pipeline rerun.

Recurring runs

Besides kicking off individual pipeline runs, Kubeflow Pipelines also lets us run the pipeline according to a schedule. As shown in Figure 12-12, we can schedule runs similar to schedules in Apache Airflow.

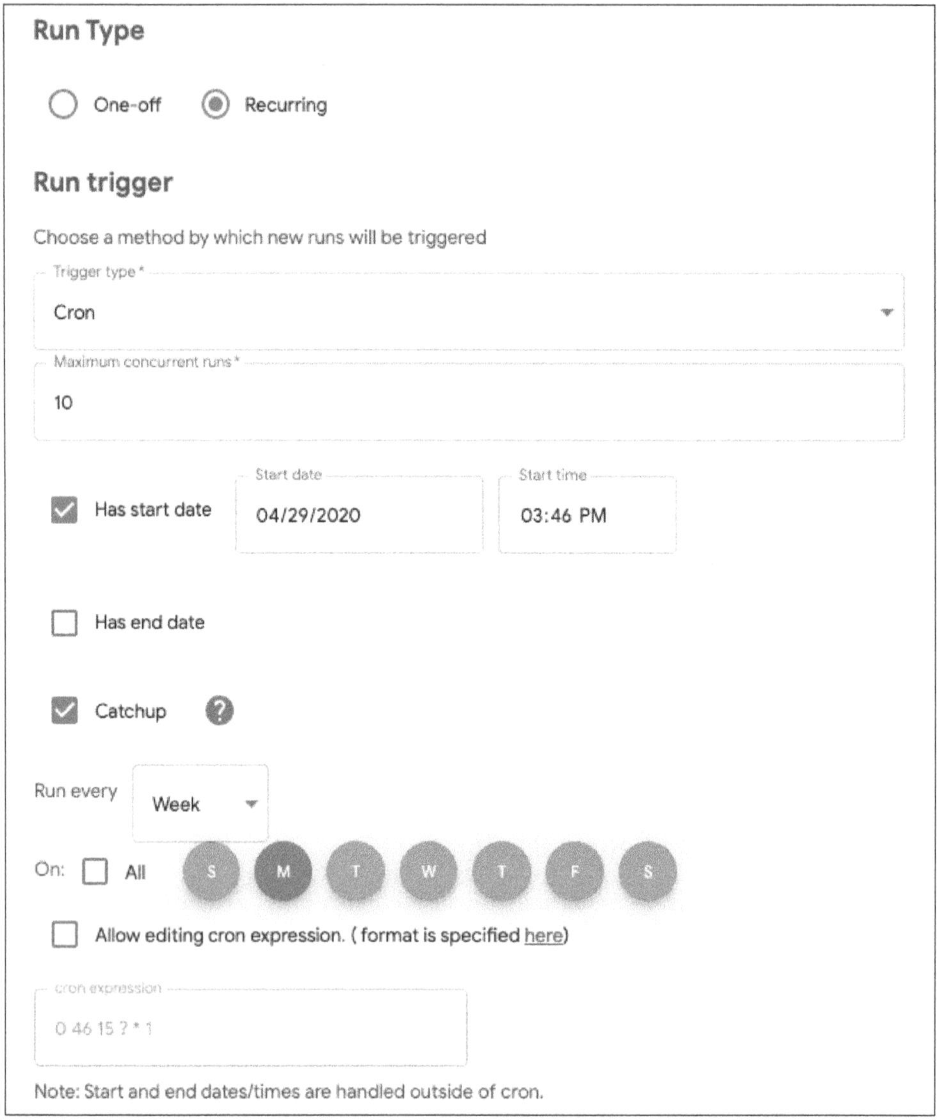

Run Type

◯ One-off   ⦿ Recurring

Run trigger

Choose a method by which new runs will be triggered

Trigger type *

Cron   ▼

Maximum concurrent runs *

10

Start date   Start time
☑ Has start date   04/29/2020   03:46 PM

☐ Has end date

☑ Catchup ❓

Run every   Week ▼

On: ☐ All   (S) (M) (T) (W) (T) (F) (S)

☐ Allow editing cron expression. (format is specified here)

cron expression

0 46 15 ? * 1

Note: Start and end dates/times are handled outside of cron.

Figure 12-12. Scheduling recurring runs with Kubeflow Pipelines

Collaborating and reviewing pipeline runs

Kubeflow Pipelines provides interfaces for data scientists to collaborate and to review the pipeline runs as a team. In Chapters 4 and 7, we discussed visualizations to show the results of the data or model validation. After the completion of these pipeline components, we can review the results of the components.

Figure 12-13 shows the results of the data validation step as an example. Since the component output is saved to a disk or to a cloud storage bucket, we can also review the pipeline runs retroactively.

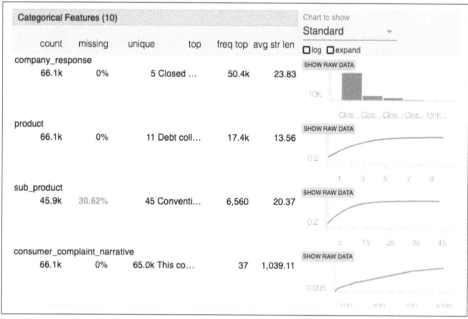

Figure 12-13. TFDV statistics available in Kubeflow Pipelines

Since the results from every pipeline run and component of those runs are saved in the ML MetadataStore, we can also compare the runs. As shown in Figure 12-14, Kubeflow Pipelines provides a UI to compare pipeline runs.

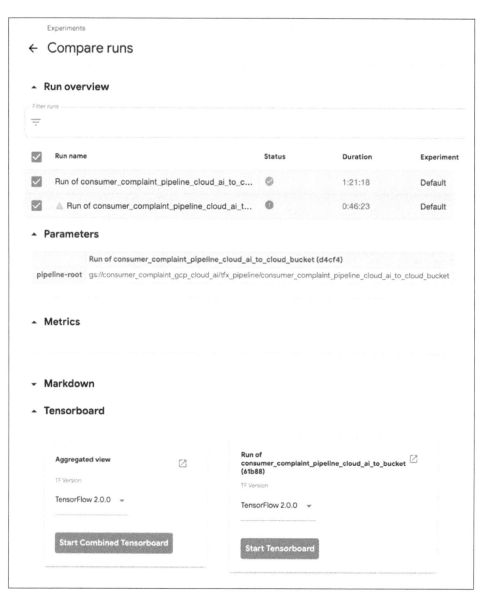

Figure 12-14. Comparing pipeline runs with Kubeflow Pipelines

Kubeflow Pipelines also integrates TensorFlow's TensorBoard nicely. As you can see in Figure 12-15, we can review the statistics from model training runs with Tensor-Board. After the creation of the underlying Kubernetes pod, we can review the statistics from model training runs with TensorBoard.

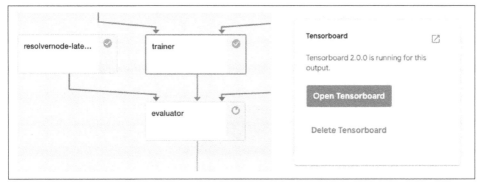

Figure 12-15. Reviewing training runs with TensorFlow's TensorBoard

Auditing the pipeline lineage

For the wider adoption of machine learning, it is critical to review the creation of the model. If, for example, data scientists observe that the trained model is unfair (as we discussed in Chapter 7), it is important to retrace and reproduce the data or hyperparameters that we used. We basically need an audit trail for each machine learning model.

Kubeflow Pipelines offers a solution for such an audit trail with the Kubeflow Lineage Explorer. It creates a UI that can query the ML MetadataStore data easily.

As shown in the lower right corner of Figure 12-16, a machine learning model was pushed to a certain location. The Lineage Explorer allows us to retrace all components and artifacts that contributed to the exported model, all the way back to the initial, raw dataset. We can retrace who signed off on the model if we use the human in the loop component (see "Human in the Loop" on page 195), or we can check the data validation results and investigate whether the initial training data started to drift.

As you can see, Kubeflow Pipelines is an incredibly powerful tool for orchestrating our machine learning pipelines. If your infrastructure is based on AWS or Azure, or if you want full control over your setup, we recommend this approach. However, if you are already using GCP, or if you would like a simpler way to use Kubeflow Pipelines, read on.

Figure 12-16. Inspecting the pipeline lineage with Kubeflow Pipelines

Pipelines Based on Google Cloud AI Platform

If you don't want to spend the time administrating your own Kubeflow Pipelines setup or if you would like to integrate with GCP's AI Platform or other GCP services like Dataflow, AI Platform training and serving, etc., this section is for you. In the following section, we will discuss how to set up Kubeflow Pipelines through Google Cloud's AI Platform. Furthermore, we will highlight how you can train your machine learning models with Google Cloud's AI jobs and scale your preprocessing with Google Cloud's Dataflow, which can be used as an Apache Beam runner.

Pipeline Setup

Google's AI Platform Pipelines (*https://oreil.ly/WAft5*) lets you create a Kubeflow Pipelines setup through a UI. Figure 12-17 shows the front page for AI Platform Pipelines, where you can start creating your setup.

Beta Product

As you can see in Figure 12-17, at the time of writing, this Google Cloud product is still in beta. The presented workflows might change.

Figure 12-17. Google Cloud AI Platform Pipelines

When you click New Instance (near the top right of the page), it will send you to the Google Marketplace, as shown in Figure 12-18.

Figure 12-18. Google Cloud Marketplace page for Kubeflow Pipelines

After selecting Configure, you'll be asked at the top of the menu to either choose an existing Kubernetes cluster or create a cluster, as shown in Figure 12-19.

Node Sizes

When creating a new Kubernetes cluster or selecting an existing cluster, consider the available memory of the nodes. Each node instance needs to provide enough memory to hold the entire model. For our demo project, we selected `n1-standard-4` as an instance type. At the time of writing, we could not create a custom cluster while starting Kubeflow Pipelines from Marketplace. If your pipeline setup requires larger instances, we recommend creating the cluster and its nodes first, and then selecting the cluster from the list of existing clusters when creating the Kubeflow Pipelines setup from GCP Marketplace.

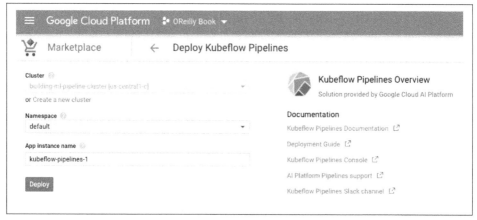

Figure 12-19. Configuring your cluster for Kubeflow Pipelines

Access Scope

During the Marketplace creation of Kubeflow Pipelines or your custom cluster creation, select "Allow full access to all Cloud APIs" when asked for the access scope of the cluster nodes. Kubeflow Pipelines require access to a variety of Cloud APIs. Granting access to all Cloud APIs simplifies the setup process.

After configuring your Kubernetes cluster, Google Cloud will instantiate your Kubeflow Pipelines setup, as shown in Figure 12-20.

Figure 12-20. Creating your Kubeflow Pipelines setup

After a few minutes, your setup will be ready for use and you can find your Kubeflow Pipelines setup as an instance listed in the AI Platform Pipelines list of deployed Kubeflow setups. If you click Open Pipelines Dashboard, as shown in Figure 12-21, you'll be redirected to your newly deployed Kubeflow Pipelines setup. From here, Kubeflow Pipelines will work as we discussed in the previous section and the UI will look very similar.

Figure 12-21. List of Kubeflow deployments

Step-By-Step Installations Available in the AI Platform Pipelines Dashboard

If you install Kubeflow Pipelines manually step by step, as discussed in "Accessing Your Kubeflow Pipelines Installation" on page 234 and Appendix B, your Kubeflow Pipelines setup will also be listed under your AI Platform Pipelines instances.

TFX Pipeline Setup

The configuration of our TFX pipelines is very similar to the configuration of the KubeflowDagRunner, which we discussed previously. In fact, if you mount a persistent volume with the required Python module and training data as discussed in "Pipeline Setup" on page 237, you can run your TFX pipelines on the AI Platform Pipelines.

In the next sections, we will show you a few changes to the earlier Kubeflow Pipelines setup that can either simplify your workflow (e.g., loading data from Google Storage buckets) or assist you with scaling pipelines beyond a Kubernetes cluster (e.g., by training a machine learning model with AI Platform Jobs).

Use Cloud Storage buckets for data exchange

In "Pipeline Setup" on page 237, we discussed that we can load the data and Python modules required for pipeline execution from a persistent volume that is mounted in the Kubernetes cluster. If you run pipelines within the Google Cloud ecosystem, you can also load data from Google Cloud Storage buckets. This will simplify the workflows, enabling you to upload and review files through the GCP web interface or the gcloud SDK.

The bucket paths can be provided in the same way as file paths on a disk, as shown in the following code snippet:

```
input_bucket = 'gs://YOUR_INPUT_BUCKET'
output_bucket = 'gs://YOUR_OUTPUT_BUCKET'
data_dir = os.path.join(input_bucket, 'data')

tfx_root = os.path.join(output_bucket, 'tfx_pipeline')
pipeline_root = os.path.join(tfx_root, pipeline_name)
serving_model_dir = os.path.join(output_bucket, 'serving_model_dir')
module_file = os.path.join(input_bucket, 'components', 'module.py')
```

It is often beneficial to split the buckets between input (e.g., the Python module and training data) and output data (e.g., trained models), but you could also use the same buckets.

Training models with an AI Platform job

If you want to scale model training through a GPU or TPU, you can configure your pipeline to run the training step of the machine learning model on this hardware:

```
project_id = 'YOUR_PROJECT_ID'
gcp_region = 'GCP_REGION>'  ❶

ai_platform_training_args = {
    'project': project_id,
    'region': gcp_region,
    'masterConfig': {
```

```
        'imageUri': 'gcr.io/oreilly-book/ml-pipelines-tfx-custom:0.22.0'} ❷
        'scaleTier': 'BASIC_GPU', ❸
}
```

❶ For example, us-central1.

❷ Provide a custom image (if required).

❸ Other options include BASIC_TPU, STANDARD_1, and PREMIUM_1.

For the Trainer component to observe the AI Platform configuration, you need to configure the component executor and swap out the GenericExecutor we have used with our Trainer component so far. The following code snippet shows the additional arguments required:

```
from
tfx.extensions.google_cloud_ai_platform.trainer import executor \
as ai_platform_trainer_executor

trainer = Trainer(
    ...
    custom_executor_spec=executor_spec.ExecutorClassSpec(
        ai_platform_trainer_executor.GenericExecutor),
    custom_config = {
            ai_platform_trainer_executor.TRAINING_ARGS_KEY:
                ai_platform_training_args}
)
```

Instead of training machine learning models inside a Kubernetes cluster, you can distribute the model training using the AI Platform. In addition to the distributed training capabilities, the AI Platform provides access to accelerated training hardware like TPUs.

When the Trainer component is triggered in the pipeline, it will kick off a training job in the AI Platform Jobs, as shown in Figure 12-22. There you can inspect log files or the completion status of a training task.

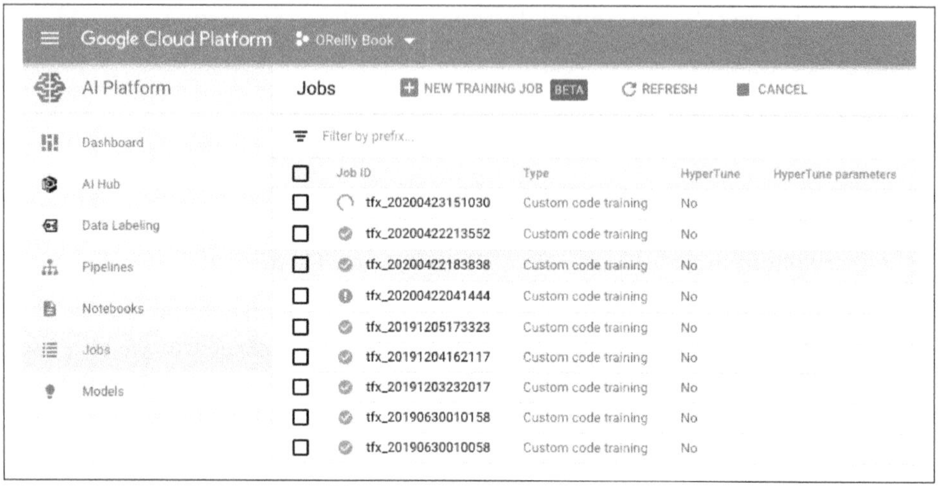

Figure 12-22. AI Platform training jobs

Serving models through AI Platform endpoints

If you run your pipelines within the Google Cloud ecosystem, you can also deploy machine learning models to endpoints of the AI Platform. These endpoints have the option to scale your model in case the model experiences spikes of inferences.

Instead of setting a `push_destination` as we discussed in "TFX Pusher Component" on page 126, we can overwrite the executor and provide Google Cloud details for the AI Platform deployment. The following code snippet shows the required configuration details:

```
ai_platform_serving_args = {
    'model_name': 'consumer_complaint',
    'project_id': project_id,
    'regions': [gcp_region],
}
```

Similar to the setup of the `Trainer` component, we need to exchange the component's executor and provide the `custom_config` with the deployment details:

```
from tfx.extensions.google_cloud_ai_platform.pusher import executor \
    as ai_platform_pusher_executor

pusher = Pusher(
    ...
    custom_executor_spec=executor_spec.ExecutorClassSpec(
        ai_platform_pusher_executor.Executor),
    custom_config = {
        ai_platform_pusher_executor.SERVING_ARGS_KEY:
            ai_platform_serving_args
    }
)
```

If you provide the configuration of the Pusher component, you can avoid setting up and maintaining your instance of TensorFlow Serving by using the AI Platform.

Deployment Limitations

At the time of writing, models were restricted to a maximum size of 512 MB for deployments through the AI Platform. Our demo project is larger than the limit and, therefore, can't be deployed through AI Platform endpoints at the moment.

Scaling with Google's Dataflow

So far, all the components that rely on Apache Beam have executed data processing tasks with the default DirectRunner, meaning that the processing tasks will be executed on the same instance where Apache Beam initiated the task run. In this situation, Apache Beam will consume as many CPU cores as possible, but it won't scale beyond the single instance.

One alternative is to execute Apache Beam with Google Cloud's Dataflow. In this situation, TFX will process jobs with Apache Beam and the latter will submit tasks to Dataflow. Depending on each job's requirements, Dataflow will spin up compute instances and distribute job tasks across instances. This is a pretty neat way of scaling data preprocessing jobs like statistics generation or data preprocessing.[5]

In order to use the scaling capabilities of Google Cloud Dataflow, we need to provide a few more Beam configurations, which we'll pass to our pipeline instantiation:

```
tmp_file_location = os.path.join(output_bucket, "tmp")
beam_pipeline_args = [
    "--runner=DataflowRunner",
    "--experiments=shuffle_mode=auto",
    "--project={}".format(project_id),
    "--temp_location={}".format(tmp_file_location),
    "--region={}".format(gcp_region),
    "--disk_size_gb=50",
]
```

Besides configuring DataflowRunner as the runner type, we also set the shuffle_mode to auto. This is an interesting feature of Dataflow. Instead of running transformations like GroupByKey in the Google Compute Engine's VM, the operation will be processed in the service backend of Dataflow. This reduces the execution time and the CPU/memory costs of the compute instances.

---

5 Dataflow is only available through Google Cloud. Alternative distribution runners are Apache Flink and Apache Spark.

Pipeline Execution

Executing the pipeline with the Google Cloud AI Platform is no different than what we discussed in "Orchestrating TFX Pipelines with Kubeflow Pipelines" on page 235. The TFX script will generate the Argo configuration. The configuration can then be uploaded to the Kubeflow Pipelines setup on the AI Platform.

During the pipeline execution, you can inspect the training jobs as discussed in "Training models with an AI Platform job" on page 256 and you can observe the Dataflow jobs in detail, as shown in Figure 12-23.

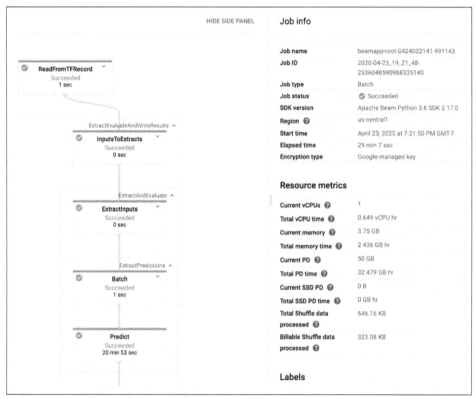

Figure 12-23. Google Cloud Dataflow job details

The Dataflow dashboard provides valuable insights into your job's progress and scaling requirements.

Summary

Running pipelines with Kubeflow Pipelines provides great benefits that we think offset the additional setup requirements. We see the pipeline lineage browsing, the seamless integration with TensorBoard, and the options for recurring runs as good reasons to choose Kubeflow Pipelines as the pipeline orchestrator.

As we discussed earlier, the current workflow for running TFX pipelines with Kubeflow Pipelines is different than the workflows we discussed for pipelines running on Apache Beam or Apache Airflow in Chapter 11. However, the configuration of the TFX components is the same, as we discussed in the previous chapter.

In this chapter, we walked through two Kubeflow pipeline setups: the first setup can be used with almost any managed Kubernetes service, such as AWS Elastic Kubernetes Service or Microsoft Azure Kubernetes Service. The second setup can be used with Google Cloud's AI Platform.

In the following chapter, we will discuss how you can turn your pipeline into a cycle using feedback loops.

Feedback Loops

Now that we have a smooth pipeline for putting a machine learning model into production, we don't want to run it only once. Models shouldn't be static once they are deployed. New data is collected, the data distribution changes (described in Chapter 4), models drift (discussed in Chapter 7), and most importantly, we would like our pipelines to continuously improve.

Adding feedback of some kind into the machine pipeline changes it into a life cycle, as shown in Figure 13-1. The predictions from the model lead to the collection of new data, which continuously improves the model.

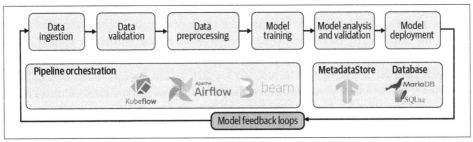

Figure 13-1. Model feedback as part of ML pipelines

Without fresh data, the predictive power of a model may decrease as inputs change over time. The deployment of the ML model may in fact alter the training data that comes in because user experiences change; for example, in a video recommendation system, better recommendations from a model lead to different viewing choices from the user. Feedback loops can help us collect new data to refresh our models. They are particularly useful for models that are personalized, such as recommender systems or predictive text.

At this point, it is extremely important to have the rest of the pipeline set up robustly. Feeding in new data should cause the pipeline to fail only if the influx of new data causes the data statistics to fall outside the limits set in data validation, or if it causes the model statistics to move outside the boundaries set in model analysis. This can then trigger events such as model retraining, new feature engineering, and so on. If one of these triggers occurs, the new model should receive a new version number.

In addition to the collection of new training data, feedback loops can also provide information on the real-world use of the model. This can include the number of active users, the times of day when they interact with it, and many other pieces of data. This type of data is extremely useful for demonstrating the value of the model to business stakeholders.

Feedback Loops Can Be Dangerous

Feedback loops can also have negative consequences and should be approached with caution. If you are feeding the model's predictions back into new training data with no human input, the model will be learning from its mistakes as well as its correct predictions. Feedback loops can also amplify any biases or inequalities that are present in the original data. Careful model analysis can help you spot some of these situations.

Explicit and Implicit Feedback

We can divide our feedback into two main types: implicit and explicit.[1] *Implicit* feedback is where people's actions in their normal usage of a product give the model feedback—for example, by buying something suggested by a recommender system or by watching a suggested movie. User privacy needs careful consideration with implicit feedback because it's tempting to just track every action that a user takes. *Explicit* feedback is where a user gives some direct input on a prediction—for example, giving a thumbs-up or thumbs-down to a recommendation or correcting a prediction.

The Data Flywheel

In some situations, you may have all the data you need to create a new product powered by machine learning. But in other cases, you may need to collect more. This happens particularly often when dealing with supervised learning problems. Supervised learning is more mature than unsupervised learning and generally provides more robust results, so the majority of models deployed in production systems are supervised models. Frequently, the situation arises that you have large amounts of

---

1 For more details, see Google's PAIR manual (*https://oreil.ly/N__j4*).

unlabelled data but insufficient labelled data. However, the growth of *transfer learning*, as we used in our example project, is starting to remove the need for vast amounts of labelled data for some machine learning problems.

In the case where you have a lot of unlabelled data and need to collect more labels, the *data flywheel* concept is especially useful. This data flywheel allows you to grow your training dataset by setting up an initial model using preexisting data from a product, hand-labelled data, or public data. By collecting feedback on the initial model from users, you can label the data, which improves the model predictions and thus attracts more users to the product, who label more data, and so on, as illustrated in Figure 13-2.

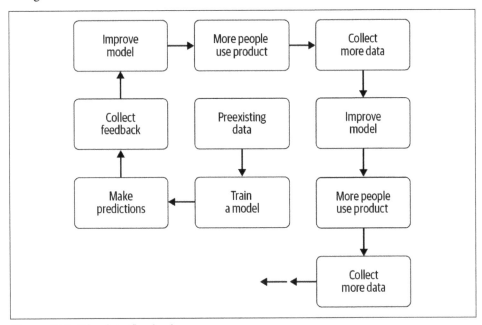

Figure 13-2. The data flywheel

Feedback Loops in the Real World

Some of the most familiar examples of feedback loops in machine learning systems occur when a model's predictions are exposed to a customer. This is particularly common in recommender systems, where a model predicts the top *k* most relevant choices for a specific user. It's often difficult to collect training data for recommender systems in advance of launching a product, so these systems are often heavily dependent on feedback from their users.

Netflix's movie recommendation system (*https://oreil.ly/uX9Oo*) is a classic example of a feedback loop. The user gets movie recommendations and then provides feedback by rating the predictions. As the user rates more movies, they receive recommendations that are more closely tailored to their tastes.

Originally, when the main business of Netflix was shipping DVDs in the mail, it used a one to five star rating system to collect DVD ratings, which signaled that the customer had actually watched the DVD. In this situation, Netflix was only able to collect explicit feedback. But when its business changed to streaming movies online, the company was also able to collect the implicit feedback of whether a user watched the movies that were recommended to them and whether the user watched the whole movie. Netflix then switched from the one to five star rating system to a simpler thumbs-up or thumbs-down system, which allowed it to collect more feedback because the system required less time from users. In addition, the finer-grained ratings may not have been so actionable: how should a model respond if a movie is rated three stars? A three-star review doesn't signal that the prediction is correct or incorrect, whereas a thumbs-up or thumbs-down gives a clear signal to the model.[2]

Another example of a feedback loop—in this case a negative one—is Microsoft's infamous Twitter bot TAY (*https://oreil.ly/YM21r*). This hit the news in 2016 when, within 16 hours of its launch, it was taken offline because of its offensive and sometimes racist tweets. Before it was taken offline, it had tweeted over 96,000 times. It was retrained automatically based on replies to its tweets, which were deliberately provocative. The feedback loop in this situation was that the system took the replies to its initial tweets and incorporated them into its training data. This was probably intended to make the bot sound more human, but the outcome was that it picked up on the worst replies and became extremely offensive.

What Could Go Wrong?

It's important to think about what might go wrong with a feedback loop, as well as the best-case scenario. What is the worst thing that your users might do? How do you protect against bad actors who may want to disrupt your system in an organized or automated way?

A third example of real-world feedback loops comes from Stripe, the online payment company.[3] Stripe built a binary classifier to predict fraud on credit card transactions, and its system would block transactions if the model predicted that they were likely

---

2 Feedback should be easy to collect and give actionable results.

3 See Michael Manapat's talk, "Counterfactual Evaluation of Machine Learning Models," (Presentation, PyData Seattle 2015), *https://oreil.ly/rGCHo*.

fraudulent. The company obtained a training set from past transaction data and trained a model on it, which produced good results on the training set. However, it was impossible to know the precision and recall of the production system because if the model predicted that the transaction was fraudulent, it was blocked. We can't be sure whether it was in fact fraudulent because it never happened.

A larger problem arose when the model was retrained on new data: its accuracy decreased. In this case, the feedback loop caused all the original types of fraudulent transactions to be blocked, so they were unavailable for new training data. The new model was being trained on the residual fraudulent transactions that hadn't been caught. Stripe's solution was to relax the rules and allow a small number of charges to go through, even if the model predicted that they would be fraudulent. This allowed it to evaluate the model and provide new, relevant training data.

Consequences of Feedback Loops

Feedback loops will often have some consequences that weren't apparent during their design. It's essential to keep monitoring the system after it has been deployed to check that the feedback loop is leading to positive change rather than a negative spiral. We suggest using the techniques in Chapter 7 to keep a close eye on the system.

In the preceding example from Stripe, the feedback loop caused the model's accuracy to decrease. However, an increase in accuracy can also be an undesirable effect. YouTube's recommendation system (*https://oreil.ly/QDCC2*) is designed to increase the amount of time that people spend watching videos. The feedback from the users means that the model accurately predicts what they will watch next. And it's been incredibly successful: people watch over one billion hours (*https://oreil.ly/KVF4M*) of video on YouTube every day. However, there are concerns that this system leads people toward watching videos with increasingly extreme content (*https://oreil.ly/_Iubw*). When systems become very large, it's extremely hard to anticipate all the consequences of the feedback loop. So proceed with caution and ensure there are safeguards for your users.

As these examples show, feedback loops can be positive and help us obtain more training data that we can use to improve a model and even build a business. However, they can also lead to serious problems. If you have carefully chosen the metrics for your model that ensure your feedback loop will be a positive one, the next step is to learn how to collect feedback, which we will discuss in the next section.

Design Patterns for Collecting Feedback

In this section, we'll discuss some common ways of collecting feedback. Your choice of method will depend on a few things:

- The business problem you're trying to solve
- The type and design of the app or product
- The type of machine learning model: classification, recommender system, etc.

If you're planning to collect feedback from the users of your product, it's very important to inform the user what's happening so that they can consent to providing feedback. This can also help you collect more feedback: if the user is invested in improving the system, they are more likely to provide feedback.

We will break down the different options for collecting feedback in the following sections:

- "Users Take Some Action as a Result of the Prediction"
- "Users Rate the Quality of the Prediction"
- "Users Correct the Prediction"
- "Crowdsourcing the Annotations"
- "Expert Annotations"
- "Producing Feedback Automatically"

While your choice of design pattern will be driven to some extent by the problem that your machine learning pipeline is trying to solve, your choice will affect how you track the feedback and also how you incorporate it back into your machine learning pipeline.

Users Take Some Action as a Result of the Prediction

In this method, our model's predictions are shown directly to a user, who takes some online action as a result. We record this action, and this record provides some new training data to the model.

An example of this would be any kind of product recommendation system, such as the one used by Amazon to recommend a next purchase to their users. The user is shown a set of products that the model has predicted will be of interest. If the user clicks on one of these products or goes on to buy the product, the recommendation was a good one. However, there is no information on whether the other products that the user didn't click on were good recommendations. This is implicit feedback: it does not provide exactly the data that we need to train the model (this would be ranking every single prediction). Instead, the feedback needs to be aggregated over many different users to provide new training data.

Users Rate the Quality of the Prediction

With this technique, a model's prediction is shown to the user, who gives some kind of signal to show that they like or dislike the prediction. This is an example of explicit feedback, where some extra action must be taken by the user to provide new data. The feedback could be a star rating or a simple binary thumbs-up or thumbs-down. This is a good fit for recommender systems and is especially useful for personalization. Care must be taken that the feedback is actionable: a rating of three stars out of five (such as the preceding Netflix example) does not give much information about whether a model's predictions are useful or accurate.

One limitation of this method is that the feedback is indirect—in the recommender system situation, users say what are poor predictions but do not tell you what the correct prediction should be. Another limitation of this system is that there are a number of ways that the feedback can be interpreted. What a user "likes" may not necessarily be something that they want to see more of. For example, in a movie recommendation system, a user may give a thumbs-up to show that they want to see more movies of the genre, by the same director, or starring the same actors. All these nuances are lost when it's only possible to give binary feedback.

Users Correct the Prediction

This method is an example of explicit feedback, and it works as follows:

- Predictions from a lower-accuracy model are shown to the user.
- The user accepts the prediction if it is correct or updates it if it is incorrect.
- The predictions (now verified by a user) can be used as new training data.

This works best in cases where the user is highly invested in the outcome. A good example of this would be a banking app through which a user can deposit checks. An image recognition model automatically fills in the check amount. If the amount is correct, the user confirms it; if it is incorrect, the user inputs the correct value. In this case, it's in the user's interests to enter the correct amount so that the money is deposited into their account. The app becomes more accurate over time as more training data is created by its users. If your feedback loop can use this method, this can be an excellent way to collect a lot of high-quality, new data quickly.

Care must be taken to only use this method in cases where the objectives of the machine learning system and the user are strongly aligned. If the user accepts incorrect responses because there is no reason for them to put in effort to change it, the training data becomes full of errors and the model does not become more accurate with time. And if there is some gain to the user if they provide incorrect results, this will bias the new training data.

Crowdsourcing the Annotations

This method is particularly useful if you have a large amount of unlabelled data and it's not possible to collect labels from users through the normal usage of a product. Many problems in the NLP and computer vision domains fall into this category: it's easy to collect a large corpus of images, but the data isn't labelled for the specific use case of your machine learning model. For example, if you want to train an image classification model that classifies cellphone images as either documents or nondocuments, you might have your users take many photos but not supply your labels.

In this case, a large pool of unlabelled data is usually collected, which is then passed to a crowdsourcing platform, such as AWS Mechanical Turk or Figure Eight. Human annotators are then paid (usually a small amount) to label the data. This is most suitable for tasks that do not require special training.

With this method, it's necessary to control for varying quality of labelling, and the annotation tool is usually set up so that multiple people label the same data example. The Google PAIR guide (*https://oreil.ly/6FMFD*) gives some excellent, detailed suggestions for designing annotation tools, but the key thing to consider is that the incentives of the annotators need to be aligned with the model outcomes. The main advantage of this method is that it's possible to be extremely specific about the new data that's created so it can exactly fit the needs of a complex model.

However, there are a number of drawbacks to this approach—for example, it may not be suitable for private or sensitive data. Also, be careful to ensure that there is a diverse pool of raters that reflect the users of your product and society as a whole. There can be a high cost to this approach too, which may not scale to a large number of users.

Expert Annotations

Expert annotations are set up similar to crowdsourcing, but with carefully chosen annotators. This could be you (the person building the pipeline), using an annotation tool such as Prodigy (*https://prodi.gy*) for text data. Or it may be a domain expert—for example, if you are training an image classifier on medical images. This method is especially suitable for the following situations:

- The data requires some specialist knowledge to annotate.
- The data is private or sensitive in some way.
- Only a small number of labels are required (e.g., transfer learning or semi-supervised learning).

- Mistakes in annotations have high, real-world consequences for people.

This method allows the collection of high-quality feedback, but it is expensive, manual, and doesn't scale well.

Producing Feedback Automatically

In some machine learning pipelines, no human is required for feedback collection. The model makes a prediction, and some future event happens that tells us whether the model was correct or not. In this case, new training data is collected automatically by the system. While this does not involve any separate infrastructure to collect the feedback, it still requires care: unexpected things can happen because the presence of the predictions can perturb the system. The preceding example from Stripe illustrates this well: the model influences its own future training data.[4]

How to Track Feedback Loops

Once you've decided which type of feedback loop best fits your business and your type of model, it's time to incorporate it into your machine learning pipeline. This is where model validation, as we discussed in Chapter 7, becomes absolutely essential: new data will propagate through the system, and, as it does so, it must not cause the system performance to decline against the metrics you are tracking.

The key concept here is that every prediction should receive a tracking ID, as shown in Figure 13-3. This can be implemented with some kind of prediction register in which each prediction is stored along with a tracking ID. The prediction and the ID are passed to the application, and then the prediction is shown to the user. If the user gives feedback, the process continues.

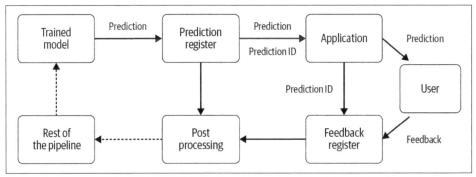

Figure 13-3. Tracking feedback

---

4 More on this can be found in D. Sculley et al.'s "Hidden Technical Debt in Machine Learning Systems," in *Advances in Neural Information Processing Systems 28* (NIPS, 2015), *https://oreil.ly/eUyZM*.

When feedback is collected, it is stored in a feedback register along with that prediction's tracking ID. A data processing step joins the feedback with the original prediction. This allows you to track the feedback through the data and model validation steps so that you know which feedback is powering the new model version.

Tracking Explicit Feedback

If the system is collecting explicit feedback, as described previously, there are two possibilities for how to track it:

Binary feedback
> In most situations, only the feedback that tells you that a prediction is correct can give you new training data with an associated tracking ID. For example, in a multiclass classification system, user feedback only tells you whether the predicted class is correct or not. If the predicted class is marked as incorrect, you don't know which of the other classes it should be. If the predicted class is correct, the pairing of the data plus the prediction form a new training example. A binary classification problem is the only situation where you can use the feedback that a prediction is incorrect. In this case, this feedback tells us that the example belongs to the negative class.

Reclassification or correction
> When a user gives the model a correct answer, the pairing of the input data plus the new classification form a new training example and should receive a tracking ID.

Tracking Implicit Feedback

Implicit feedback generates binary feedback. If a recommendation system suggests a product and the user clicks on that product, the pairing of the product and the user data form a new training example and receive a tracking ID. However, if the user does not click on a product, this doesn't mean that the recommendation was bad. In this situation, it may be necessary to wait for many pieces of binary feedback for each product that is recommended before retraining the model.

Summary

Feedback loops turn a machine learning pipeline into a cycle and help it grow and improve itself. It's essential to incorporate new data into the machine learning pipeline to prevent the model from getting stale and having its accuracy drop. Make sure to choose the feedback method that is most aligned with your type of model and its success metrics.

Feedback loops need careful monitoring. Once you start collecting new data, it's very easy to violate one of the most fundamental assumptions of many machine learning algorithms: that your training and validation data are drawn from the same distribution. Ideally, both your training and validation data will be representative of the real world that you model, but in practice, this is never the case. So as you collect new data, it's important to generate new validation datasets as well as training datasets.

Feedback loops require you to work closely with the designers, developers, and UX experts involved in the product. They need to build the systems that will capture the data and improve the model. It's important that you work with them to connect the feedback to improvements users will see and to set expectations for when the feedback will change the product. This effort will help keep users invested in giving feedback.

One note of caution is that feedback loops can reinforce any harmful bias or unfairness in the initial model. Never forget that there can be a person on the end of this process! Consider offering users a method to give feedback that a model has caused harm to someone so that it's easy for them to flag situations that should be fixed immediately. This will need far more details than a one to five star rating.

Once your feedback loop is set up and you are able to track the model's predictions and responses to predictions, you have all the pieces of the pipeline.

Data Privacy for Machine Learning

In this chapter, we introduce some aspects of data privacy as they apply to machine learning pipelines. Privacy-preserving machine learning is a very active area of research that is just beginning to be incorporated into TensorFlow and other frameworks. We'll explain some of the principles behind the most promising techniques at the time of writing and show some practical examples for how they can fit into a machine learning pipeline.

We'll cover three main methods for privacy-preserving machine learning in this chapter: differential privacy, federated learning, and encrypted machine learning.

Data Privacy Issues

Data privacy is all about trust and limiting the exposure of data that people would prefer to keep private. There are many different methods for privacy-preserving machine learning, and in order to choose between them, you should try to answer the following questions:

- Who are you trying to keep the data private from?
- Which parts of the system can be private, and which can be exposed to the world?
- Who are the trusted parties that can view the data?

The answers to these questions will help you decide which of the methods described in this chapter best fits your use case.

Why Do We Care About Data Privacy?

Data privacy is becoming an important part of machine learning projects. There are many legal requirements surrounding user privacy, such as the EU's General Data Protection Regulation (GDPR), which went into effect in May 2018, and the California Consumer Privacy Act of January 2020. There are ethical considerations around the use of personal data for machine learning, and users of products powered by ML are starting to care deeply about what happens to their data. Because machine learning has traditionally been hungry for data, and because many of the predictions made by machine learning models are based on personal data collected from users, machine learning is at the forefront of debates around data privacy.

At the time of writing, there's always a cost to privacy: adding privacy comes with a cost in model accuracy, computation time, or both. At one extreme, collecting no data keeps an interaction completely private but is completely useless for machine learning. At the other extreme, knowing all the details about a person might endanger that person's privacy, but it allows us to make very accurate machine learning models. We're just now starting to see the development of privacy-preserving ML, in which privacy can be increased without such a large trade-off in model accuracy.

In some situations, privacy-preserving machine learning can help you use data that would otherwise be unavailable for training a machine learning model due to privacy concerns. It doesn't, however, give you free rein to do whatever you like with the data just because you use one of the methods in this chapter. You should discuss your plans with other stakeholders, for example, the data owners, privacy experts, and even your company's legal team.

The Simplest Way to Increase Privacy

Often, the default strategy for building a product powered by machine learning is to collect all the data possible and then decide afterward what is useful for training a machine learning model. Even though this is done with the user's consent, the simplest way to increase user privacy is to only collect the data that is necessary for the training of a particular model. In the case of structured data, fields such as name, gender, or race can simply be deleted. Text or image data can be processed to remove much personal information, such as deleting faces from images or names from text. However, in some cases this can reduce the utility of the data or make it impossible to train an accurate model. And if data on race and gender is not collected, it's impossible to tell whether a model is biased against a particular group.

Control of what data is collected can also be passed to the user: consent to collect data can be made more nuanced than a simple opt-in or opt-out selection, and the user of a product can specify exactly what data may be collected about them. This raises design challenges: should users who provide less data receive less accurate predictions than the users who contribute more data? How do we track consent through machine learning pipelines? How do we measure the privacy impact of a single feature in our models? These are all questions that need more discussion in the machine learning community.

What Data Needs to Be Kept Private?

In machine learning pipelines, data is often collected from people, but some data has a higher need for privacy-preserving machine learning. Personally identifying information (PII) is data that can directly identify a single person, such as their name, email address, street address, ID number, and so on, and this needs to be kept private. PII can appear in free text, such as feedback comments or customer service data, not just when users are directly asked for this data. Images of people may also be considered PII in some circumstances. There are often legal standards around this—if your company has a privacy team, it's best to consult them before embarking on a project using this type of data.

Sensitive data also requires special care. This is often defined as data that could cause harm to someone if it were released, such as health data or proprietary company data (e.g., financial data). Care should be taken to ensure that this type of data is not leaked in the predictions of a machine learning model.

Another category is quasi-identifying data. Quasi-identifiers can uniquely identify someone if enough of them are known, such as location tracking or credit card transaction data. If several location points are known about the same person, this provides a unique trace that can be combined with other datasets to reidentify that person. In December 2019, the *New York Times* published an in-depth piece (*https://oreil.ly/VPea0*) on reidentification using cellphone data, which represents just one of several voices questioning the release of such data.

Differential Privacy

If we have identified a need for additional privacy in the machine learning pipeline, there are different methods that can help increase privacy while retaining as much data utility as possible. The first one we'll discuss is *differential privacy*.[1] Differential privacy (DP) is a formalization of the idea that a query or a transformation of a dataset should not reveal whether a person is in that dataset. It gives a mathematical measure of the privacy loss that a person experiences by being included in a dataset and minimizes this privacy loss through the addition of noise.

> Differential privacy describes a promise, made by a data holder, or curator, to a data subject, and the promise is like this: "You will not be affected, adversely or otherwise,

---

1 Cynthia Dwork, "Differential Privacy," in *Encyclopedia of Cryptography and Security*, ed. Henk C. A. van Tilborg and Sushil Jajodia (Boston: Springer, 2006).

by allowing your data to be used in any study or analysis, no matter what other studies, datasets or information sources are available."

—Cynthia Dwork[2]

To put it another way, a transformation of a dataset that respects privacy should not change if one person is removed from that dataset. In the case of machine learning models, if a model has been trained with privacy in mind, then the predictions that a model makes should not change if one person is removed from the training set. DP is achieved by the addition of some form of noise or randomness to the transformation.

To give a more concrete example, one of the simplest ways of achieving differential privacy is the concept of randomized response, as shown in Figure 14-1. This is useful in surveys that ask sensitive questions, such as "Have you ever been convicted of a crime?" To answer this question, the person being asked flips a coin. If it comes up heads, they answer truthfully. If it comes up tails, they flip again and answer "Yes" if the coin comes up heads, and "No" if the coin comes up tails. This gives them deniability—they can say that they gave a random answer rather than a truthful answer. Because we know the probabilities for a coin flip, if we ask a lot of people this question, we can calculate the proportion of people who have been convicted of a crime with reasonable accuracy. The accuracy of the calculation increases when larger numbers of people participate in the survey.

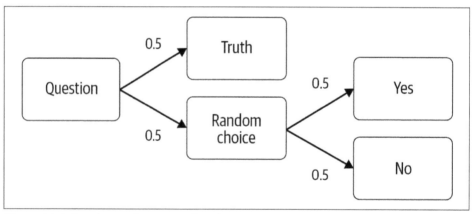

Figure 14-1. Randomized response flowchart

These randomized transformations are the key to DP.

---

2 Cynthia Dwork and Aaron Roth, "The Algorithmic Foundations of Differential Privacy," *Foundations and Trends* in *Theoretical Computer Science* 9, no.3–4: 211–407, (2014), https://www.cis.upenn.edu/~aaroth/Papers/privacybook.pdf.

Assume One Training Example Per Person

Throughout this chapter, for simplicity, we assume that each training example in a dataset is associated with or collected from one individual person.

Local and Global Differential Privacy

DP can be divided into two main methods: local and global DP. In local DP, noise or randomness is added at the individual level, as in the randomized response example earlier, so privacy is maintained between an individual and the collector of the data. In global DP, noise is added to a transformation on the entire dataset. The data collector is trusted with the raw data, but the result of the transformation does not reveal data about an individual.

Global DP requires us to add less noise compared to local DP, which leads to a utility or accuracy improvement of the query for a similar privacy guarantee. The downside is that the data collector must be trusted for global DP, whereas for local DP only individual users see their own raw data.

Epsilon, Delta, and the Privacy Budget

Probably the most common way of implementing DP is using ϵ - δ (epsilon-delta) DP ϵ. When comparing the result of a randomized transformation on a dataset that includes one specific person with another result that does not contain that person, e^{ϵ} describes the maximum difference between the outcomes of these transformations. So, if ϵ is 0, both transformations return exactly the same result. If the value of ϵ is smaller, the probability that our transformations will return the same result is greater —a lower value of ϵ is more private because ϵ measures the strength of the privacy guarantee. If you query a dataset more than once, you need to sum the epsilons of each query to get your total privacy budget.

δ is the probability that ϵ does not hold, or the probability that an individual's data is exposed in the results of the randomized transformation. We generally set δ to be approximately the inverse of the population size: for a dataset containing 2,000 people, we would set δ to be 1/1,000.[3]

---

3 More details on the math behind this can be found in Dwork and Roth, "The Algorithmic Foundations of Differential Privacy."

What value of epsilon should you choose? ϵ allows us to compare the privacy of different algorithms and approaches, but the absolute value that gives us "sufficient" privacy depends on the use case.[4]

To decide on a value to use for ϵ, it can be helpful to look at the accuracy of the system as ϵ is decreased. Choose the most private parameters possible while retaining acceptable data utility for the business problem. Alternatively, if the consequences of leaking data are very high, you may wish to set the acceptable values of ϵ and δ first, and then tune your other hyperparameters to get the best model accuracy possible. One weakness of ϵ - δ DP is that ϵ is not easily interpretable. Other approaches are being developed to help with this, such as planting secrets within a model's training data and measuring how likely it is that they are exposed in a model's predictions.[5]

Differential Privacy for Machine Learning

If you want to use DP as part of your machine learning pipeline, there are a few current options for where it can be added, though we expect to see more in the future. First, DP can be included in a federated learning system (see "Federated Learning" on page 283), and this can use either global or local DP. Second, the TensorFlow Privacy library is an example of global DP: raw data is available for model training.

A third option is the Private Aggregation of Teacher Ensembles (PATE) approach.[6] This is a data-sharing scenario: in the case that 10 people have labelled data, but you haven't, they train a model locally and each make a prediction on your data. A DP query is then performed to generate the final prediction on each example in your dataset so that you don't know which of the 10 models has made the prediction. A new model is then trained from these predictions—this model includes the information from the 10 hidden datasets in such a way that it's not possible to learn about those hidden datasets. The PATE framework shows how ϵ is being spent in this scenario.

Introduction to TensorFlow Privacy

TensorFlow Privacy (*https://oreil.ly/vlcIy*) (TFP) adds DP to an optimizer during model training. The type of DP used in TFP is an example of global DP: noise is added during training so that private data is not exposed in a model's predictions.

---

4 Further details may be found in Justin Hsu et al., "Differential Privacy: An Economic Method for Choosing Epsilon" (Paper presentation, 2014 IEEE Computer Security Foundations Symposium, Vienna, Austria, February 17, 2014), *https://arxiv.org/pdf/1402.3329.pdf*.

5 Nicholas Carlini et al., "The Secret Sharer," July 2019. *https://arxiv.org/pdf/1802.08232.pdf*.

6 Nicolas Papernot et al., "Semi-Supervised Knowledge Transfer for Deep Learning from Private Training Data," October 2016, *https://arxiv.org/abs/1610.05755*.

This lets us offer the strong DP guarantee that an individual's data has not been memorized while still maximizing model accuracy. As shown in Figure 14-2, in this situation, the raw data is available to the trusted data store and model trainer, but the final predictions are untrusted.

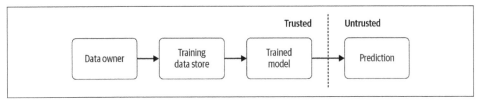

Figure 14-2. Trusted parties for DP

Training with a Differentially Private Optimizer

The optimizer algorithm is modified by adding random noise to the gradients at each training step. This compares the gradient's updates with or without each individual data point and ensures that it is not possible to tell whether a specific data point was included in the gradient update. In addition, gradients are clipped so that they do not become too large—this limits the contribution of any one training example. As a nice bonus, this also helps prevent overfitting.

TFP can be installed with pip. At the time of writing, it requires TensorFlow version 1.X:

```
$ pip install tensorflow_privacy
```

We start with a simple `tf.keras` binary classification example:

```
import tensorflow as tf

model = tf.keras.models.Sequential([
  tf.keras.layers.Dense(128, activation='relu'),
  tf.keras.layers.Dense(128, activation='relu'),
  tf.keras.layers.Dense(1, activation='sigmoid')
])
```

The differentially private optimizer requires that we set two extra hyperparameters compared to a normal `tf.keras` model: the noise multiplier and the L2 norm clip. It's best to tune these to suit your dataset and measure their impact on ϵ:

```
NOISE_MULTIPLIER = 2
NUM_MICROBATCHES = 32    ❶
LEARNING_RATE = 0.01
POPULATION_SIZE = 5760   ❷
L2_NORM_CLIP = 1.5
BATCH_SIZE = 32          ❸
EPOCHS = 70
```

❶ The batch size must be exactly divisible by the number of microbatches.

❷ The number of examples in the training set.

❸ The population size must be exactly divisible by the batch size.

Next, initialize the differentially private optimizer:

```
from tensorflow_privacy.privacy.optimizers.dp_optimizer \
    import DPGradientDescentGaussianOptimizer

optimizer = DPGradientDescentGaussianOptimizer(
    l2_norm_clip=L2_NORM_CLIP,
    noise_multiplier=NOISE_MULTIPLIER,
    num_microbatches=NUM_MICROBATCHES,
    learning_rate=LEARNING_RATE)

loss = tf.keras.losses.BinaryCrossentropy(
    from_logits=True, reduction=tf.losses.Reduction.NONE) ❶
```

❶ Loss must be calculated on a per-example basis rather than over an entire minibatch.

Training the private model is just like training a normal `tf.keras` model:

```
model.compile(optimizer=optimizer, loss=loss, metrics=['accuracy'])

model.fit(X_train, y_train,
          epochs=EPOCHS,
          validation_data=(X_test, y_test),
          batch_size=BATCH_SIZE)
```

Calculating Epsilon

Now, we calculate the differential privacy parameters for our model and our choice of noise multiplier and gradient clip:

```
from tensorflow_privacy.privacy.analysis import compute_dp_sgd_privacy


compute_dp_sgd_privacy.compute_dp_sgd_privacy(n=POPULATION_SIZE,
                                              batch_size=BATCH_SIZE,
                                              noise_multiplier=NOISE_MULTIPLIER,
                                              epochs=EPOCHS,
                                              delta=1e-4) ❶
```

❶ The value of delta is set to 1/the size of the dataset, rounded to the nearest order of magnitude.

The final output of this calculation, the value of epsilon, tells us the strength of the privacy guarantee for our particular model. We can then explore how changing the L2 norm clip and noise multiplier hyperparameters discussed earlier affects both epsilon and our model accuracy. If the values of these two hyperparameters are increased, keeping all others fixed, epsilon will decrease (so the privacy guarantee becomes stronger). At some point, accuracy will begin to decrease and the model will stop being useful. This trade-off can be explored to get the strongest possible privacy guarantees while still maintaining useful model accuracy.

Federated Learning

Federated learning (FL) is a protocol where the training of a machine learning model is distributed across many different devices and the trained model is combined on a central server. The key point is that the raw data never leaves the separate devices and is never pooled in one place. This is very different from the traditional architecture of gathering a dataset in a central location and then training a model.

FL is often useful in the context of mobile phones with distributed data, or a user's browser. Another potential use case is in the sharing of sensitive data that is distributed across multiple data owners. For example, an AI startup may want to train a model to detect skin cancer. Images of skin cancer are owned by many hospitals, but they can't be centralized in one location due to privacy and legal concerns. FL lets the startup train a model without the data leaving the hospitals.

In an FL setup, each client receives the model architecture and some instructions for training. A model is trained on each client's device, and the weights are returned to a central server. This increases privacy slightly, in that it's more difficult for an interceptor to learn anything about a user from model weights than from raw data, but it doesn't provide any guarantee of privacy. The step of distributing the model training doesn't provide the user with any increased privacy from the company collecting the data because the company can often work out what the raw data would have been with a knowledge of the model architecture and the weights.

However, there is one more very important step to increase privacy using FL: the secure aggregation of the weights into the central model. There are a number of algorithms for doing this, but they all require that the central party has to be trusted to not attempt to inspect the weights before they are combined.

Figure 14-3 shows which parties have access to the personal data of users in the FL setting. It's possible for the company collecting the data to set up secure averaging such that they don't see the model weights that are returned from users. A neutral third party could also perform the secure aggregation. In this case, only the users would see their data.

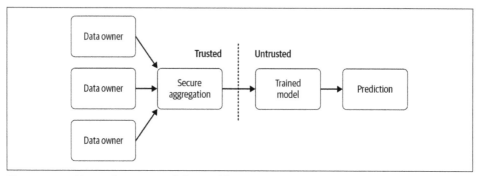

Figure 14-3. Trusted parties in federated learning

An additional privacy-preserving extension to FL is the incorporation of DP into this technique. In this situation, DP limits the amount of information that each user can contribute to the final model. Research has shown that the resulting models are almost as accurate as non-DP models if the number of users is large.[7] However, as yet, this hasn't been implemented for either TensorFlow or PyTorch.

An example of FL in production is Google's Gboard keyboard for Android mobile phones (*https://oreil.ly/LXtSN*). Google is able to train a model to make better next-word predictions without learning anything about users' private messaging. FL is most useful in use cases that share the following characteristics:[8]

- The data required for the model can only be collected from distributed sources.
- The number of data sources is large.
- The data is sensitive in some way.
- The data does not require extra labelling—the labels are provided directly by the user and do not leave the source.
- Ideally, the data is drawn from close to identical distributions.

---

7 Robin C. Geyer et al., "Differentially Private Federated Learning: A Client Level Perspective," December 2017, *https://arxiv.org/abs/1712.07557*.

8 This is covered in more detail in the paper by H. Brendan McMahan et al., "Communication-Efficient Learning of Deep Networks from Decentralized Data," Proceedings of the 20th International Conference on Artificial Intelligence and Statistics, *PMLR* 54 (2017): 1273–82, *https://arxiv.org/pdf/1602.05629.pdf*.

FL introduces many new considerations into the design of a machine learning system: for example, not all data sources may have collected new data between one training run and the next, not all mobile devices are powered on all the time, and so on. The data that is collected is often unbalanced and practically unique to each device. It's easiest to get sufficient data for each training run when the pool of devices is large. New secure infrastructure must be developed for any project using FL.[9]

Care must be taken to avoid performance issues on devices that train an FL model. Training can quickly drain the battery on a mobile device or cause large data usage, leading to expense for the user. Even though the processing power of mobile phones is increasing rapidly, they are still only capable of training small models, so more complex models should be trained on a central server.

Federated Learning in TensorFlow

TensorFlow Federated (TFF) simulates the distributed setup of FL and contains a version of stochastic gradient descent (SGD) that can calculate updates on distributed data. Conventional SGD requires that updates are computed on batches of a centralized dataset, and this centralized dataset doesn't exist in a federated setting. At the time of writing, TFF is mainly aimed at research and experimentation on new federated algorithms.

PySyft (*https://oreil.ly/qlAWh*) is an open source Python platform for privacy-preserving machine learning developed by the OpenMined organization. It contains an implementation of FL using secure multiparty computation (explained further in the following section) to aggregate data. It was originally developed to support PyTorch models, but a TensorFlow version has been released (*https://oreil.ly/01yw2*).

Encrypted Machine Learning

Encrypted machine learning is another area of privacy-preserving machine learning that's currently receiving a lot of attention from both researchers and practitioners. It leans on technology and research from the cryptographic community and applies these techniques to machine learning. The major methods that have been adopted so far are homomorphic encryption (HE) and secure multiparty computation (SMPC). There are two ways to use these techniques: encrypting a model that has already been trained on plain text data and encrypting an entire system (if the data must stay encrypted during training).

---

9 For more details on system design for FL, refer to the paper by Keith Bonawitz et al., "Towards Federated Learning at Scale: System Design" (Presentation, Proceedings of the 2nd SysML Conference, Palo Alto, CA, 2019), *https://arxiv.org/pdf/1902.01046.pdf*.

HE is similar to public-key encryption but differs in that data does not have to be decrypted before a computation is applied to it. The computation (such as obtaining predictions from a machine learning model) can be performed on the encrypted data. A user can provide their data in its encrypted form using an encryption key that is stored locally and then receive the encrypted prediction, which they can then decrypt to get the prediction of the model on their data. This provides privacy to the user because their data is not shared with the party who has trained the model.

SMPC allows several parties to combine data, perform a computation on it, and see the results of the computation on their own data without knowing anything about the data from the other parties. This is achieved by *secret sharing (https://oreil.ly/kIeOx)*, a process in which any single value is split into shares that are sent to separate parties. The original value can't be reconstructed from any share, but computations can still be carried out on each share individually. The result of the computations is meaningless until all the shares are recombined.

Both of these techniques come with a cost. At the time of writing, HE is rarely used for training machine learning models: it causes several orders of magnitudes of slowdown in both training and predictions. Because of this, we won't discuss HE any further. SMPC also has an overhead in terms of networking time when the shares and the results are passed between parties, but it is significantly faster than HE. These techniques, along with FL, are useful for situations which data can't be gathered in one place. However, they do not prevent models from memorizing sensitive data— DP is the best solution for that.

Encrypted ML is provided for TensorFlow by TF Encrypted (*https://tf-encrypted.io*) (TFE), primarily developed by Cape Privacy (*https://capeprivacy.com*). TFE can also provide the secure aggregation required for FL (*https://oreil.ly/VVPJx*).

Encrypted Model Training

The first situation in which you might want to use encrypted machine learning is training models on encrypted data. This is useful when the raw data needs to be kept private from the data scientist training the model or when two or more parties own the raw data and want to train a model using all parties' data, but don't want to share the raw data. As shown in Figure 14-4, only the data owner or owners are trusted in this scenario.

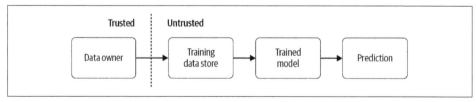

Figure 14-4. Trusted parties with encrypted model training

TFE can be used to train an encrypted model for this use case. It's installed using `pip` as usual:

```
$ pip install tf_encrypted
```

The first step in building a TFE model is to define a class that yields training data in batches. This class is implemented locally by the data owner(s). It is converted to encrypted data using a decorator:

```
@tfe.local_computation
```

Writing model training code in TFE is almost identical to regular Keras models—simply replace `tf` with `tfe`:

```
import tf_encrypted as tfe

model = tfe.keras.Sequential()
model.add(tfe.keras.layers.Dense(1, batch_input_shape=[batch_size, num_features]))
model.add(tfe.keras.layers.Activation('sigmoid'))
```

The only difference is that the argument `batch_input_shape` must be supplied to the `Dense` first layer.

Working examples of this are given in the TFE documentation (*https://oreil.ly/ ghGnu*). At the time of writing, not all functionality of regular Keras was included in TFE, so we can't show our example project in this format.

Converting a Trained Model to Serve Encrypted Predictions

The second scenario where TFE is useful is when you'd like to serve encrypted models that have been trained on plain-text data (*https://oreil.ly/HBUBj*). In this case, as shown in Figure 14-5, you have full access to the unencrypted training data, but you want the users of your application to be able to receive private predictions. This provides privacy to the users, who upload encrypted data and receive an encrypted prediction.

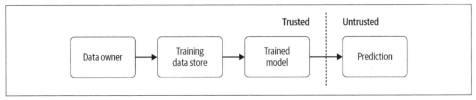

Figure 14-5. Trusted parties when encrypting a trained model

This method may be the best fit with today's machine learning pipelines, as models can be trained as normal and converted to an encrypted version. It can also be used for models that have been trained using DP. The main difference from unencrypted models is that multiple servers are required: each one hosts a share of the original model. If anyone views a share of the model on one server or one share of the data that is sent to any one server, it reveals nothing about the model or the data.

Keras models can be converted to TFE models via:

```
tfe_model = tfe.keras.models.clone_model(model)
```

In this scenario, the following steps need to be carried out:

- Load and preprocess the data locally on the client.
- Encrypt the data on the client.
- Send the encrypted data to the servers.
- Make a prediction on the encrypted data.
- Send the encrypted prediction to the client.
- Decrypt the prediction on the client and show the result to the user.

TFE provides a series of notebooks (*https://oreil.ly/r0cKP*) showing how to serve private predictions.

Other Methods for Data Privacy

There are many other techniques for increasing privacy for the people who have their data included in machine learning models. Simply scrubbing text data for names, addresses, phone numbers, and so on, can be surprisingly easy using regular expressions and named-entity recognition models.

K-Anonymity

K-anonymity (*https://oreil.ly/sxQet*), often simply known as *anonymization*, is not a good candidate for increasing privacy in machine learning pipelines. *K*-anonymity requires that each individual in a dataset is indistinguishable from $k - 1$ others with respect to their quasi-identifiers (data that can indirectly identify individuals, such as gender, race, and zip code). This is achieved by aggregating or removing data until the dataset satisfies this requirement. This removal of data generally causes a large decrease in the accuracy of machine learning models.[10]

---

10 In addition, individuals in "anonymized" datasets can be reidentified using outside information; see Luc Rocher et al., "Estimating the Success of Re-identifications in Incomplete Datasets Using Generative Models," *Nature Communications* 10, Article no. 3069 (2019), *https://www.nature.com/articles/s41467-019-10933-3*.

Summary

When you're working with personal or sensitive data, choose the data privacy solution that best fits your needs regarding who is trusted, what level of model performance is required, and what consent you have obtained from users.

All of the techniques described in this chapter are extremely new, and their production use is not yet widespread. Don't assume that using one of the frameworks described in this chapter ensures complete privacy for your users. There is always a substantial additional engineering effort involved in adding privacy to a machine learning pipeline. The field of privacy-preserving machine learning is evolving rapidly, and new research is being undertaken right now. We encourage you to look for improvements in this field and support open source projects around data privacy, such as PySyft (*https://oreil.ly/rj0_c*) and TFE (*https://oreil.ly/L5zik*).

The goals of data privacy and machine learning are often well aligned, in that we want to learn about a whole population and make predictions that are equally good for everyone, rather than learning only about one individual. Adding privacy can stop a model from overfitting to one person's data. We expect that, in the future, privacy will be designed into machine learning pipelines from the start whenever models are trained on personal data.

The Future of Pipelines and Next Steps

In the past 14 chapters, we have captured the current state of machine learning pipelines and given our recommendations on how to build them. Machine learning pipelines are a relatively new concept, and there's much more to come in this space. In this chapter, we will discuss a few things that we feel are important but don't fit well with current pipelines, and we also consider future steps for ML pipelines.

Model Experiment Tracking

Throughout this book, we have assumed that you've already experimented and the model architecture is basically settled. However, we would like to share some thoughts on how to track experiments and make experimentation a smooth process. Your experimental process may include exploring potential model architectures, hyperparameters, and feature sets. But whatever you explore, the key point we would like to make is that your experimental process should fit closely with your production process.

Whether you optimize your models manually or you tune the models automatically, capturing and sharing the results of the optimization process is essential. Team members can quickly evaluate the progress of the model updates. At the same time, the author of the models can receive automated records of the performed experiments. Good experiment tracking helps data science teams become more efficient.

Experiment tracking also adds to the audit trail of the model and may be a safeguard against potential litigations. If a data science team is facing the question of whether an edge case was considered while training a model, experiment tracking can assist in tracing the model parameters and iterations.

Tools for experiment tracking include Weights and Biases (*https://www.wandb.com*) and Sacred (*https://oreil.ly/6zK3V*). Figure 15-1 shows an example of Weights and

Biases in action, with the loss for each model training run plotted against the training epoch. Many different visualizations are possible, and we can store all the hyperparameters for each model run.

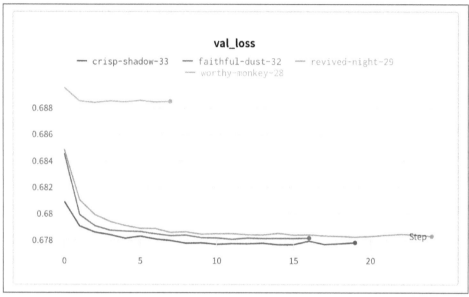

Figure 15-1. Experiment tracking in Weights and Biases

In the future, we expect to see the experiment and the production process become more tightly linked so that a data scientist can smoothly switch from trying out a new model architecture to adding it to their pipeline.

Thoughts on Model Release Management

In software engineering, there are well established procedures for versioning code and managing releases. Large changes that may be backward-incompatible get a major version change (from 0.x to 1.0, for example). Smaller feature additions get a minor version change (1.0 to 1.1). But what does this mean in the machine learning world? From one ML model to the next, the input format of the data may be the same and the output format of the predictions remains the same, so there is no breaking change. The pipeline still runs; no errors are thrown. But the performance of the new model may be completely different from the one that came before. Standardization of machine learning pipelines requires model versioning practices.

We suggest the following strategy for model release management:

- If the input data is changed, the model version gets a minor change.

- If the hyperparameters are changed, the model version gets a major change. This includes the number of layers in a network or the number of nodes in a layer.

- If the model architecture is completely changed (e.g., from a recurrent neural network [RNN] to a Transformer architecture), this becomes an entirely new pipeline.

The model validation step controls whether the release happens by validating that the new model's performance is an improvement on the previous model's performance. At the time of writing, only a single metric is used in this step by a TFX pipeline. We expect that the validation step will become more sophisticated in the future to include other factors such as inference time or accuracy on different slices of the data.

Future Pipeline Capabilities

In this book, we've captured the state of machine learning pipelines at the time of writing. But what will machine learning pipelines look like in the future? Some of the capabilities that we'd like to see include:

- Privacy and fairness becoming first-class citizens: at the time of writing, the assumption is that the pipeline does not include privacy-preserving ML. Analysis for fairness is included, but the ModelValidator step can only use overall metrics.

- Incorporation of FL, as we discussed in Chapter 14. If data preprocessing and model training happen on a large number of individual devices, a machine learning pipeline would need to look very different from the one we've described in this book.

- The ability to measure the carbon emissions of our pipelines. As models become larger, their energy usage becomes significant. Although this is often more relevant during the experimentation process (especially searching for model architectures), it would be very useful to integrate emissions tracking into pipelines.

- Ingestion of data streams: in this book, we have only considered pipelines that are trained on data batches. But with more sophisticated data pipelines, machine learning pipelines should be able to consume data streams.

Future tools may further abstract some of the processes in this book, and we expect that future pipelines will be even smoother to use and more automated.

We also predict that future pipelines will need to tackle some of the other types of machine learning problems. We have only discussed supervised learning, and almost exclusively classification problems. It makes sense to start with supervised classification problems because these are some of the easiest to understand and build into pipelines. Regression problems and other types of supervised learning such as image captioning or text generation will be easy to substitute into most components of the pipeline we describe in this book. But reinforcement learning problems and unsupervised problems may not fit so well. These are still rare in production systems, but we anticipate that they will become more common in the future. The data ingestion, validation, and feature engineering components of our pipeline should still work with these problems, but the training, evaluation, and validation parts will need significant changes. The feedback loops will also look very different.

TFX with Other Machine Learning Frameworks

The future of machine learning pipelines will also likely include openness regarding underlying machine learning frameworks, so that a data scientist doesn't need to choose between building their model in TensorFlow, PyTorch, scikit-learn, or any other future framework.

It is great to see that TFX is moving toward removing pure TensorFlow dependency. As we discussed in Chapter 4, some TFX components can be used with other ML frameworks. Other components are going through a transition to allow the integration with other ML frameworks. For example, the Trainer component now provides an executor that allows training models independently from TensorFlow. We hope that we will see more generic components that integrate frameworks like PyTorch or scikit-learn easily.

Testing Machine Learning Models

An emerging topic in machine learning engineering is the testing of machine learning models. Here, we don't mean model validation, as we discussed in Chapter 7, but rather a test of the model inference. These tests can be unit tests for the model or complete end-to-end tests of the model's interactions with an app.

As well as testing that the system runs end to end, other tests may center around:

- Inference time
- Memory consumption
- Battery consumption on mobile devices
- The trade-off between model size and accuracy

We are looking forward to seeing best practices from software engineering merge with data science practices, and model testing will be part of this.

CI/CD Systems for Machine Learning

With machine learning pipelines becoming more streamlined in the coming months, we will see machine learning pipelines moving toward more complete CI/CD workflows. As data scientists and machine learning engineers, we can learn from software engineering workflows. For example, we are looking forward to better integrations of data versioning in ML pipelines or best practices to facilitate deployment rollbacks of machine learning models.

Machine Learning Engineering Community

As the field of machine learning engineering is forming, the community around the topic will be vital. We are looking forward to sharing best practices, custom components, workflows, use cases, and pipeline setups with the machine learning community. We hope this publication is a small contribution to the emerging field. Similar to DevOps in software engineering, we hope to see more data scientists and software engineers becoming interested in the discipline of machine learning engineering.

Summary

This book contains our recommendations for how to turn your machine learning model into a smooth pipeline. Figure 15-2 shows all the steps that we believe are necessary and the tools that we think are best at the time of writing. We encourage you to stay curious about this topic, to follow new developments, and to contribute to the various open source efforts around machine learning pipelines. This is an area of extremely active development, with new solutions being released frequently.

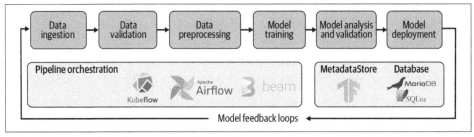

Figure 15-2. Machine learning pipeline architecture

Figure 15-2 has three extremely important features: it is *automated*, *scalable*, and *reproducible*. Because it is automated, it frees up data scientists from maintaining models and gives them time to experiment with new ones. Because it is scalable, it can expand to deal with large quantities of data. And because it is reproducible, once you have set it up on your infrastructure for one project, it will be easy to build a second one. These are all essential for a successful machine learning pipeline.

Introduction to Infrastructure for Machine Learning

This appendix gives a brief introduction to some of the most useful infrastructure tools for machine learning: containers, in the form of Docker or Kubernetes. While this may be the point at which you hand your pipeline over to a software engineering team, it's useful for anyone building machine learning pipelines to have an awareness of these tools.

What Is a Container?

All Linux operating systems are based on the filesystem, or the directory structure that includes all hard drives and partitions. From the root of this filesystem (denoted as /), you can access almost all aspects of a Linux system. Containers create a new, smaller root and use it as a "smaller Linux" within a bigger host. This lets you have a whole separate set of libraries dedicated to a particular container. On top of that, containers let you control resources like CPU time or memory for each container.

Docker is a user-friendly API that manages containers. Containers can be built, packaged, saved, and deployed multiple times using Docker. It also allows developers to build containers locally and then publish them to a central registry that others can pull from and immediately run the container.

Dependency management is a big issue in machine learning and data science. Whether you are writing in R or Python, you're almost always dependent on third-party modules. These modules are updated frequently and may cause breaking changes to your pipeline when versions conflict. By using containers, you can prepackage your data processing code along with the correct module versions and avoid these problems.

Introduction to Docker

To install Docker on Mac or Windows, visit *https://docs.docker.com/install* and download the latest stable version of Docker Desktop for your operating system.

For a Linux operating system, Docker provides a very convenient script to install Docker with just a couple of commands:

```
$ curl -fsSL https://get.docker.com -o get-docker.sh
$ sudo sh get-docker.sh
```

You can test whether your Docker installation is working correctly using the command:

```
docker run hello-world
```

Introduction to Docker Images

A Docker image is the basis of a container, and it consists of a collection of changes to the root filesystem and the execution parameters to run the container. The image must first be "built" before it can be run.

A useful concept behind Docker images is storage layers. Building an image means installing almost a whole dedicated Linux OS for your package. To avoid running this operation every time, Docker uses a layered filesystem. Here is how it works: if the first layer contains Files A and B, and the second layer adds File C, the resulting filesystems show A, B, and C. If we want to create a second image that uses Files A, B, and D, we only need to change the second layer to add File D. This means that we can have base images that have all the basic packages, and then we can focus on changes specific to your image, as shown in Figure A-1.

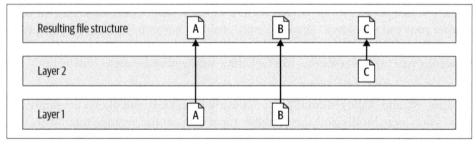

Figure A-1. Example of a layered filesystem

Docker image names are called *tags*. They follow the pattern *docker registry/ docker namespace/image name:tag*. For example, *docker.io/tensorflow/tensorflow:nightly* would point to the `tensorflow` image in DockerHub in the `tensorflow` namespace. The tag is usually used to mark versions of a particular image. In our example, the tag `nightly` is reserved for nightly builds of TensorFlow.

Docker images are built based on a `Dockerfile`. Each line in a *Dockerfile* starts with one of a few clauses. The most important are:

FROM
> Indicates the Docker base container to build from. We will always want to use this clause. There are many base containers available to download, such as `ubuntu`.

RUN
> Runs bash. This is the bread and butter of most Docker images. This is where we want to do package installations, directory creation, etc. Because each line will create a layer in the image, it's good to have package installations and other long tasks as one of the first lines in *Dockerfile*. This means that during rebuilds, Docker will try to use layers from the cache.

ARG
> Builds arguments. It's useful if you want to have multiple flavors of the same image, for example *dev* and *production*.

COPY
> Copies files from a context. The path to the context is an argument used in `docker build`. The context is a set of local files that are exposed to Docker during the build, and it only uses them in the process. This can be used to copy your source code to a container.

ENV
> Sets an environment variable. This variable will be part of the image and will be visible in build and run.

CMD
> This is the default command for a container. A good practice in Docker is to run one command per container. Docker will then monitor this command, exit when it exits, and post STDOUT from it to `docker logs`. Another way to specify this command is by using `ENTRYPOINT`. There are several subtle differences between these, but here we'll focus on `CMD`.

USER
> The default user in the container. This is different from host system users. You should create a user during the build if you want to run commands as one.

WORKDIR
> The default directory in the image. This will be the directory the default command will be run from.

EXPOSE

Specifies ports the container will use. For example, HTTP services should have
EXPOSE 80.

Building Your First Docker Image

Let's build our first image!

First, we need to create a new directory for our small Docker project:

```
$ mkdir hello-docker
$ cd hello-docker
```

In this directory, create a file called *Dockerfile* with the following contents:

```
FROM ubuntu
RUN apt-get update
RUN apt-get -y install cowsay
CMD /usr/games/cowsay "Hello Docker"
```

To build it, use the command docker build . -t hello-docker. The -t flag specifies the tag for this image. You will see a series of commands that are run in the container. Each layer in our image (corresponding to each command in the Dockerfile)
is called in the temporary container running the previous layers. The difference is
saved, and we end up with a full image. The first layer (which we don't build) is based
on Ubuntu Linux. The FROM command in Dockerfile tells Docker to pull this image
from a registry, in our case DockerHub, and use it as the base image.

After the build is finished, calling docker images should show something like this:

```
REPOSITORY      TAG      IMAGE ID       CREATED        SIZE
hello-docker    latest   af856e494ed4   2 minutes ago  155MB
ubuntu          latest   94e814e2efa8   5 weeks ago    88.9MB
```

We should see the base Ubuntu image and our new image.

Even though we have built this image, that doesn't mean it's ready to use. The next
step is to run the image. docker run is arguably the most important command in
Docker. It creates a new container from an existing image (or, if an image is not
present on the system, it will try to pull it from the registry). To run our image, we
should call docker run -it hello-docker. This should show us the output of our
cowsay command.

Docker Registries

One of the great strengths of Docker is the ease of publishing a built image. The repository of Docker images is called the *registry*. The default Docker registry, called DockerHub, is supported by Docker, Inc. An account on DockerHub is free and lets you push public images to it.

Diving into the Docker CLI

The Docker CLI is the main way to interact with images and containers on your local machine. In this section, we'll discuss the most important commands and options for it. Let's start with `docker run`.

There are many important options we could pass to `docker run`. With these, we can override most of the options set in the `Dockerfile`. This is important because many Docker images will have a set basic default command, but often that's not exactly how we want to run them. Let's look at our `cowsay` example:

```
docker run -it hello-docker /usr/games/cowsay "Our own message"
```

The argument that comes after the image tag will override the default command we have set in `Dockerfile`. This is the best way to specify our own command-line flags to the default binaries. Other useful flags for `docker run` include:

`-it`

Means "interactive" (i) and `tty` (t), which allows us to interact with the command being run from our shell.

`-v`

Mounts a Docker volume or host directory into the container—for example, a directory containing datasets.

`-e`

Passes configurations through environment variables. For example, `docker run -e MYVARNAME=value image` will create the `MYVARNAME` env variable in a container.

`-d`

Allows the container to be run in detached mode, making it perfect for long running tasks.

`-p`

Forwards a host's port to a container to allow external services to interact with the container over a network. For example, `docker run -d -p 8080:8080 imagename` would forward `localhost:8080` to the container's port 8080.

Docker Compose

`docker run` can get pretty complex when you start mounting directories, managing container links, and so on. *Docker Compose* is a project to help with that. It allows you to create a *docker-compose.yaml* file in which you can specify all your Docker options for any number of containers. You can then link containers together over a network or mount the same directories.

Other useful Docker commands include:

`docker ps`
Shows all the running containers. To also show exited containers, add the `-a` flag.

`docker images`
Lists all images present on the machine.

`docker inspect` *container id*
Allows us to examine the container's configuration in detail.

`docker rm`
Deletes containers.

`docker rmi`
Deletes images.

`docker logs`
Displays the STDOUT and STDERR information produced by a container, which is very useful for debugging.

`docker exec`
Allows you to call a command within a running container. For example, `docker exec -it` *container id* `bash` will allow you to enter into the container environment with bash and examine it from inside. The `-it` flag works in the same way as in `docker run`.

Introduction to Kubernetes

Up to now, we've just talked about Docker containers running on a single machine. What happens if you want to scale up? Kubernetes is an open source project, initially developed by Google, that manages scheduling and scaling for your infrastructure. It dynamically scales loads to many servers and keeps track of computing resources. Kubernetes also maximizes efficiency by putting multiple containers on one machine (depending on their size and needs), and it manages the communications between containers. It can run on any cloud platform—AWS, Azure, or GCP.

Some Kubernetes Definitions

One of the hardest parts of getting started with Kubernetes is the terminology. Here are a few definitions to help you:

Cluster
> A cluster is a set of machines that contains a central node controlling the Kubernetes API server and many worker nodes.

Node
> A node is a single machine (either a physical machine or a virtual machine) within a cluster.

Pod
> A pod is a group of containers that run together on the same node. Often, a pod only contains a single container.

Kubelet
> A kubelet is the Kubernetes agent that manages communication with the central node on each worker node.

Service
> A service is a group of pods and the policies to access them.

Volume
> A volume is a storage space shared by all containers in the same pod.

Namespace
> A namespace is the virtual cluster that divides up the space in a physical cluster into different environments. For example, we can divide a cluster into development and production environments or environments for different teams.

ConfigMap
> A ConfigMap provides an API for storing nonconfidential configuration information (environment variables, arguments, etc.) in Kubernetes. ConfigMaps are useful to separate the configuration from container images.

kubectl
> kubectl is the CLI for Kubernetes.

Getting Started with Minikube and kubectl

We can create a simple, local Kubernetes cluser using a tool called Minikube. Minikube makes it easy to set up Kubernetes on any operating system. It creates a virtual machine, installs Docker and Kubernetes on it, and adds a local user connected to it.

Don't Use Minikube in Production

Minikube should not be used in production; rather, it is designed to be a quick and easy local environment. The easiest way to gain access to a production-quality Kubernetes cluer is by purchasing managed Kubernetes as a service from any major public cloud provider.

First, install kubectl, the Kubernetes CLI tool.

For Mac, kubectl can be installed using `brew`:

```
brew install kubectl
```

For Windows, see their resources (*https://oreil.ly/AhAwc*).

For Linux:

```
curl -LO https://storage.googleapis.com/kubernetes-release\
/release/v1.14.0/bin/linux/amd64/kubectl
chmod +x ./kubectl
sudo mv ./kubectl /usr/local/bin/kubectl
```

To install Minikube, we'll first need to install a *hypervisor* that creates and runs virtual machines, such as VirtualBox (*https://oreil.ly/LJgFJ*).

On a Mac, Minikube can be installed using `brew`:

```
brew install minikube
```

For Windows, see the resources (*https://oreil.ly/awtxY*).

For Linux machines, use the following steps:

```
curl -Lo minikube \
https://storage.googleapis.com/minikube/releases/latest/minikube-linux-amd64
chmod +x minikube
sudo cp minikube /usr/local/bin && rm minikube
```

Once installation is complete, start a simple Kubernetes cluster in a single command:

```
minikube start
```

To quickly check if Minikube is good to go, we can try to list the nodes in the cluster:

```
kubectl get nodes
```

Interacting with the Kubernetes CLI

The Kubernetes API is based on *resources*. Almost everything in the Kubernetes world is represented as a resource. `kubectl` is built with this in mind, so it will follow a similar pattern for most of the resource interactions.

For example, a typical `kubectl` call to list all pods would be:

```
kubectl get pods
```

This should produce a list of all the running pods, but since we haven't created any, the listing will be empty. That doesn't mean that no pods are currently running on our cluster. Most of the resources in Kubernetes can be placed in a namespace, and unless you query the specific namespace, they won't show up. Kubernetes runs its internal services in a namespace called `kube-system`. To list all pods in any namespace, you can use the `-n` option:

```
kubectl get pods -n kube-system
```

This should return several results. We can also use `--all-namespaces` to show all pods regardless of namespace.

You can use the name only to display one pod:

```
kubectl get po mypod
```

You can also filter out by label. For example, this call should show all pods that have the label `component` with the value `etcd` in `kube-system`:

```
kubectl get po -n kube-system -l component=etcd
```

The information displayed by `get` can also be modified. For example:

```
# Show nodes and addresses of pods.
kubectl get po -n kube-system -o wide
# Show the yaml definition of pod mypod.
kubectl get po mypod -o yaml
```

To create a new resource, `kubectl` offers two commands: `create` and `apply`. The difference is that `create` will always try to create a new resource (and fail if it already exists), whereas `apply` will either create or update an existing resource.

The most common way to create a new resource is by using a YAML (or JSON) file with the resource definition, as we'll see in the next section. The following kubectl commands allow us to create of update Kubernetes resources, (e.g., pods):

```
# Create a pod that is defined in pod.yaml.
kubectl create -f pod.yaml
# This can also be used with HTTP.
kubectl create -f http://url-to-pod-yaml
# Apply will allow making changes to resources.
kubectl apply -f pod.yaml
```

To delete a resource, use `kubectl delete`:

```
# Delete pod foo.
kubectl delete pod foo
# Delete all resources defined in pods.yaml.
kubectl delete -f pods.yaml
```

You can use kubectl edit to update an existing resource quickly. This will open an editor where you can edit the loaded resource definition:

```
kubectl edit pod foo
```

Defining a Kubernetes Resource

Kubernetes resources are most often defined as YAML (although JSON can also be used). Basically, all resources are data structures with a few essential sections.

apiVersion

Every resource is part of an API, either supplied by Kubernetes itself or by third parties. The version number shows the maturity of the API.

kind

The type of resource (e.g., pod, volume, etc.).

metadata

The data required for any resource.

name

The key that every resource can be queried by, which must be unique.

labels

Each resource can have any number of key-value pairs called labels. These labels can then be used in selectors, for querying resources, or just as information.

annotations

Secondary key-value pairs that are purely informational and cannot be used in queries or selectors.

namespace

A label that shows a resource belongs to a particular namespace or team.

spec

Configuration of the resource. All information required for the actual runtime should be in spec. Each spec schema is unique to a particular resource type.

Here is an example *.yaml* file using these definitions:

```
apiVersion: v1
kind: Pod
metadata:
  name: myapp-pod
  labels:
    app: myapp
spec:
  containers:
  - name: myapp-container
```

```
image: busybox
command: ['sh', '-c', 'echo Hello Kubernetes! && sleep 3600']
```

In this file, we have `apiVersion` and `kind`, which define what this resource is. We have `metadata` that specifies the name and the label, and we have `spec`, which makes up the body of the resource. Our pod consists of a single container, running the command `sh -c echo Hello Kubernetes! && sleep 3600` in the image busybox.

Deploying Applications to Kubernetes

In this section, we will walk through the full deployment of a functional Jupyter Notebook using Minikube. We will create a persistent volume for our notebooks and create a NodePort service to allow us access to our notebook.

First, we need to find the correct Docker image. *jupyter/tensorflow-notebook* is an official image maintained by the Jupyter community. Next, we will need to find out which port our application will listen on: in this case, it's 8888 (the default port for Jupyter Notebooks).

We want our notebook to persist between sessions, so we need to use PVC (persistent volume claim). We create a *pvc.yaml* file to do this for us:

```
kind: PersistentVolumeClaim
apiVersion: v1
metadata:
  name: notebooks
spec:
  accessModes:
    — ReadWriteOnce
  resources:
    requests:
      storage: 3Gi
```

Now we can create this resource by calling:

```
kubectl apply -f pvc.yaml
```

This should create a volume. To confirm, we can list all volumes and PVCs:

```
kubectl get pv
kubectl get pvc
kubectl describe pvc notebooks
```

Next up, we create our deployment *.yaml* file. We will have one pod that will mount our volume and expose port 8888:

```
apiVersion: apps/v1
kind: Deployment
metadata:
  name: jupyter
  labels:
    app: jupyter
```

```
spec:
  selector:
    matchLabels:
      app: jupyter    ❶
  template:
    metadata:
      labels:
        app: jupyter
    spec:
      containers:
        - image: jupyter/tensorflow-notebook    ❷
        name: jupyter
        ports:
        - containerPort: 8888
          name: jupyter
        volumeMounts:
        - name: notebooks
          mountPath: /home/jovyan
      volumes:
      - name: notebooks
        persistentVolumeClaim:
          claimName: notebooks
```

❶   It's important that this selector matches the labels in the template.

❷   Our image.

By applying this resource (in the same way we did with PVC), we will create a pod with a Jupyter instance:

```
# Let's see if our deployment is ready.
kubectl get deploy
# List pods that belong to this app.
kubectl get po -l app=jupyter
```

When our pod is in the Running state, we should grab a token with which we'll be able to connect to our notebook. This token will appear in logs:

```
kubectl logs deploy/jupyter
```

To confirm that the pod is working, let's access our notebook with port-forward:

```
# First we need the name of our pod; it will have a randomized suffix.
kubectl get po -l app=jupyter
kubectl port-forward jupyter-84fd79f5f8-kb7dv 8888:8888
```

With this, we should be able to access a notebook on *http://localhost:8888*. The problem is, nobody else will be able to since it's proxied through our local kubectl. Let's create a NodePort service to let us access the notebook:

```
apiVersion: v1
kind: Service
metadata:
  name: jupyter-service
  labels:
    app: jupyter
spec:
  ports:
    - port: 8888
      nodePort: 30888
  selector:
    app: jupyter
  type: NodePort
```

When this is created, we should be able to access our Jupyter! But first, we need to find the IP address of our pod. We should be able to access Jupyter under this address and port 30888:

```
minikube ip
# This will show us what is our kubelet address is.
192.168.99.100:30888
```

Others can now access the Jupyter Notebook by using the obtained IP address and the service port (see Figure A-2). Once you access the address with your browser, you should see the Jupyter Notebook instance.

Figure A-2. Jupyter Notebook running on Kubernetes

This was a brief overview of Kubernetes and its parts. The Kubernetes ecosystem is very extensive, and a brief appendix can't provide a holistic overview. For more details regarding Kubeflow's underlying architecture Kubernetes, we highly recommend the O'Reilly publication *Kubernetes: Up and Running* by Brendan Burns et al.

Setting Up a Kubernetes Cluster on Google Cloud

This appendix provides a brief overview of how to create a Kubernetes cluster on Google Cloud that can run our example project. If Kubernetes is new to you, take a look at Appendix A and our suggested reading at the end of Chapter 9. While the exact commands we will cover only apply to Google Cloud, the overall setup process is the same with other managed Kubernetes services like AWS EKS or Microsoft Azure's AKS.

Before You Get Started

For the following installation steps, we assume you have an account with Google Cloud. If you don't have an account, you can create one (*https://oreil.ly/TFM-4*). Furthermore, we assume that you have installed Kubernetes kubectl (client version 1.18.2 or higher) on your local computer and that you can also execute Google Cloud's SDK gcloud (version 289.0.0 or higher).

Watch Your Cloud Infrastructure Costs

Operating Kubernetes clusters can accumulate significant infrastructure costs. Therefore, we highly recommend to watch your infrastructure costs by setting billing alerts and budgets. Details can be found in the Google Cloud documentation (*https://oreil.ly/ubjAa*). We also recommend turning off idling compute instances because they accrue costs even if they are idling and no pipeline task is being computed.

Steps on how to install a `kubectl` client for your operating system can be found as part of the Kubernetes documentation (*https://oreil.ly/syf_v*). The Google Cloud documentation (*https://oreil.ly/ZmhG5*) provides step-by-step details on how to install their client for your operating system.

Kubernetes on Google Cloud

In the following five sections, we take you through the step-by-step process of creating a Kubernetes cluster from scratch with Google Cloud.

Selecting a Google Cloud Project

For the Kubernetes cluster, we need to create a new Google Cloud project or select an existing project in the Google Cloud Project dashboard (*https://oreil.ly/LQS99*).

Please note the project ID for the following steps. We will deploy our cluster in the project with the ID `oreilly-book`, as shown in Figure B-1.

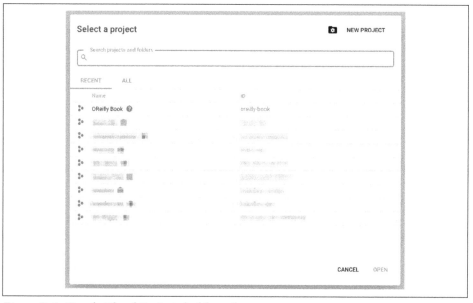

Figure B-1. Google Cloud Project dashboard

Setting Up Your Google Cloud Project

Before creating a Kubernetes cluster, let's set up your Google Cloud project. In the terminal of your operating system, you can authenticate your Google Cloud SDK client with:

```
$ gcloud auth login
```

Then update the SDK client with:

```
$ gcloud components update
```

After you have successfully authenticated and updated the SDK client, let's configure a few basics. First, we'll set the GCP project as the default project and pick a compute zone as a default zone. In our example, we have chosen us-central-1. You can find a list of all available zones in the Google Cloud documentation (*https://oreil.ly/5beJg*). Pick a zone either closest to your physical location or where the required Google Cloud services are available (not all services are available in all zones).

By setting these default values, we don't have to specify them later on in following commands. We also will request to enable Google Cloud's container APIs. The last step is only needed once per project:

```
$ export PROJECT_ID=<your gcp project id> ❶
$ export GCP_REGION=us-central1-c ❷
$ gcloud config set project $PROJECT_ID
$ gcloud config set compute/zone $GCP_REGION
$ gcloud services enable container.googleapis.com ❸
```

❶ Replace with the project ID from the previous step.

❷ Select your preferred zone or region.

❸ Enable APIs.

Creating a Kubernetes Cluster

With our Google Cloud project ready to go, we can now create a Kubernetes cluster with a number of compute nodes as part of the cluster. In our example cluster called kfp-oreilly-book, we allow the cluster to run between zero and five nodes at any point in time in our pool called kfp-pool, and the desired number of available nodes is three. We also assign a service account to the cluster. Through the service account, we can control access permissions for requests from the cluster nodes. To learn more about service accounts at Google Cloud, we recommend the online documentation (*https://oreil.ly/7Ar4X*):

```
$ export CLUSTER_NAME=kfp-oreilly-book
$ export POOL_NAME=kfp-pool
$ export MAX_NODES=5
$ export NUM_NODES=3
$ export MIN_NODES=0
$ export SERVICE_ACCOUNT=service-account@oreilly-book.iam.gserviceaccount.com
```

With the cluster parameters now defined in an environment variable, we can execute the following command:

```
$ gcloud container clusters create $CLUSTER_NAME \
    --zone $GCP_REGION \
    --machine-type n1-standard-4 \
    --enable-autoscaling \
    --min-nodes=$MIN_NODES \
    --num-nodes=$NUM_NODES \
    --max-nodes=$MAX_NODES \
    --service-account=$SERVICE_ACCOUNT
```

For our demo pipeline, we selected the instance type n1-standard-4, which provides 4 CPUs and 15 GB of memory per node. These instances provide enough compute resources to train and evaluate our machine learning model and its datasets. You can find a complete list of available instance types by running the following SDK command:

```
$ gcloud compute machine-types list
```

If you would like to add a GPU to the cluster, you can specify the GPU type and the number of GPUs by adding the accelerator argument, as shown in the following example:

```
$ gcloud container clusters create $CLUSTER_NAME \
    ...
    --accelerator=type=nvidia-tesla-v100,count=1
```

The creation of the Kubernetes cluster can take a few minutes until all the resources are fully assigned to your project and available. The time depends on your requested resources and the number of nodes. For our demo cluster, you can expect to wait approximately 5 minutes until all the resources are available.

Accessing Your Kubernetes Cluster with kubectl

When your newly created cluster is available, you can set up your kubectl to access the cluster. The Google Cloud SDK provides a command to register the cluster with your local kubectl configuration:

```
$ gcloud container clusters get-credentials $CLUSTER_NAME --zone $GCP_REGION
```

After updating the kubectl configuration, you can check if the correct cluster is selected by running the following command:

```
$ kubectl config current-context
gke_oreilly-book_us-central1-c_kfp-oreilly-book
```

Using Your Kubernetes Cluster with kubectl

Because your local kubectl can connect with your remote Kubernetes cluster, all kubectl commands, such as our Kubeflow Pipelines steps mentioned in the following and in Chapter 12, will be executed on the remote cluster:

```
$ export PIPELINE_VERSION=0.5.0
$ kubectl apply -k "github.com/kubeflow/pipelines/manifests/kustomize/"\
                "cluster-scoped-resources?ref=$PIPELINE_VERSION"
$ kubectl wait --for condition=established \
            --timeout=60s crd/applications.app.k8s.io
$ kubectl apply -k "github.com/kubeflow/pipelines/manifests/kustomize/"\
                "env/dev?ref=$PIPELINE_VERSION"
```

Persistent Volume Setups for Kubeflow Pipelines

In "Exchange Data Through Persistent Volumes" on page 319, we'll discuss the setup of persistent volumes in our Kubeflow Pipelines setup. The complete configuration of the persistent volume and its claim can be seen in the following code blocks. The presented setup is specific to the Google Cloud environment.

Example B-1 shows the configuration of the persistent volume for our Kubernetes cluster:

Example B-1. Persistent volume configuration

```
apiVersion: v1
kind: PersistentVolume
metadata:
  name: tfx-pv
  namespace: kubeflow
  annotations:
    kubernetes.io/createdby: gce-pd-dynamic-provisioner
    pv.kubernetes.io/bound-by-controller: "yes"
    pv.kubernetes.io/provisioned-by: kubernetes.io/gce-pd
spec:
  accessModes:
  - ReadWriteOnce
  capacity:
    storage: 20Gi
  claimRef:
    apiVersion: v1
    kind: PersistentVolumeClaim
    name: tfx-pvc
    namespace: kubeflow
  gcePersistentDisk:
    fsType: ext4
    pdName: tfx-pv-disk
  nodeAffinity:
    required:
      nodeSelectorTerms:
      - matchExpressions:
        - key: failure-domain.beta.kubernetes.io/zone
          operator: In
          values:
          - us-central1-c
```

```
      - key: failure-domain.beta.kubernetes.io/region
        operator: In
        values:
        - us-central1
  persistentVolumeReclaimPolicy: Delete
  storageClassName: standard
  volumeMode: Filesystem
status:
  phase: Bound
```

Once the persistent volume is created, we can claim a portion or all of the available storage through a persistent volume claim. The configuration file can be seen in Example B-2:

Example B-2. Persistent volume claim configuration

```
kind: PersistentVolumeClaim
apiVersion: v1
metadata:
  name: tfx-pvc
  namespace: kubeflow
spec:
  accessModes:
    - ReadWriteOnce
  resources:
    requests:
      storage: 20Gi
```

With the presented configuration, we have now created a persistent volume and its claim in the Kubernetes cluster. The volume can now be mounted as discussed in "Pipeline Setup" on page 237 or used as discussed in the section "Exchange Data Through Persistent Volumes" on page 319 of the following appendix.

Tips for Operating Kubeflow Pipelines

When you operate your TFX pipelines with Kubeflow Pipelines, you might want to customize the underlying container images of your TFX components. Custom TFX images are required if your components rely on additional Python dependencies outside of the TensorFlow and TFX packages. In the case of our demo pipeline, we have an additional Python dependency, the TensorFlow Hub library, for accessing our language model.

In the second half of this appendix, we want to show you how to transfer data to and from your local computer and your persistent volume. The persistent volume setup is beneficial if you can access your data via a cloud storage provider (e.g., with an on-premise Kubernetes cluster). The presented steps will guide you through the process of copying data to and from your cluster.

Custom TFX Images

In our example project, we use a language model provided by TensorFlow Hub. We use the `tensorflow_hub` library to load the language model efficiently. This particular library isn't part of the original TFX image; therefore, we need to build a custom TFX image with the required library. This is also the case if you plan to use custom components like the ones we discussed in Chapter 10.

Fortunately, as we discussed in Appendix A, Docker images can be built without much trouble. The following *Dockerfile* shows our custom image setup:

```
FROM tensorflow/tfx:0.22.0

RUN python3.6 -m pip install "tensorflow-hub" ❶
RUN ... ❷

ENTRYPOINT ["python3.6", "/tfx-src/tfx/scripts/run_executor.py"] ❸
```

❶ Install required packages.

❷ Install additional packages if needed.

❸ Don't change the container entry point.

We can easily inherit the standard TFX image as a base for our custom image. To avoid any sudden changes in the TFX API, we highly recommend pinning the version of the base image to a specific build (e.g., *tensorflow/tfx:0.22.0*) instead of the common `latest` tag. The TFX images are built on the Ubuntu Linux distribution and come with Python installed. In our case, we can simply install the additional Python package for the Tensorflow Hub models.

It is very important to provide the same entry point as configured in the base image. Kubeflow Pipelines expects that the entry point will trigger the component's executor.

Once we have defined our Docker image, we can build and push the image to a container registry. This can be AWS Elastic, GCP or Azure Container Registry. It's important to ensure that the running Kubernetes cluster can pull images from the container registry and has permission to do so for private containers. In the following code, we demonstrate those steps for the GCP Container Registry:

```
$ export TFX_VERSION=0.22.0
$ export PROJECT_ID=<your gcp project id>
$ export IMAGE_NAME=ml-pipelines-tfx-custom

$ gcloud auth configure-docker
$ docker build pipelines/kubeflow_pipelines/tfx-docker-image/. \
    -t gcr.io/$PROJECT_ID/$IMAGE_NAME:$TFX_VERSION
$ docker push gcr.io/$PROJECT_ID/$IMAGE_NAME:$TFX_VERSION
```

Once the built image is uploaded, you can see the image available in the cloud provider's container registry, as shown in Figure C-1.

Component-Specific Images

At the time of writing, it isn't possible to define custom images for specific component containers. At the moment, the requirements for all components need to be included in the image. However, there are currently proposals being discussed to allow component-specific images in the future.

Figure C-1. Google Cloud's Container Registry

We can now use this container image for all of our TFX components in our Kubeflow Pipelines setup.

Exchange Data Through Persistent Volumes

As we discussed earlier, we need to provide containers to mount a filesystem to read from and write data to locations outside of the container filesystem. In the Kubernetes world, we can mount filesystems through *persistent volumes* (PVs) and *persistent volume claims* (PVCs). In simple terms, we can provision a drive to be available inside of a Kubernetes cluster and then claim that filesystem in its entirety or a portion of its space.

You can set up such PVs through the Kubernetes configurations that we provide in "Persistent Volume Setups for Kubeflow Pipelines" on page 315. If you would like to use this setup, you will need to create a disk with your cloud provider (e.g., AWS Elastic Block Storage or GCP Block Storage). In the following example, we create a disk drive with a size of 20 GB named *tfx-pv-disk*:

```
$ export GCP_REGION=us-central1-c
$ gcloud compute disks create tfx-pv-disk --size=20Gi --zone=$GCP_REGION
```

We can now provision the disk to be used as a PV in our Kubernetes cluster. The following kubectl command will facilitate the provisioning:

```
$ kubectl apply -f "https://github.com/Building-ML-Pipelines/"\
    "building-machine-learning-pipelines/blob/master/pipelines/"\
    "kubeflow_pipelines/kubeflow-config/storage.yaml"
$ kubectl apply -f "https://github.com/Building-ML-Pipelines/"\
    "building-machine-learning-pipelines/blob/master/pipelines/"\
    "kubeflow_pipelines/kubeflow-config/storage-claim.yaml"
```

After the provisioning is completed, we can check if the execution worked by calling `kubectl get pvc`, as shown in the following example:

```
$ kubectl -n kubeflow get pvc
NAME            STATUS   VOLUME    CAPACITY   ACCESS MODES   STORAGECLASS   AGE
tfx-pvc         Bound    tfx-pvc   20Gi       RWO            manual         2m
```

Kubernetes' `kubectl` provides a handy `cp` command to copy data from our local machines to the remote PV. In order to copy the pipeline data (e.g., the Python module for the transform and training steps, as well as the training data), we need to mount the volume to a Kubernetes pod. For the copy operations, we created a simple app that basically just idles and allows us to access the PV. You can create the pod with the following *kubectl* command:

```
$ kubectl apply -f "https://github.com/Building-ML-Pipelines/"\
    "building-machine-learning-pipelines/blob/master/pipelines/"\
    "kubeflow_pipelines/kubeflow-config/storage-access-pod.yaml"
```

The pod `data-access` will mount the PV, and then we can create the necessary folders and copy the required data to the volume:

```
$ export DATA_POD=`kubectl -n kubeflow get pods -o name | grep data-access`
$ kubectl -n kubeflow exec $DATA_POD -- mkdir /tfx-data/data
$ kubectl -n kubeflow exec $DATA_POD -- mkdir /tfx-data/components
$ kubectl -n kubeflow exec $DATA_POD -- mkdir /tfx-data/output

$ kubectl -n kubeflow cp \
    ../building-machine-learning-pipelines/components/module.py \
    ${DATA_POD#*/}:/tfx-data/components/module.py
$ kubectl -n kubeflow cp \
    ../building-machine-learning-pipelines/data/consumer_complaints.csv \
    ${DATA_POD#*/}:/tfx-data/data/consumer_complaints.csv
```

After all the data is transferred to the PV, you can delete the `data-access` pod by running the following command:

```
$ kubectl delete -f \
    pipelines/kubeflow_pipelines/kubeflow-config/storage-access-pod.yaml
```

The `cp` command also works in the other direction, in case you want to copy the exported model from your Kubernetes cluster to a different location outside of your cluster.

TFX Command-Line Interface

TFX provides a CLI to manage your TFX projects and their orchestration runs. The CLI tool provides you *TFX Templates*, a predefined folder and file structure. Projects that use the provided folder structure can then be managed through the CLI tool instead of a web UI (in the case of Kubeflow and Airflow). It also incorporated the Skaffold library to automate the creation and publication of custom TFX images.

TFX CLI Under Active Development

The TFX CLI is under active development at the time of writing this section. The commands might change or more functionality might be added. Also, more TFX templates might become available in the future.

TFX and Its Dependencies

TFX CLI requires the *Kubeflow Pipelines SDK* and the Skaffold (*https://skaffold.dev*), a Python tool for continuously building and deploying Kubernetes applications.

If you haven't installed or updated TFX and the Python SDK from Kubeflow Pipelines, run the two `pip install` commands:

```
$ pip install -U tfx
$ pip install -U kfp
```

The installation of Skaffold depends on your operating system:

Linux

```
$ curl -Lo skaffold \
https://storage.googleapis.com/\
skaffold/releases/latest/skaffold-linux-amd64
$ sudo install skaffold /usr/local/bin/
```

MacOS

```
$ brew install skaffold
```

Windows

```
$ choco install -y skaffold
```

After the installation of Skaffold, make sure the execution path of the tool is added to the PATH of the terminal environment where you are executing the TFX CLI tool. The following bash example shows how Linux users can add the Skaffold path to their PATH bash variable:

```
$ export PATH=$PATH:/usr/local/bin/
```

Before we discuss how to use the TFX CLI tool, let's discuss TFX templates briefly.

TFX Templates

TFX provides project templates to organize machine learning pipeline projects. The templates provide a predefined folder structure and a blueprint for your feature, model, and preprocessing definitions. The following `tfx template copy` command will download the *taxi cab* example project of the TFX project:

```
$ export PIPELINE_NAME="customer_complaint"
$ export PROJECT_DIR=$PWD/$PIPELINE_NAME
$ tfx template copy --pipeline-name=$PIPELINE_NAME \
```

```
--destination-path=$PROJECT_DIR \
--model=taxi
```

When the copy command completes its execution, you can find a folder structure, as seen in the following bash output:

```
$ tree .
.
├── __init__.py
├── beam_dag_runner.py
├── data
│   └── data.csv
├── data_validation.ipynb
├── kubeflow_dag_runner.py
├── model_analysis.ipynb
├── models
│   ├── __init__.py
│   ├── features.py
│   ├── features_test.py
│   ├── keras
│   │   ├── __init__.py
│   │   ├── constants.py
│   │   ├── model.py
│   │   └── model_test.py
│   ├── preprocessing.py
│   └── preprocessing_test.py
├── pipeline
│   ├── __init__.py
│   ├── configs.py
│   └── pipeline.py
└── template_pipeline_test.tar.gz
```

We have taken the *taxi cab* template[1] and tuned our book example project to match the template. The results can be found in the book's GitHub repository (*https://oreil.ly/bmlp-git*). If you want to follow along with this example, please copy the CSV file *consumer_complaints.csv* into the folder:

```
$pwd/$PIPELINE_NAME/data
```

Also, double check the file *pipelines/config.py*, which defines the GCS bucket and other pipeline details. Update the GCS bucket path with a bucket you created or use the GCS buckets that were created when you created the Kubeflow Pipelines installation through GCP's AI Platform. You can find the path with the following command:

```
$ gsutil -l
```

---

1 At the time of writing, this was the only template available.

Publishing Your Pipeline with TFX CLI

We can publish the TFX pipeline, which we created based on the TFX template, to our Kubeflow Pipelines application. To access our Kubeflow Pipelines setup, we need to define our GCP Project, a path for our TFX container image and the URL of our Kubeflow Pipelines endpoint. In "Accessing Your Kubeflow Pipelines Installation" on page 234, we discussed how to obtain the endpoint URL. Before publishing our pipeline with TFX CLI, let's set up the required environment variables for our example:

```
$ export PIPELINE_NAME="<pipeline name>"
$ export PROJECT_ID="<your gcp project id>"
$ export CUSTOM_TFX_IMAGE=gcr.io/$PROJECT_ID/tfx-pipeline
$ export ENDPOINT="<id>-dot-<region>.pipelines.googleusercontent.com"
```

With the details defined, we can now create the pipeline through the TFX CLI with the following command:

```
$ tfx pipeline create --pipeline-path=kubeflow_dag_runner.py \
                      --endpoint=$ENDPOINT \
                      --build-target-image=$CUSTOM_TFX_IMAGE
```

The `tfx pipeline create` command performs a variety of things. With the assistance of Skaffold, it creates a default docker image and publishes the container image via the Google Cloud Registry. It also runs the Kubeflow Runner, as we discussed in Chapter 12, and uploads the Argo configuration to the pipeline endpoint. After the command completes the execution, you will find two new files in the template folder structure: *Dockerfile* and *build.yaml*.

The *Dockerfile* contains an image definition similar to the *Dockerfile* we discussed in "Custom TFX Images" on page 317. The *build.yaml* file configures Skaffold and sets the docker images registry details and tag policy.

You will be able to see the pipeline now registered in your Kubeflow Pipelines UI. You can start a pipeline run with the following command:

```
$ tfx run create --pipeline-name=$PIPELINE_NAME \
                 --endpoint=$ENDPOINT

Creating a run for pipeline: customer_complaint_tfx
Detected Kubeflow.
Use --engine flag if you intend to use a different orchestrator.
Run created for pipeline: customer_complaint_tfx
+-------------------------+----------+----------+---------------------------+
| pipeline_name           | run_id   | status   | created_at                |
+=========================+==========+==========+===========================+
| customer_complaint_tfx  | <run-id> |          | 2020-05-31T21:30:03+00:00 |
+-------------------------+----------+----------+---------------------------+
```

You can check on the status of the pipeline run with the following command:

```
$ tfx run status --pipeline-name=$PIPELINE_NAME \
                 --endpoint=$ENDPOINT \
                 --run_id <run_id>

Listing all runs of pipeline: customer_complaint_tfx
+-----------------------+----------+------------+--------------------------+
| pipeline_name         | run_id   | status     | created_at               |
+=======================+==========+============+==========================+
| customer_complaint_tfx | <run-id> | Running    | 2020-05-31T21:30:03+00:00 |
+-----------------------+----------+------------+--------------------------+
```

A list of all runs for a given pipeline can be obtained with the following command:

```
$ tfx run list --pipeline-name=$PIPELINE_NAME \
               --endpoint=$ENDPOINT

Listing all runs of pipeline: customer_complaint_tfx
+-----------------------+----------+------------+--------------------------+
| pipeline_name         | run_id   | status     | created_at               |
+=======================+==========+============+==========================+
| customer_complaint_tfx | <run-id> | Running    | 2020-05-31T21:30:03+00:00 |
+-----------------------+----------+------------+--------------------------+
```

Stop and Delete Pipeline Runs

You can stop a pipeline run with `tfx run terminate`. Pipeline runs can be deleted with `tfx run delete`.

TFX CLI is a very useful tool in the TFX toolchain. It supports not only Kubeflow Pipelines but also Apache Airflow and Apache Beam orchestrators.

Index

A

A/B testing of models, using TensorFlow Serving, 152

access scope for Kubernetes cluster nodes, 254

accuracy, 102
- equal accuracy for all groups, 110

AI Platform (see Google Cloud AI Platform)

AirflowDagRunner, 226, 226

AirflowPipelineConfig, 226

ai_platform_trainer_executor.GenericExecutor, 89

analysis, 99
- (see also model analysis and validation)
- analysis step in TensorFlow Transform execution, 68
- model explainability versus, 120

annotations
- crowdsourcing, 270
- expert, 270

anonymization, 288

Apache Airflow, 214, 220-228
- installation and initial setup, 220-222
- orchestrating TFX pipelines with, 225-228
  - pipeline execution, 227
  - setting up TFX pipeline, 225
- setting up basic pipeline, 222-225
  - project-specific configurations, 222
  - putting it all together, 224-225
  - task definitions, 223
  - task dependencies, 223
- simple interactive pipeline conversion for, 217

Apache Beam, 13, 21-25, 45, 218-220
- basic data pipeline, 22

classes and function decorators for data ingestion via Apache Beam pipelines, 209
- example ML pipeline, 24
- executing with Google Cloud's Dataflow, 259
- executing your basic pipeline, 25
- installation and setup, 21
- orchestrating TFX pipelines with, 219-220
- as pipeline orchestrator, 214
- simple interactive pipeline conversion for, 217
- use with TensorFlow Transform, 64
- using TensorFlow Transform on local setup, 73

Apache Flink, 220

Apache Spark, 220

APIs
- creating for model deployment in Python web app, 130
- gRPC versus REST, 147
- lack of code separation between model and API, 132

Argo
- configuration for output from Kubeflow Pipelines orchestrating TFX pipeline, 241
- conversion of Python TFX scripts to Argo instructions, 235
- in Kubeflow Pipelines, 232

artifacts
- defined, 17
- input artifacts, registration in metadata store, 204

using the custom component, 207

D

DAG objects
    Airflow configuration options for, 222
    KubeflowDagRunnerConfig, 238
    turning on a DAG in Airflow, 227
DAGs (see directed acyclic graphs)
data flywheel, 264
data ingestion, 4, 27-42
    concepts, 27
    directly from databases, 34
        Google Cloud BigQuery, 34
        Presto databases, 35
    ingesting local data files, 28-33
        converting Avro-serialized data to
            tf.Example, 31
        converting CSV data to tf.Example, 29
        converting Parquet-serialized data to
            tf.Example, 30
        converting your custom data to TFRe-
            cord data structures, 31
        importing existing TFRecord files, 30
    ingesting remote data files, 34
    preparing data for, 36-40
        spanning datasets, 38
        splitting datasets, 36
        versioning datasets, 39
    reusing existing components, 208
    strategies for, 40-42
        image data for computer vision prob-
            lems, 41
        structured data, 40
        text data for natural language problems,
            40
data preprocessing, 5, 63-78
    image data for computer vision problems,
        41
    in machine learning pipelines, 63
    reasons for performing, 64-66
        avoiding training-serving skew, 65
        checking preprocessing results in ML
            pipeline, 66
        deploying preprocessing steps and
            model as one artifact, 66
        processing data in context of entire data-
            set, 64
        scaling preprocessing steps, 64
    using TensorFlow Transform, 67-78

best practices, 70
    functions in TFT, 70
    installing TFT, 68
    preprocessing strategies, 68
    standalone execution of TFT, 73
data privacy, 7, 275-289
    differential privacy, 277-280
        epsilon, delta, and the privacy budget,
            279
        local and global, 279
        for machine learning, 280
    encrypted machine learning, 285
        converting trained model to serve
            encrypted predictions, 287
        encrypted model training, 286
    federated learning, 283-285
        in TensorFlow, 285
    issues, 275-277
        simplest way to increase privacy, 276
        what data should be kept private, 277
        why care about data privacy, 276
    model deployment and, 130
    other methods for, 288
    TensorFlow Privacy, 280-283
        calculating epsilon, 282
        training with differentially private opti-
            mizer, 281
data types
    considering in TFT, 70
    in tf.Estimator model, 90
    neural network weights stored as float 32-
        bit data types, 175
data validation, 4, 43-62
    benefits of, 44
    integrating TFDV into machine learning
        pipeline, 60
    processing large datasets with GCP, 57-59
    recognizing problems in your data, 49-57
        biased datasets, 54
        comparing datasets, 50
        data skew and drift, 52
        slicing data, 55
        updating the schema, 52
    TensorFlow Data Validation (TFDV), 45-49
Data Version Control (DVC), 40
databases
    ingesting data directly from, 34
        Presto databases, 35
    initializing Airflow database, 221

export_saved_model method, 134
ExternalArtifact channel, 200

F

Fairness Indicators project
  checking false positives for equal opportunity, 112
  documentation, 110
  loading Fairness Indicators in TFX Evaluator, 125
fairness, model analysis for, 109-119
  checking decision thresholds with Fairness Indicators, 112
  defining numerically the meaning of fairness, 109
  going deeper with What-If Tool, 116-119
  slicing model predictions in TFMA, 111
false negatives, 101
false positives, 101
  false positive rate (FPR), 102
feature attributions, 122
features
  converting to one-hot, 77
  feature names in TFT, 70
  slicing datasets on, 55
  tf.train.Feature object, 32
federated learning, 283-285
  in TensorFlow, 285
feedback loops, 7, 263-273
  design patterns for collecting feedback, 268-271
    crowdsourcing annotations, 270
    expert annotations, 270
    feedback produced automatically by the system, 271
    users correct the prediction, 269
    users rate quality of the prediction, 269
    users take an action as result of prediction, 268
  explicit and implicit feedback, 264-267
    data flywheel, 264
    feedback loops in the real world, 265
  monitoring for unexpected consequences, 267
  negative consequenes of, 264
  tracking, 271
    explicit feedback, 272
    implicit feedback, 272
FileBasedExampleGen, 208, 211

floating point numbers, quantization of, 175
function decorators, 209
future of pipelines and next steps, 291-295
  CI/CD systems for machine learning, 295
  future pipeline capabilities, 293
  machine learning engineering community, 295
  model experiment tracking, 291
  model realease management, 292
  testing of machine learning models, 294
  TFX with other ML frameworks, 294

G

GCP (Google Cloud Platform), 311
  accessing models from GCP buckets, 174
  adding GCP credentials of TFX component containers, 240
  AI Platform (see Google Cloud AI Platform)
  container registry, 318
  Google Cloud Credentials, 34
  Kubernetes on, 312-315
    accessing your cluster with kubectl, 314
    creating a Kubernetes cluster, 313
    selecting Google Cloud project, 312
    setting up Google Cloud project, 312
    using your Kubernetes cluster with kubectl, 314
  persistent volume setup for Kubeflow Pipelines, 315
  processing large datasets with, 57-59
  storage buckets, 34
  TensorFlow Serving deployment on Kubernetes, 185
  training models on AI Platform, 89
GenericExecutor, 89
get_model function, 86
get_serve_tf_examples_fn function, 87, 88
global differential privacy, 279
global explanations, 120
Google Cloud AI Platform
  example model deployment with, 163-168
    model deployment, 163
    model inference, 166
  feature attributions, 122
  Kubeflow Pipelines on, 215
  managed Kubeflow Pipelines installations, 233
  pipelines based on, 252-260

training steps (TFX Trainer), 86
training-serving skew, 65
transfer learning, 265
Transform component, 216
transformations (Apache Beam), 22
true negatives, 101
true positives, 101
    true positive rate (TPR), 102
Tuner component, 96
tuning models (see model tuning)

U

Ubuntu
    installing TensorFlow Serving on, 141
    packages for TensorFlow Serving, 142
URLs
    for HTTP requests to model server, 148
    randomly changing request URL for model
        inference in REST API, 153

V

valency, 49
vector representations
    bag-of-words vector, 72
    defining difference between two vectors, 53
    features embedded from string to vector
        representation, 75
    TFIDF, 72
version labels, 146
versioning
    configuring specific model versions for
        TensorFlow Serving, 146

lack of model version control in deployment
    with Python app, 132
of datasets, 39
TensorFlow Serving loading model with
    highest version, 144
visualizations
    basic TensorBoard visualization, 91
    offered in TensorFlow Data Validation, 45
    TFMA visualization comparing two models,
        108

W

warm start model training, 194
Weights and Biases, experiment tracking in,
    292
What-If Tool (WIT), 116-119
    counterfactuals, 117
    decision thresholds, 119
    extra steps for running in standalone note-
        book, 117
    generating model explanations with,
        121-122
    partial dependence plots, 118

Y

YouTube's recommendation system, 267

Z

zip codes represented as strings, converting to
    float values, 76

About the Authors

Hannes Hapke is a senior data scientist for Concur Labs at SAP Concur, where he explores innovative ways to use machine learning to improve the experience of a business traveller. Prior to joining SAP Concur, Hannes solved machine learning infrastructure problems in various industries, including healthcare, retail, recruiting, and renewable energy. Additionally, he has coauthored a publication about natural language processing and deep learning and presented at various conferences about deep learning and Python. Hannes is also the creator of *wunderbar.ai*. He holds a master of science in electrical engineering from Oregon State University.

Catherine Nelson is also a senior data scientist for Concur Labs at SAP Concur. She is particularly interested in privacy-preserving machine learning and applying deep learning to enterprise data. In her previous career as a geophysicist, she studied ancient volcanoes and explored for oil in Greenland. Catherine has a PhD in geophysics from Durham University and a masters of Earth sciences from Oxford University.

Colophon

The animal on the cover of *Building Machine Learning Pipelines* is a mudpuppy salamander (*Necturus maculosus*). These nocturnal amphibians live in North America's eastern lakes, rivers, and ponds, breathing through distinctive bushy red gills and sleeping under detritus in the water during the day.

Mudpuppy salamanders usually have slimy brown skin with blackish-blue spots. From flat head to flat tail, a mature mudpuppy measures about 13 inches long. On average, mudpuppy salamanders live 11 years in the wild and 20 in captivity. Salamanders have three different sets of teeth. Mudpuppy salamanders often prey on small fish, crayfish, other amphibians, and insects. Because of their limited eyesight, they rely on smell to feed.

These salamanders rely on a stable environment to thrive, so they can be bioindicators of their ecosystems, warning us of changes in water quality. Mudpuppy salamanders have a conservation status of Least Concern. Many of the animals on O'Reilly's covers are endangered; all of them are important to the world.

The cover illustration is by Karen Montgomery, based on a black and white engraving from *Wood's Illustrated Natural History*. The cover fonts are Gilroy Semibold and Guardian Sans. The text font is Adobe Minion Pro; the heading font is Adobe Myriad Condensed; and the code font is Dalton Maag's Ubuntu Mono.

O'REILLY®

There's much more where this came from.

Experience books, videos, live online training courses, and more from O'Reilly and our 200+ partners—all in one place.

Learn more at oreilly.com/online-learning

Milton Keynes UK
Ingram Content Group UK Ltd.
UKHW031810170124
436207UK00003B/4